Robert Burn

Old Rome

A Handbook to the Ruins of the City and the Campagna

Robert Burn

Old Rome
A Handbook to the Ruins of the City and the Campagna

ISBN/EAN: 9783744776509

Printed in Europe, USA, Canada, Australia, Japan

Cover: Foto ©Andreas Hilbeck / pixelio.de

More available books at **www.hansebooks.com**

OLD ROME:

A HANDBOOK TO THE RUINS OF THE CITY AND THE CAMPAGNA.

BY

ROBERT BURN, M.A.,
FELLOW OF TRINITY COLLEGE, CAMBRIDGE.

BEING AN EPITOME OF HIS LARGER WORK 'ROME AND THE CAMPAGNA.'

LONDON: GEORGE BELL AND SONS, YORK STREET,
COVENT GARDEN.
CAMBRIDGE: DEIGHTON, BELL, & CO.
1880.

[The Right of Translation is reserved.]

LONDON:
PRINTED BY WILLIAM CLOWES AND SONS,
STAMFORD STREET AND CHARING CROSS.

PREFACE.

This book is intended to serve as a handbook to the actually-existing ruins and monuments of ancient Rome and the Campagna. It is divided into topographical sections for the convenience of travellers visiting Rome, and the monuments which exist in each section have been briefly described, and a summary given of their history and archæological value.

The introductory section contains general remarks upon the site, monumental history, and architecture of Rome; and in a section prefixed to Chapter IX. the nature of the soil and configuration of the hills and valleys of the district surrounding the city are stated.

In the Appendix to the eighth chapter will be found a list of the chief monumental antiquities in the museums, galleries, and other public places. This has been thought to be useful, as these are often difficult to recognise from being mixed with so many other attractive and important objects of more modern art and history. All speculative conjectures as to the probable sites or constructions of ancient buildings or places have been avoided. Such questions require more space than can be spared in so small a volume, and have been fully treated of in my larger work, "Rome and the Campagna."

I have confined myself in this handbook to a brief topographical, archæological, and historical description of each existing ruin or monument. The references given have been restricted to modern treatises and to a few of the more rarely read Greek and Latin authors. Full classical authorities are given in "Rome and the Campagna," and are referred to in the foot-notes of this handbook.

The importance of topographical and archaeological knowledge, in enabling us to realise the history of ancient life, both national and social, is fortunately becoming more and more generally recognised. The early growth and characteristic features of the Roman commonwealth can be traced in great measure to the conformation of the ground on which the community was first developed. Such local influences are among the highest and most philosophical parts of historical investigation, and have a most important value in enabling us to form an estimate of the truth of statements made by the ancient writers of history.

Besides this interest which pervades the early stage of Roman history, there is also a natural connection, by way of cause or explanation, between the events of later times and the localities in which they occurred; and this in social as well as in national history. Many Roman customs and usages, now extinct, are illustrated and realised by the knowledge gained from monuments of ancient architecture and art. And again, the spirit of Roman literature is more fully sympathised with, and its difficult passages and allusions are frequently elucidated by the light of archaeological knowledge.

Thus there is not only the poetical and imaginative satisfaction, which is usually felt most vividly in treading the soil, surveying the scenes, and breathing the air in which great historical persons lived and events occurred, but also an element of fact which gives a firm basis of incontestable truth to our knowledge, and which no speculative interpretation can dissolve.

It is hoped, therefore, that even such an abridged description of ruins, and such a summary of archaeological results as that which forms the basis of the present volume, will not be without use to the student of history, as well as a guide to the traveller.

In the chapter on the ruins of the Campagna I have inserted some statements on the geological formations, and on the climate, which appear to have influenced the history and the architecture of that district.

The books from which useful information has been derived are, in addition to those mentioned in the list given in "Rome and the Campagna," some of the later numbers of "Annali dell' Instituto," a small treatise called "Guida del Palatino," by C. L. Visconti and R. A. Lanciani, and "A Topographical Study of the Roman Forum," by Mr. F. M. Nichols.

ROBERT BURN.

CAMBRIDGE.
Sept. 24, 1879.

CONTENTS.

	PAGE
INTRODUCTION	1

CHAPTER I.

| THE PALATINE AND VELIA | 14 |

CHAPTER II.

| THE FORUM ROMANUM | 38 |

CHAPTER III.

| THE COLISEUM AND ESQUILINE | 58 |

CHAPTER IV.

| THE IMPERIAL FORA AND THE CAPITOLIUM | 83 |

CHAPTER V.

| THE VELABRUM AND THE CIRCUS FLAMINIUS | 103 |

CHAPTER VI.

| PANTHEON, COLUMN OF MARCUS AURELIUS, MAUSOLEUM OF AUGUSTUS, MAUSOLEUM OF HADRIAN, AND NEIGHBOURHOOD | 127 |

CHAPTER VII.

| THE QUIRINAL HILL—BATHS OF DIOCLETIAN—AGGER OF SERVIUS—CASTRA PRÆTORIA | 153 |

CHAPTER VIII.

	PAGE
THE AVENTINE AND CÆLIAN HILLS.	161

APPENDIX TO CHAPTER VIII. MONUMENTAL ANTIQUITIES IN THE MUSEUMS, PIAZZAS, AND OTHER PLACES 177

INTRODUCTION TO CHAPTER IX. 185

CHAPTER IX.

A. THE VIA APPIA AND THE ALBAN HILLS 194
B. THE VIA LATINA AND TUSCULUM 210
C. GABII AND PRÆNESTE 219
D. OSTIA AND PORTO 229
E. TIBUR 235
F. NORTH-WESTERN CAMPAGNA 256

LIST OF ILLUSTRATIONS.

	PAGE
Temple of Jupiter	Title page.
Temple of Saturn, etc.	47
Arch of Severus	53
Coliseum, from the Palatine Hill	62
Column of Trajan	85
Forum of Nerva, in 1600	95
Palatine Hill, Temple of Hercules, and Cloaca Maxima	109
Theatre of Marcellus	113
Pantheon	130
The Quirinal Hill from the Palatine	154
Arch of Dolabella	175
Pedestal of Antonine Column	179
Cone from the top of Hadrian's Mausoleum	180
Circus of Maxentius	213
Temple of Vesta at Tibur	250
Ponte Nomentano	258

MAPS, PLANS, &c.

Plan of Ancient Rome, with Railways	1
Plan of the Hills of Rome	2
Most Ancient Rome	2
Rome, the present Walls, and Walls of Aurelian	4
Plan of the Palatine Hill	14

	PAGE
Plan of Ruins in the Forum Romanum	38
Plan of Mons Oppius	73
Fora of the Cæsars	82
The Circus Flaminius	122
Fragments of Pianta Capitolina—Theatre of Pompey	124
The Thermæ of Diocletian	154
The Servian Walls	156
The Baths of Caracalla	166
Geological Map of Rome	185
Plan of the Alban Hills and Gabii	202
Plan of the Area of the Temple of Jupiter on Monte Cavo	206
Plan of the Temple of Fortune at Præneste	224
Plan of Ostia and Porto	229
Plan of Hadrianeum, near Tivoli	236
Plan of Tivoli	248
Map of Ancient Roads	256
Ichnographia	261

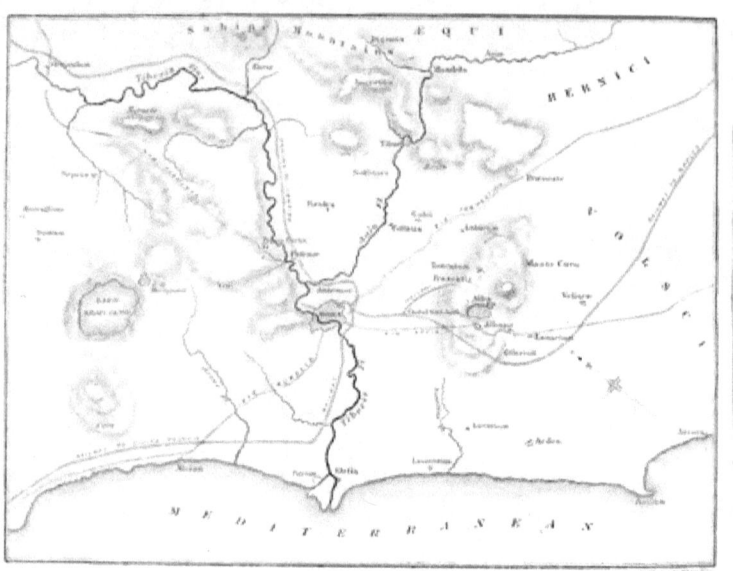

OLD ROME:

A HANDBOOK TO THE RUINS OF THE CITY AND THE CAMPAGNA.

INTRODUCTION.

I.—THE SITE OF ROME AND THE WALLS OF ROME.

ONE of the principal points in the early history of every nation is the effect of the natural configuration of the country in which their first settlements are formed upon the subsequent character of the people.

The site of Rome consists of several separate hills, upon which distinct groups of original settlers established themselves. These groups after a temporary rivalry seem to have agreed to form a confederation, in which the leading part was assigned to the Palatine settlement. Such was the origin of that special aptitude shown by the Romans for forming coalitions with rival states, and also of that most valuable trait in their political character, their reverence for law as laid down by a central authority, for each group was taught by their confederate union to regard itself as sharing that central authority. Hence, the historian Livy remarks that under the Roman Republic which built up the power of Rome, the command of law was superior to that of men. But besides this aptitude for confederate union and respect for central authority which the nature of the site seems to have instilled into them, the Romans were also taught by it a readiness to meet their enemies in the open field, and not to trust much to the protection of steep crags or fortified posts. None of the hills of Rome afforded a strong acropolis, such as most other ancient cities possessed. The Capitol of

Rome was by no means impregnable. Its central depression rendered it always more or less accessible and liable to be seized by a powerful enemy. The Palatine, though partially fortified, was never considered a strong position. Hence we find that the Servian walls were the only fortifications erected to protect Rome for more than eight hundred years, from the time of Servius down to that of Aurelian. The statement of Strabo, that the absence of fortifications round Rome was to be accounted for by the native spirit of the Romans, which was "to defend their walls by their men, and not their men by their walls," is evidently full of meaning.

II.—Monumental History.

Relics of the two great public works executed during the regal period of Roman history still remain in the venerable stone arches of the main drain which was constructed to make the Forum valley more habitable, and in the rough portions of the Servian walls which have been found on the Aventine and Quirinal Hills. It is probable that the ruined walls at the edge of the Palatine are anterior to the monuments of the time of Servius.

Of the earlier republican period of Roman history there are no monumental ruins now existing. The ruins which have been excavated on the Capitoline Hill and the basement of the Temple of Vesta in the Forum date from the regal epoch. And this is what might be naturally expected from the dislike of a republican government to require the forced labour anciently called for in the erection of large buildings.

But in the later period of the Roman republic some of the oligarchical leaders and successful generals constructed large buildings, of which traces can now be found. Thus the foundations of the temples and of the portico built in the Campus Martius by Metellus Macedonicus and by Cn. Octavius can be still recognised, and ruins of the immense stone theatre of Pompeius Magnus remain to the present day. But the greater portion of the ruins of Rome dates from the Augustan age and the subsequent imperial ages. First among them stands the Pantheon, which has kept its roof and its original structure uninjured through the storms

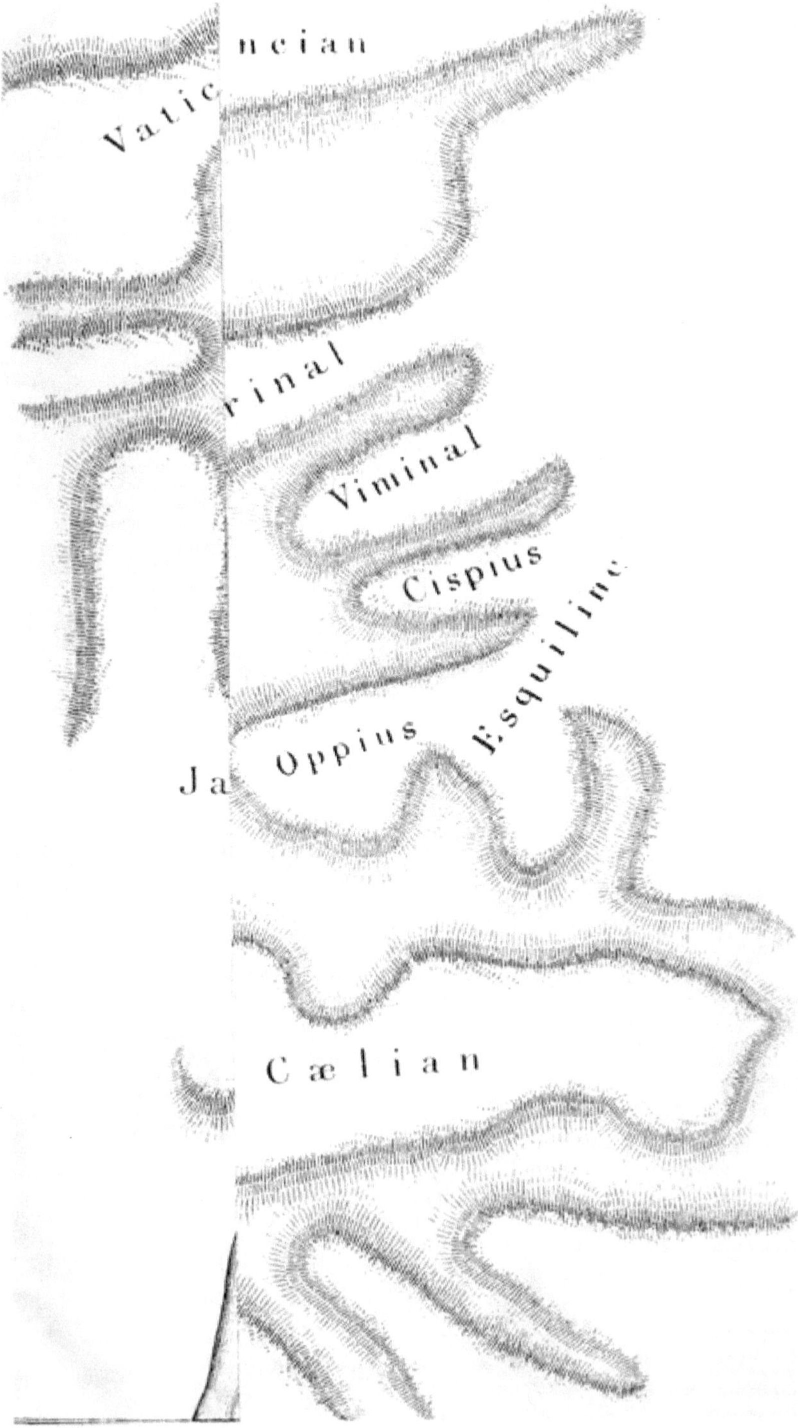

Vatican
ncian
rinal
Viminal
Cispius
Ja Oppius Esquiline
Cælian

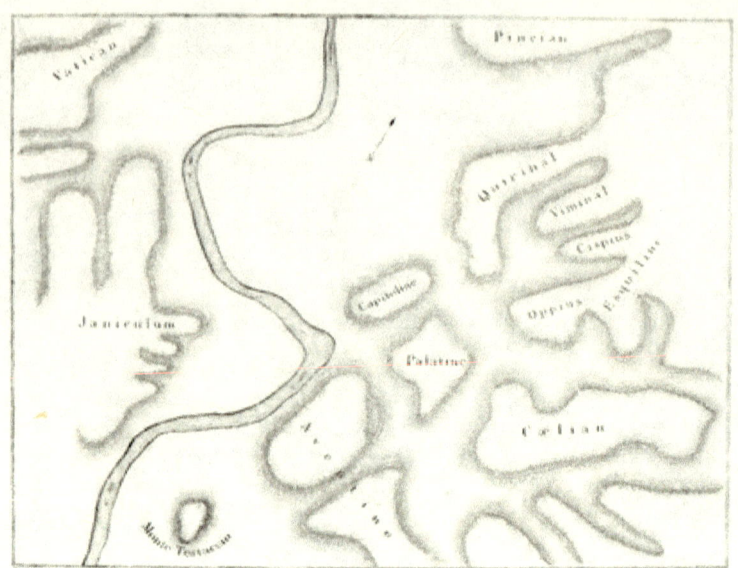

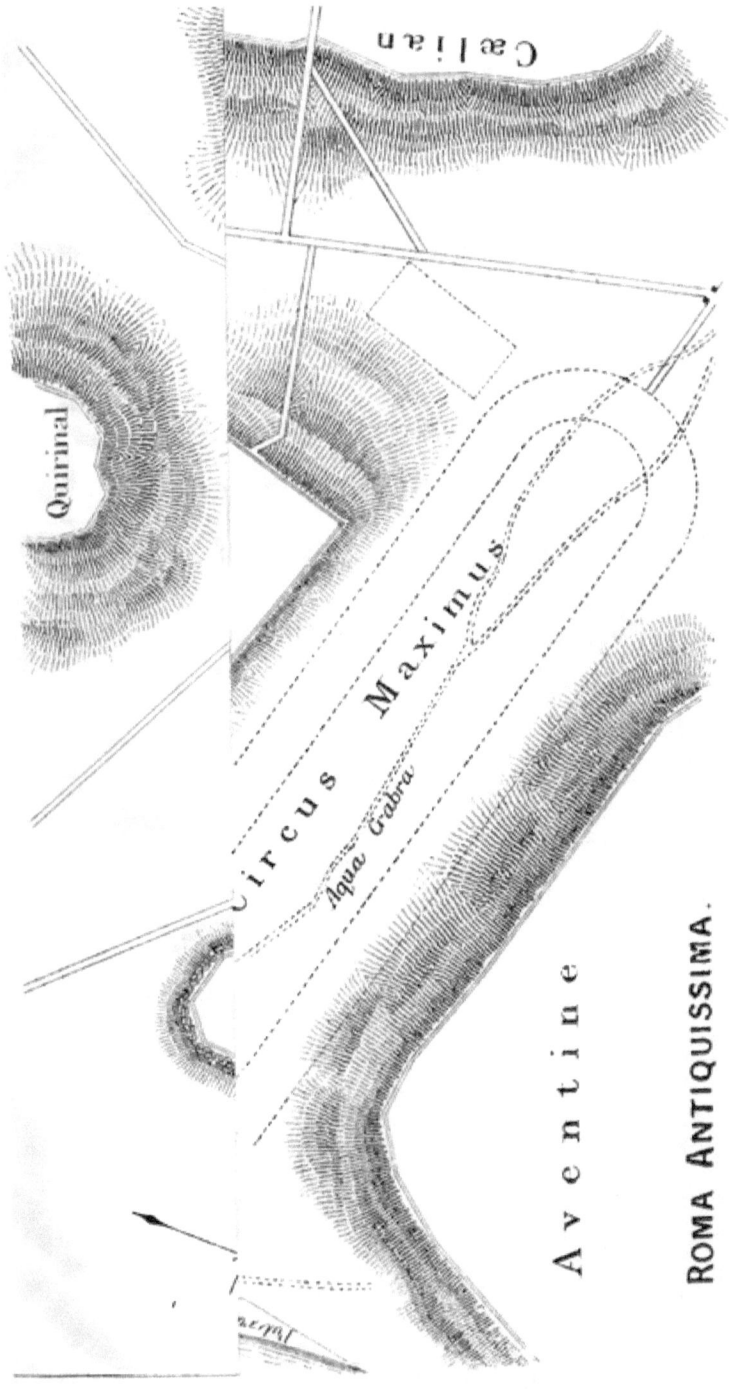

ROMA ANTIQUISSIMA.

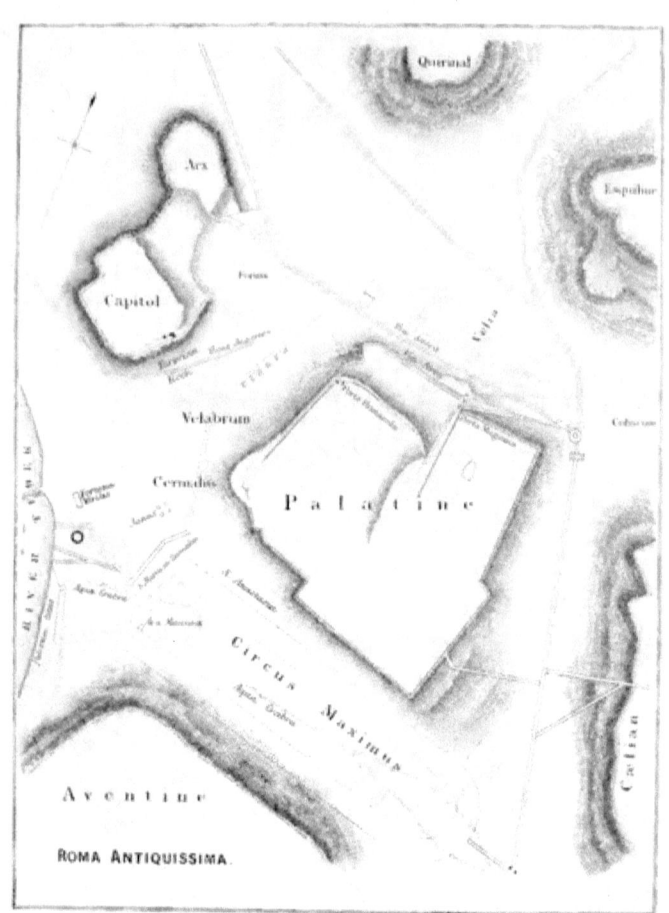

and earthquakes and the wasting hand of time during more than nineteen centuries. It bears the date of B.C. 27 on the frieze of its portico. The Theatre of Marcellus must be next mentioned, and the Mausoleum of Augustus. To the Julian dynasty may be also ascribed the colossal columns of the Temple of Mars Ultor, with the huge wall adjoining them, and the Egyptian obelisks which still decorate some of the piazzas. To the same dynasty we owe the vast arches of the Claudian aqueduct, and the massive brick foundation of the Palatine palace.

The Flavian dynasty, Vespasian, Titus, and Domitian changed the characteristic features of the city of Rome. Where Caligula and Nero had covered the ground with costly palaces and pleasure-grounds, the Flavian emperors built the resorts of military and of national life. The Coliseum and the Arch of Titus were the fit accompaniments of their world-subduing, blood-thirsty legions, and the Baths of Titus, and the public reception rooms on the Palatine, encouraged the citizen life of Rome once more to develop itself.

The political aims and imperial ideas of Trajan, Hadrian and the Antonines are nobly illustrated by the modifications and enlargements they introduced in the structure and extent of the city of Rome. Trajan in his magnificent Forum and library sought to encourage the metropolitan life and literary tastes of the nation, while on his storied column he recorded their world-wide triumphs and reminded them of their enormous power.

The Mausoleum of Hadrian remains to commemorate the vast and ponderous strength of his rule, and the Aurelian Column stands to attest the lofty magnificence of the Antonine dynasty.

In the reign of Commodus, between the Antonine era and the time of Severus, a great fire devastated the central districts of Rome. The restorations effected by Severus and the popular policy of his successors are commemorated in the Arch of Severus, the Portico of the Pantheon, and the huge ruins of the Baths of Caracalla. The defensive power of the Roman nation then became gradually weaker and weaker, till in sixty years after the time of Caracalla, Aurelian commenced the sad task of home fortification. His walls, which were completed a hundred years later by Honorius, still surround the greater part of Rome. During these hundred years the power of the Constantinian rule, of which the great basilica and arch remain monuments, and the warlike courage of Diocletian revived for a time the imperial spirit at Rome.

The last and most familiar of the monuments which follow the transfer of power from Rome to Constantinople is the Column of Phocas in the Forum, erected when three centuries of desolation had followed the grandeur of Constantine and his dynasty.

The Vatican Hill and the northern end of the Transtiberine district were not enclosed within walls till the time of Pope Leo IV. He undertook in A.D. 848 the enclosure of St. Peter's and the Vatican Hill, thus forming that district into a separate town, which was named after the Pope Civitas Leoniana. The western wall of this enclosure may still be traced by its ruins in the garden of the Vatican palace. After the successive destructions and minor repairs of the tenth, eleventh, twelfth, and thirteenth centuries, in 1527 the architect San Gallo was employed to erect huge bastions on the wall of Rome, which he placed chiefly between the Porta Ostiense and the Porta Appia. In 1628 Pope Urban VIII. restored the walls on the left bank, and subsequently in 1642 he proceeded to erect the walls which now stand between the Porta Portese and the Porta Cavallegieri, where the arms of that Pope are still affixed to the walls. This was the final important addition to the main walls of the city.

III.—ROMAN BUILDING AND ARCHITECTURE.

The earliest form of Roman masonry, consisting of rectangular tufa blocks placed in layers alternately parallel to and across the line of the wall, so as to bind the mass together firmly, may be best seen in the ancient fragments of the Servian wall on the Aventine and the Quirinal Hills and in the ruins on the western slope of the Palatine. This kind of building is the natural product of the peculiar parallel

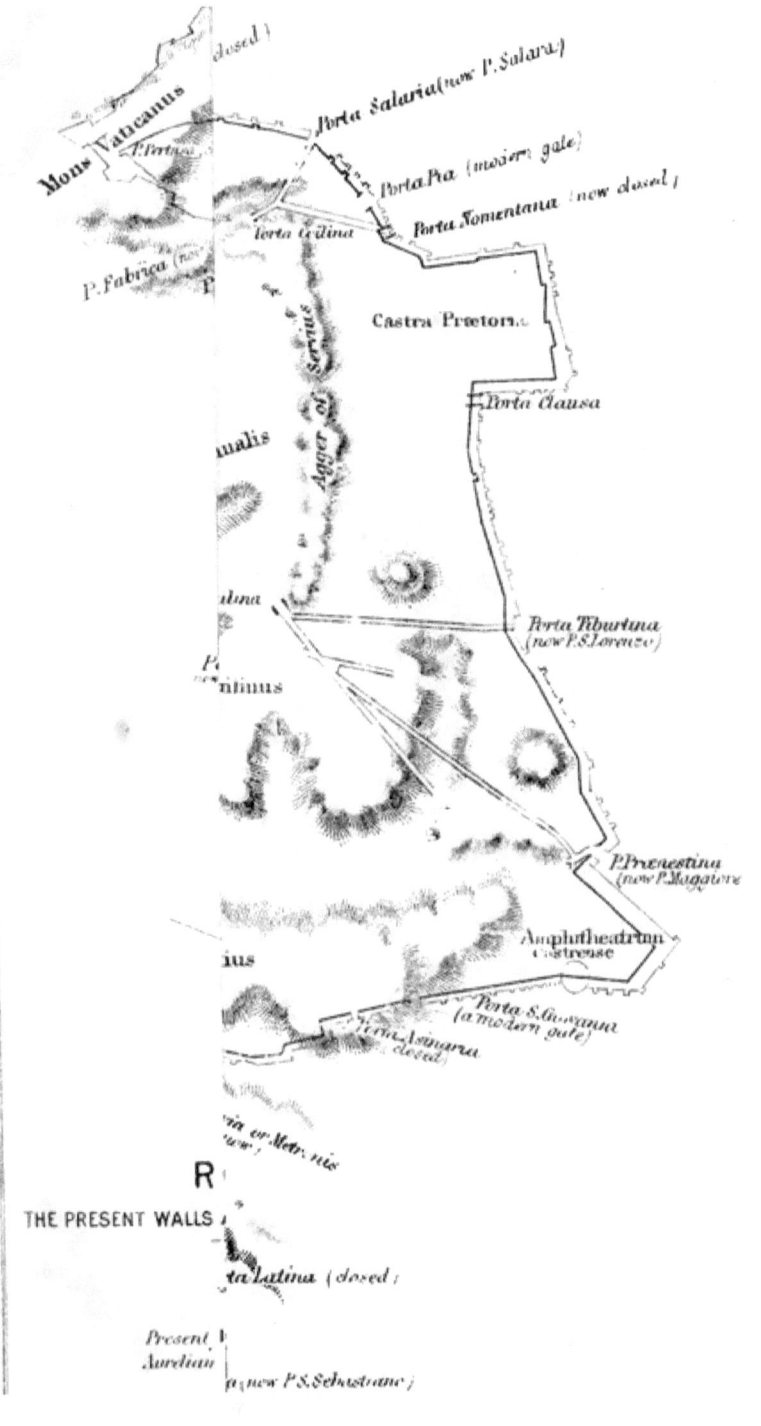

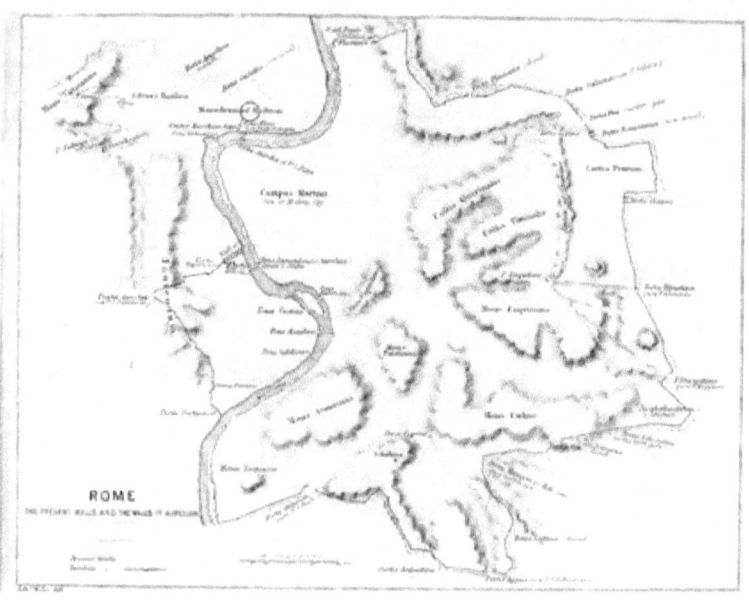

cleavage in the tufaceous rocks of the Roman hills. In those parts of the Campagna where basalt rather than tufa becomes the usual material, as at Præneste, we find polygonal masonry. One specimen of a mode of construction anterior to the introduction of the arch into Roman masonry is left us at Rome. This is the vault of the old well-house near the Capitol called the Mamertine Prison, where we find overlapping horizontal blocks of stone which originally met in a conical roof, but are now truncated and capped by a mass of stones cramped together with iron. That the principle of the arch was known in the regal period of Rome is shown by the great arch of the Cloaca Maxima. But no arches remain of so early a date which are not subterranean, and it is not likely that the arch was used in the early temples at Rome. These were, as we learn from Vitruvius, constructed in the so-called Tuscan style, which was the Italian contemporary of the Greek Doric. It is possible that the columns in the walls of S. Maria in Cosmedin, which are placed at unusual distances from each other, may have been an imperial restoration of the Temple of Ceres, after the old Tuscan fashion (Fig. 1). The next modification of architectural style, which is usually called, from the general influence of the Greek colonists on Latin art, the Tusco-Doric order, may be seen in the lowest range of columns and bases in the Theatre of Marcellus. The shaft of these columns is much more slender than in the Grecian Doric, and only partially fluted, if at all; while a cima recta is substituted for the echinus of the capitals (Figs. 2 and 3). The position of the triglyphs and the proportions of the cornice were also much changed, and the whole effect became less massive and bold than that of the Tuscan temples.

The ancient Tuscan arrangement of the interior of temples remained after this modification of their columns and capitals. The three ruins which now occupy the most prominent place at the northern end of the Forum, the Temples of Saturn, of Concord, and of Vespasian, all retain the plan called prostylos by Vitruvius. The Temple of Concord is especially remarkable for the union of a broad Tuscan cella with a narrow Greek portico. An alteration peculiarly Roman was made in the cella of the Greek temple. Instead of surrounding this part of a temple with rows of columns, the Romans clothed it with pilasters, thus introducing the mode of construction deservedly stigmatised by Vitruvius, under the name pseudoperipteral (Fig. 4). This may be seen in the ruin commonly called by the name of the Temple of Fortuna Virilis at Rome.

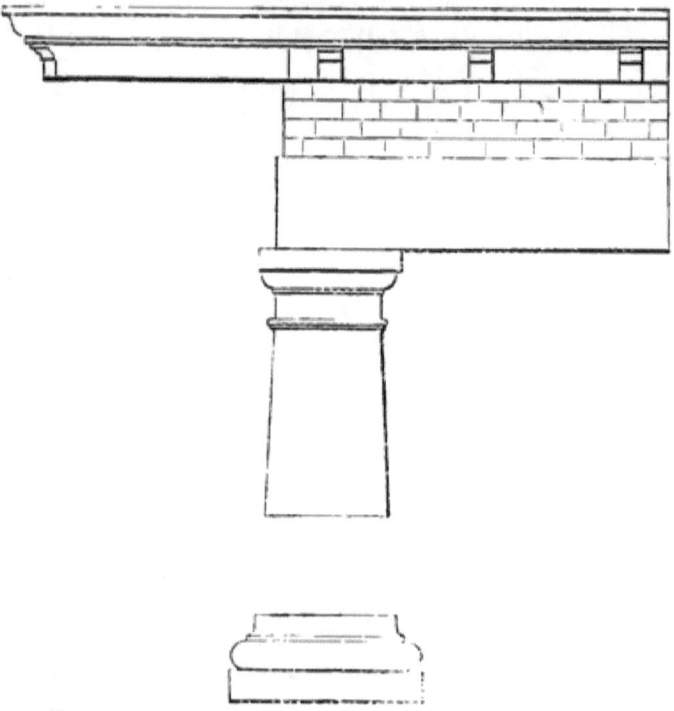

Fig. 1.

The Greek Ionic order became known and employed by the Romans early in the third century B.C. The Tomb of Scipio Barbatus shows the Ionic volute and dentil mixed with the Doric triglyph and gutta. The Roman alterations in the Ionic capital may be best seen in the pillars of the Temple of Saturn, and in the second range of columns surrounding the Theatre of Marcellus and the Coliseum. Specimens may also be seen in the basilica of S. Lorenzo fuori le Mura, and in the church of S. Maria in Trastevere, which have been transferred from the ancient temples. The distinctive Roman modification was the position of the volutes diagonally instead of laterally (Figs. 5 and 6).

It is supposed that the first introduction of the Greek

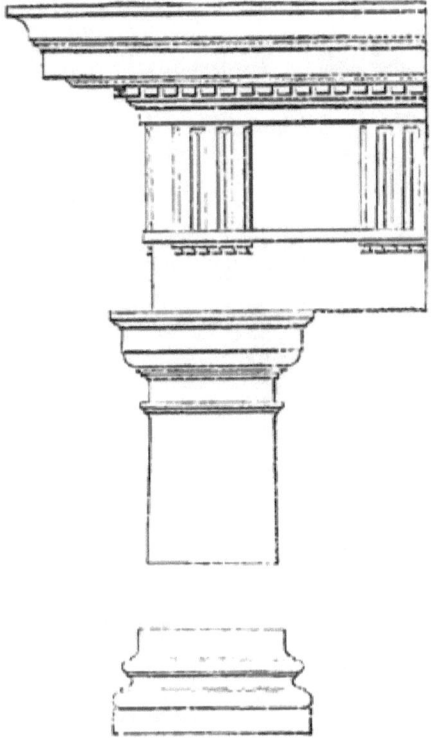

Fig. 2.

Corinthian order into Rome was brought about by the barbarian act of Sulla, in transporting the columns of the Temple of Zeus from Athens to the Capitoline Temple of Jupiter. Of the remaining specimens of this order in Rome, the portico of the Pantheon is the oldest. In that building the capitals appear somewhat shorter and broader than in the later examples, at the ruins of the Temple of Castor in the

Forum (Fig. 7), and in the peristyle of Nerva's Forum called the Colonnacce.

The Composite capital, for it can hardly be called an order, as there is nothing in the entablature or the base to distinguish it from the Corinthian, was formed probably under the patronage of the early emperors. The earliest instance we

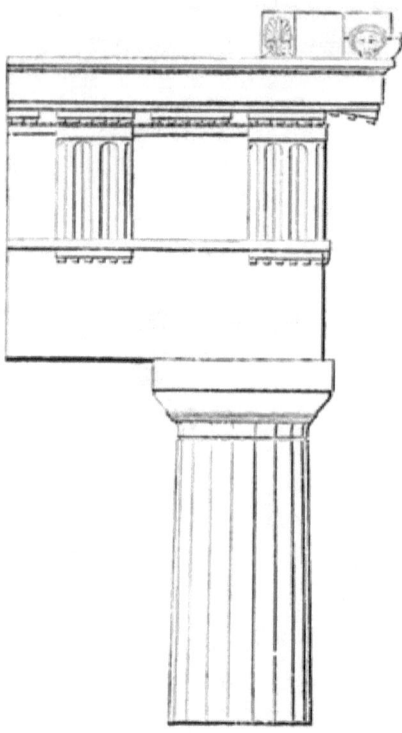

Fig. 3.

have of it now extant in Rome, is in the Arch of Titus (Fig. 8) and there are only three other ruins where it is found. These are, the Arch of Septimius Severus, the Arch of the Goldsmiths, and the Baths of Diocletian, at Sta. Maria degli Angeli, where it is mixed up with Corinthian capitals. The peculiar combination of which it consists, the superposition of the Ionic volutes upon two rings of Corinthian acanthus leaves, is not generally considered a very happy artistic design. Hope says of it, that "instead of being a new creation of genius, it gave evidence of poverty to invent and ignorance to combine," and Fergusson is hardly more complimentary to the Roman architects.

But though we must deny to this Roman adaptation of Greek forms the credit of originality, or even of symmetrical design, yet its rich appearance was peculiarly suited to the lavish ornamentation with which the Roman emperors delighted to trick out their palaces and halls, and it well represents to us the character of the Roman imperial architecture, with its indiscriminate combination of mouldings and profusion of gaudy detail.

The three great triumphal arches of Titus, Septimius Severus, and Constantine at Rome, and also the Arch of Drusus, are decorated with an unmeaning and foreign dress. In the Arch of Constantine alone, the columns which stand in front are in some measure justified by the statues they support.

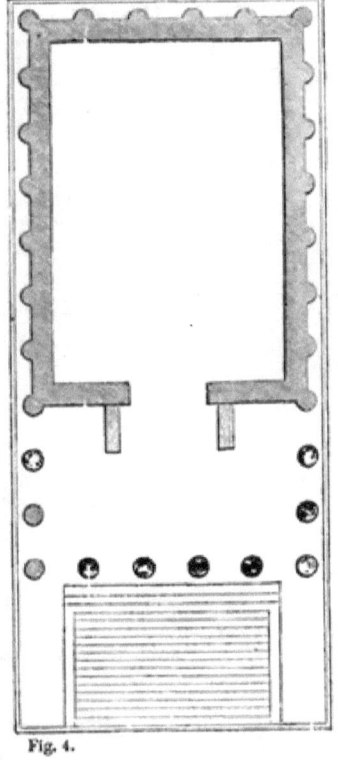

Fig. 4.

Of the minor archways at Rome, that of Gallienus has Corinthian pilasters in the roughest style of art, the Janus Quadrifrons probably had rows of Corinthian columns between its niches, and the small gateway near it has decorative pilasters with Composite capitals. On the other hand, the Arch of Dolabella on the Cælian, which has a single line as cornice, and the Porta S. Lorenzo are examples of the striking effect of a simple arch without Greek ornament. The unmeaning pediments and tasteless columns with which most of these arches are adorned, remind us of Pope's recipe for the front of a villa, "Clap four slices of pilaster on't; that, laid with bits of rustic, makes a front."

Colossal columns were as genuine a creation of Imperial

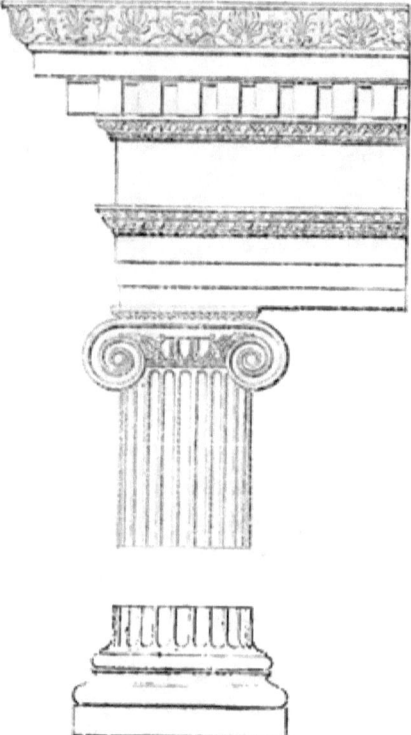

Fig. 5.

Rome as triumphal arches. In both the sculpture had become subordinate to the pedestal. The idea of placing a statue upon the top of a column was probably unknown to the Greeks, or at least, never carried out on the immense scale of the two great Roman Columns of Trajan and Marcus Aurelius. It must not, however, be forgotten, that the Column of Trajan, and probably also that of Marcus Aurelius, was enclosed within a narrow court, and that the bas-reliefs were intended to be seen from the roofs and windows of the surrounding buildings.

Some of the most characteristic remains of the Roman national taste in architecture are the Mausoleum of Hadrian, and the Tombs of Cæcilia Metella and of Plautius. The ponderous walls of these massive and indestructible marvels

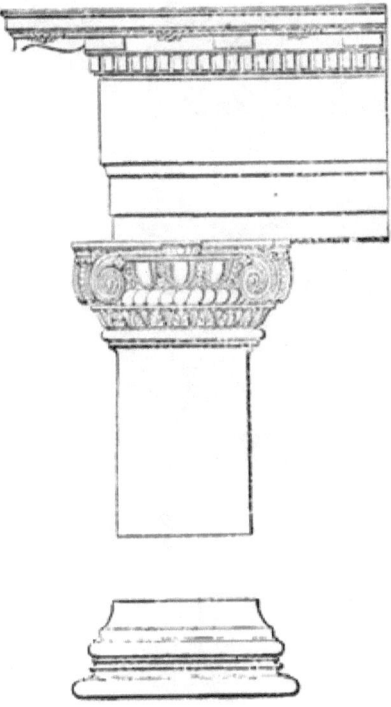

Fig. 6.

of masonry were essentially Roman, but in their external decorations we find a strange combination of foreign designs. The Mausoleum of Hadrian was dressed up with an array of pilasters, columns, and statues, and the Mausoleum of Augustus was covered with terraces and trees, in imitation of the Temple of Belus at Babylon.

The most conspicuous among the Roman appropriations of

foreign monumental designs were the oriental obelisks which were brought from Egypt, and erected in the Circi at Rome and in front of some of the buildings, and some of which still stand in the piazzas of modern Rome. The remains of eleven of these have been found. The Romans often misused

Fig. 7.

them by placing them alone, and not following the Egyptian method of always setting them in pairs.

The huge vaulted arches of brick-work and concrete which remain in the Baths of Caracalla, and the Basilica of Constantine, and the massive arches of the Claudian Aqueduct, are the glory of Roman architecture. For the Coliseum, astounding as are its durability and massive grandeur, is not so illustrative of the special Roman development of the use of the arch and of brick-work as are the other great ruins just mentioned. We see embodied in them the indomitable energy which bridged the valleys and tunnelled through the hills, but which possessed no eye for fine proportion of outline or symmetrical and harmonious combination of

Fig. 8.

details. Brickwork was the material in which the characteristic Roman ruins were executed. The Coliseum and the Theatre of Marcellus are dressed in Greek robes, while the brick arches of the aqueducts, and the massive structure of the Baths of Caracalla reflect the peculiar genius and character of the Roman imperial power.

CHAPTER I.

THE PALATINE AND VELIA.

THE entrance to the ruins on the Palatine Hill is now made through a gateway opposite to the Basilica of Constantine. This gateway was erected by the architect Vignola in the sixteenth century as an approach to the Farnese Gardens, which formerly occupied the north-western part of the Palatine Hill. On the right and left hand of the gateway are placed two ancient pedestals, which were discovered near the Arch of Septimius Severus in 1547. One of these, which stands on the right hand, supported an equestrian statue of Constantius, erected by Neratius Cerealis, prefect of the city in A.D. 353, in commemoration of the expulsion from Italy and death of Maxentius.[1] On the left side pedestal, a representation of the Suovetaurilia is sculptured in bas-relief, and the decennalia vota, or ten years' good wishes to Constantius and Galerius are mentioned. The side of the hill at the back of the gateway of Vignola is terraced at several levels, on the third of which ascending from the entrance, a part of the pavement of an old road, probably the Clivus Victoriæ, leads to the right. The line of this clivus is represented in the marble plan now on the staircase of the Capitoline Museum which plan was made in the time of Septimius Severus.

Clivus Victoriæ.

The basalt paving stones of this road are well preserved. On the right hand proceeding towards the northern angle of the hill lie a number of fragments of ancient houses, among which were probably the house bought by Clodius and that of Cicero. These houses appear to have looked down upon the Forum, since Cicero speaks of raising his house in order to exclude Clodius from the sight of the city which he had

---

[1] See Corp. Inscr. Lat. vol. vi. 1, No. 1158.

INDEX TO THE PLAN OF THE PALATINE RUINS.

1, 2. Entrance.
3. Clivus Victoriæ.
4. Museum.
5. Water reservoir.
6. Fragments of ruins.
7. Altar of Calvinus.
8. Fragments of ruin.
9. Domus Gelotiana.
10. Figure of crucified ass.
11. Stadium Palatinum.
12. Exedra.
13. Baths.
14. Palatine Belvedere.
15. Imperial Box over Circus.
16. Augustan Palace.
17. Ruin called the Academy.
18. Triclinium.
19. Viridarium.
20. Peristylium.
21. Smaller chambers.
22. Basilica.
23. Imperial reception hall.
24. Lararium.
25. Area Palatina.
26. Fragment of ancient ruin.
27. Clivus Palatinus.
28. Porta Mugionia.
29. Temple of Jupiter Stator.
30. Walls of substruction.
31. Cryptoporticus.
32. Subterranean passage.
33. Piscina.
34. House of Tiberius.
35. Well.
36. Unknown ruins.
37. So-called Temple of Jupiter Victor.
38. Uncertain basements. Scala Caci.
39. So-called Auguratorium.
40. Soldiers' quarters.
41. Garden.
42, 43. Staircase and substructions of Caligula's buildings.
44. Ruins of lavacrum of Heliogabalus.

⇉ Path to be followed.

To face Plan on p. 14.

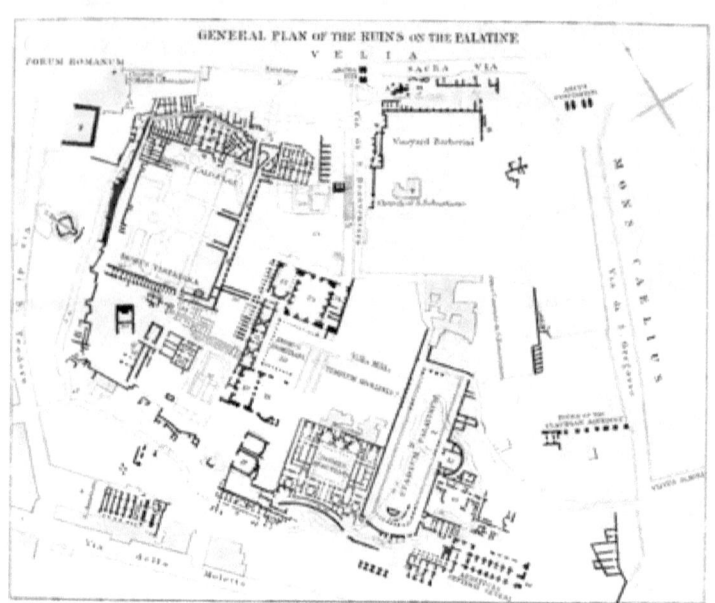

hoped to destroy.[1] Other houses of the Roman nobility of the later republican times were probably placed on this side of the Palatine, in order to be near the Forum and the places of political and social meetings.[2]

The Museum in which are collected the various fragments of statuary and antiquarian interest which have been found in the late excavations on the Palatine has been placed in the ground-floor of the casina which stands near the Clivus Victoriæ. The ancient road is then overreached and arched over by the extensions of the Palatine imperial palace built by Caligula, under which it passes to the site of the ancient Porta Romanula.[3] Most of the chambers on the left were probably occupied by the guards of the gateway, and the graffiti they contain are of a character which confirms this supposition. *Porta Romanula.*

Outside the Porta Romanula the road bends round the hill along the side which looks towards the Capitoline. The first ruins to be seen under the slope of the hill here are the remains of a portico of the republican era, constructed of tufa with reticular-work facings. This portico has been supposed to be possibly that which Lutatius Catulus built after his victory over the Cimbri in the Area Flacciana, mentioned by Valerius Maximus and by Cicero as being near his house.[4] But there seems to be nothing left which can identify this ruin with the Porticus Catuli.

Beyond this so-called Area Flacciana the line of walls presents some projecting masses, which appear to be built upon the ancient substructions of towers such as would be formed in fortified buildings. A great part of the walls erected here in imperial times were built of concrete framed and supported by beams and planks of timber. These beams having now rotted away, have left their impressions on the *Area Flacciana.*

---

[1] Cic. de Har. Resp. xv., 33. Vettius, in Cic. ad Att. ii. 24, calls Cicero "vicinus consulis," i.e. near the Regia.
[2] See 'Rome and the Campagna,' ch. viii. p. 160.
[3] Festus, p. 262, " infimo clivo Victoriæ."
[4] A descent to the right to the Forum has been observed by a French architect. See 'Le Forum Romain,' par Dutert; Lévy, Paris, 1876, p. 14. 'Guida del Palatino,' p. 71. Valerius Maximus, vi. 3, 1. Cic. pro Dom. 38. 102.

concrete, and hence the vertical and horizontal grooves which form so conspicuous a part of these walls. Two remarkable fragments of antiquity must be noticed here. The first is a conical aperture in the side of the hill which supplied a cistern placed below with water. Such cisterns are to be found elsewhere in the hills, and may be supposed to have been constructed previous to the great supplies of water having been brought by the aqueducts.

At the western corner of the hill opposite to the Janus Quadrifrons stands a large fragment of the most ancient walls of the Palatine. It is constructed of masses of tufa, taken from the hill behind it, and roughly laid together without cement or mortar. These stones appear to have been split from the rock, and not cut by chisel, which shows the antiquity of their construction. The wall of Romulus is the name by which this and the other portions of massive tufa walls round the Palatine are now known. They undoubtedly belong to the earliest defences of the Palatine settlement.

Altar.

Not far from this ancient fragment of wall stands a most interesting relic of primitive superstition, an altar of travertine stone cut in archaic fashion, with volutes resembling those in the well-known tomb of Scipio in the Vatican Museum. The inscription on this altar is as follows: SEI DEO SEI DEIVÆ SAC. C. SEXTIUS, C. F. CALVINUS, PR. DE SENATI SENTENTIA RESTITUIT. This is supposed by some antiquarians to be the altar mentioned by Cicero and Livy, as having been erected in consequence of the voice heard before the Gallic invasion predicting disastrous times.[1]

But that altar is said to have been placed above the Temple of Vesta at the end of the Nova Via, which was on the other side of the Palatine. This mode of dedication to an unknown Deity was not uncommon at Rome, and is mentioned by Cato and commented upon by Gellius. The form of the word DEIVÆ shows that the inscription belongs to the earlier Latin.[2]

C. Sextius Calvinus, who restored the altar, was probably

[1] Cic. de Div. i. 45; ii. 32. Liv. v. 32.
[2] Corp. Inscr. i. 632. Wordsworth, Frag. of early Latin, p. 167, 410.

son of C. S. Calvinus, the Consul of A.U.C. 630, and was the competitor of C. Servilius Glaucia in the year 654.[1]

The north-western end of the Palatine Hill, round which we have been passing, was the spot whence arose the name Germalus which Varro tells us was given to it in memory of the (germani) twin brothers, Romulus and Remus having been cast ashore here from the Tiber waters, and suckled by the wolf. How far the district called Germalus extended over the hill is not known. Cicero speaks of a house belonging to Milo which stood upon the Germalus, and Livy says that a wolf ran through the Vicus Tuscus and the Germalus to the Porta Capena.[2] The bronze figure of the wolf and twins now in the Capitoline Museum is said by Flaminius Vacca, who wrote in 1594, to have been found at no great distance from this place, and Urlichs has shown that this figure is probably the one dedicated by the Ogulnii, ædiles in B.C. 297.[3] _{Germalus.}

Further southwards at the foot of the slope we come to another fragment of the most ancient wall of the Palatine settlement. This building appears to stand at right angles to the line of the hillside, and it was therefore supposed at first to have belonged to a wall traversing the intermontium or depression which crosses the Palatine Hill from this point to the Arch of Titus, and to have confirmed the opinion of those archæologists who confine the extent of Roma quadrata to the north-western end of the hill. But subsequent exploration has shown that this wall does not pass along the intermontium, but turns off at a right angle. Another fragment of the most ancient wall was found in 1860, according to Lanciani, under the Villa Mills, showing that the wall of Roman quadrata passed round the whole hill, and not only round the north-western end.

Close to the fragment of ancient wall we come to a series of chambers excavated first in 1857, and afterwards cleared and rendered more accessible in 1869. These belonged to a building in connection with this part of the imperial palace, and were occupied by soldiers of the emperor's guard, as may _{Domus Gelotiana.}

---

[1] Cic. de Orat. ii. 249.
[2] Cic. ad Att. iv. 3, 3. Liv. xxxiii. 26.
[3] Vacca Memorie 3, Urlichs, in Rheinisches Museum, 1846.

be seen by examination of the inscriptions left on the walls. The traces of a square court, surrounded with a portico, one granite pillar of which remains, and on the side of this court towards the hill, of a number of chambers arranged on each side of a semicircular recess, are the main features of this ruin. The brickwork supports which appear here were erected by Canina, and a large quantity of remains have fallen from the higher levels of the hill.

The inscriptions which are most remarkable are the following. On the right-hand wall near the entrance the name HILARUS, followed by the letters MI. V. D. N., which have been interpreted to mean "miles veteranus domini nostri," a veteran soldier of our Lord. Numerous other inscriptions with the letters V. D. N. will be found in the chamber to the left of the central recess. One of these in the triangular room records the name of two soldiers who belonged to the foreign troop of Peregrini: BASSUS ET SATURUS PEREG.[1] Other inscriptions allude to a paedagogium, or training school, as for example, CORINTHUS EXIT DE PEDAGOGIO. Most of these are in the triangular rooms behind the central semicircular recess, or in the furthest room on the left of it. In this last is to be seen the figure of an ass turning a mill, with the inscription, LABORA ASELLE QUOMODO EGO LABORAVI ET PRODERIT TIBI. But the most famous of these graffiti is that now shown in the Kircherian Museum representing the crucified ass, with the title "Alexamenus worshipping his god," which was taken from the room on the right of the central semicircular recess, and has been the subject of much comment. Another record of the same Alexamenus was found here in 1870, in which he is called Alexamenus fidelis.

Stadium. Passing now beneath the Villa Mills which occupy the site of the Augustan library, and the Temple of Apollo, built by Augustus, we turn to the left up the slope of the hill and find a large open space in which the later excavations have disinterred the relics of a stadium, consisting of a curved series of walls, surrounding the foundation of a meta or goal,

---

[1] See Henzen, in Bull. dell. Inst., 1867. The name of Domus Gelotiana has been given to this ruin by Visconti. See 'Rome and the Campagna,' p. 181.

and two lines of bases of columns, which ran along the sides and the end of the stadium.[1]

A large building in the form of a semicircular recess of exedra, a stand for viewing the races, is still partially remaining, and also the foundation of two entrances on the southern side. That this was a stadium connected with the imperial palace is evident from its shape and its length, which corresponds to that laid down by the ancient writers as the proper length of a stadium for foot-races. The large exedra at the southern side contains on the ground-floor a vast central saloon, and two side rooms. A few decorative paintings of the latest and least valuable kind of art remain on the walls, among which are some geographical and astronomical figures. A coat of foreign marbles covered the walls, and the pavement was of marble. This part of the Palatine buildings was probably occupied by the Frangipani in the 13th century. The right-hand chamber was apparently without decoration, but in the one on the left the wall is ornamented with fresco paintings of elegance, and the pavement is of fine mosaic. A list of names with numbers attached to them, which seem to be those of combatants in the stadium, was found among the graffiti here.

The upper level of the semicircular exedra was filled by a large chamber, the side of which, towards the stadium, was occupied by a line of granite columns, fragments of which remain in the arena below. The interior of this chamber was also ornamented with marbles and statues. Some statues of Amazons and the Hercules of Lysippus now in the Pitti at Florence, were found here according to Vacca, who wrote at the end of the sixteenth century. The brickwork and the architecture of this exedra seem to be of the time of Hadrian, and the bricks found here with labels give the date of A.D. 134, the third consulship of Ursus Servianus. The portico which ran round the stadium was apparently of later construction than the exedra, as the date on its bricks seems to refer to

[1] The marks on the bricks found here bear the names of Clonius and Ernetes, freedmen of the Gens Domitia, but the walls which stand near the meta are constructed of materials which show that they are of later date, and belong to the Restoration of Theodoric, A.D. 500.

Tertullus Scapula, Consul in A.D. 195, in the reign of Septimius Severus, under whom great alterations and extensions were carried out in this wing of the palace.

The vast ruins which remain on the south of the stadium belong chiefly to the works of Septimius Severus, and have long been celebrated as the most picturesque among the Cæsarean relics. The curved wall behind the great exedra, and the numerous passages and chambers which stand near it, seem to have belonged to a bath supplied with water from the branch of the Aqua Claudia, four arches of which are still remaining on the hill below, opposite to the church of S. Gregorio. This was a branch from the Claudian aqueduct, and crossed the valley from the opposite Cælian Hill.

Palatine Belvedere. The lofty wing of the palace, which extends along the slope of the Circus Maximus, opposite to the Aventine, is reached by a modern bridge from the ruins adjoining the stadium. From the top of this huge ruin a splendid view of the Cælian, the Aventine, and the Alban Hills may be seen, and the spot has been sometimes called the Palatine Belvedere. What the exact nature of the buildings placed upon these lofty ranges of arches was cannot be easily determined, but they correspond in some degree to the arched walls of the side between the arches of Titus and Constantine and to those of the palace of Caligula near the Capitoline, and were mainly intended to raise the imperial saloons to the higher level of the northern end of the hill. Spartianus in his 'Life of Severus' says that Severus bestowed particular pains on this part of the Palatine Hill in order to make it the chief entrance to the imperial palace, and that his reason for so doing was to produce an impression of his magnificence upon his African fellow-countrymen, who, when visiting Rome, would naturally enter at this point by the Porta Capena, which was the gate just below. The Septizonium was an imperial building near this part of the hill probably built by Severus, views of the ruins of which are to be seen in the books of the topographers Du Perac and Garrucci who wrote before the end of the sixteenth century, when the Septizonium was pulled down by Sixtus the Fifth.[1] At the

---

[1] Hist. Aug. Severus, 19, 24. See 'Rome and the Campagna,' p. 180.

western end of the long and lofty ruin, and near the end of the stadium, is a projecting portion of ruined chambers which has been generally supposed to have contained the emperor's private pulvinar, or box whence he viewed the games in the Circus Maximus. But the construction of this edifice, including its round tower, seems to be of a very late style, and it may have been built as late as the sixteenth century.

We now return along a modern path which runs under the grounds of the Villa Mills towards the domus Gelotiana described above. A curved terrace occupies the upper edge of the hill, along which probably ran a portico commanding a view over the southern part of Rome and the Trastevere. At the back of this are the buildings called the Villa Mills from their former possessors, now occupied by a nunnery, and therefore inaccessible to the public. In the year 1777, the plan of the ancient buildings which stood here was explored by Rancoureuil. They consist of a court surrounded with columns and suites of chambers. Parts of the main front looking towards the circus remained till the year 1827. The brickwork of these ruins has induced Cav. Rosa to assign them to the Augustan Age and to call them Domus Augustana. No sure evidence has, however, been discovered for this, and it seems more probable that the Domus Augustana was nearer to the Forum Romanum.[1]

Passing back again by the ruins called the Domus Gelotiana as before described, we turn to the right and ascend the side of the hill. On the higher level at this point are the ruins of two buildings to which the names of Academia and Bibliotheca have been given by Rosa. In one of these the remains of semicircular ranges of seats and a platform have been supposed to be recognizable, and here may have taken place the recitations and discussions mentioned by Pliny as constantly kept up in the imperial palace.[2]

Academia and Bibliotheca.

Behind these rooms stand the ruins of a portico, built upon substructions of an earlier period, with Corinthian columns of cipollino, probably forming the side of a small courtyard. Here it may be seen through an opening in the ground to

[1] See 'Rome and the Campagna,' pp. 174, 200.   [2] Plin. Ep. I. 13.
[3] See 'The Journal of Philology,' Cambridge 1869, vol. ii. p. 89.

Ædes Publicæ. what a depth the substructions of this part of the Palatine buildings descend into the depression or intermontium which originally separated the two parts of the hill, and was filled up by the Flavian emperors. We now enter the range of reception rooms commenced by Vespasian when he destroyed Nero's golden house, and built by Vespasian and his sons, Titus and Domitian, at the same time with the Coliseum. These are raised on gigantic constructions of opus quadratum to the level of the rest of the Palatine Hill. Many stamps on the bricks found here seem to show that the buildings were finished by Domitian.

Triclinium. The south-eastern side of the range of the Imperial Flavian buildings we are now entering is still covered by the edge of the monastery which occupies the grounds of the Villa Mills, and we can therefore only see the north-western part. But this is sufficient to convey a full idea of the extent of the suite. We are now entering at the back of the triclinium or dining hall, at the end of which is a semicircular apse, possibly intended for the emperor's table when he dined here. The form of the room corresponds to Vitruvius' description of the proper arrangements for a triclinium. Very little of the original decoration remains, except two granite columns, of which there were originally sixteen, and a portion of beautiful pavement composed of porphyry, serpentine, and giallo antico. It is possible that this may be the triclinium in which Statius dined at Domitian's table, and of the marble decorations and spacious size of which he speaks in the fourth book of his 'Silvæ.'[1]

Near the apse of this room an opening in the ground leads down to some subterranean rooms which formerly belonged to a private house situated in the depression of the hill, and afterwards covered over by the Flavian emperors. The brickwork in this house seems to be of the later republican period, and the walls retain decorations of the best style.

These decorative paintings have, of course, suffered very much from damp and neglect, and all the principal features of the house have been destroyed by the substructures of the

---

[1] Stat. Silv., iv. 2, 26.

Flavian triclinium. The name of Bagni di Livia was long used in connection with this spot by the ciceroni.

Returning to the upper level, we find, at the side of the triclinium, the remains of a nymphæum or viridarium, consisting of an elliptical basin and fountain of marble, with niches for statues and bas reliefs, and ledges for ornamental flowers and plants. On the western side of the nymphæum a garden-house was built by the Farnese, part of which still stands, the portico having some arabesques and some paintings by a pupil of Taddeo Zuccari, representing scenes on the Palatine as described by Virgil, the meeting of Æneas and Evander, and the monster Cacus. Nymphæum.

Beyond the triclinium and nymphæum we come to the remains of the largest court in the suite, which is called the peristylium, occupying a space of 140 by 154 paces, anciently surrounded by a portico of columns of Porta Santa marble. The pavement and decorations of this quadrangle would seem by the remains to have been most superb. On the northwest side of it are eight rooms of various shapes, arranged symmetrically round an octagonal central chamber, from which four large doors open, with four corresponding niches. The same plan of rooms was carried out also on the opposite side of the peristylium, as was shown by some excavations in 1869. These were waiting-rooms and offices of various kinds. From the great quadrangle of the peristylium we pass to the grand audience chamber, the position of which corresponds generally to that of the atrium of a Roman house. This was surrounded by a portico of sixteen Corinthian columns of foreign marbles, and their frieze and bases were ornamented in a most elaborate manner. Eight niches with colossal statues of basalt are said by Bianchini to have stood round this court, and in the Tribune at the southern end was placed the solium augustale, where the emperor sat on grand occasions, when meetings of the senate or other bodies were held here. The grand entrance of this atrium, which looked towards the Arch of Titus, was adorned by two huge columns of giallo antico, and the threshold stone consisted of a mass of Greek marble from which the altar of the church of the Pantheon was made. Many of the Peristylium. Vestibulum. Atrium.

marbles from this atrium were taken by the Farnese to Naples.

Lararium. On the right hand of this reception room towards the Villa Mills was a building which shows us by its position and shape that it was the lararium or shrine of the household gods where sacrifices were offered on solemn occasions. The remains of an altar were discovered here.

Basilica. Opposite to the lararium are the foundations of a building with a tribune and podium, probably used by the emperor in cases such as those described by Tacitus, when imperial constraint was exercised over a legal verdict. Two rows of columns, arranged as is commonly the case in the basilicæ, and a portion of some white marble railings have been found and preserved here.

Along the side of this tribunal hall and that of the peristylium and its adjoining offices, ran a long portico connecting the whole suite of halls together.

The history of this range of imperial buildings has been very probably supposed to be as follows. Vespasian intended them to be used in support of his revival of the Augustan imperial policy, and that a name such as Ædes Publicæ, "National Chambers," should be given to them.[1]

Accordingly, all these rooms have the character of public rather than private buildings. There is apparently no provision for domestic life, and all the sections of the edifice seem to have been public audience or banqueting rooms.

Porta Mugionia. In front of the last described buildings, which we have called the basilica, the atrium, and the lararium, is an open space, on the right hand of which, looking towards the Arch of Titus, a fragment of the earliest walls of the Palatine remains, constructed of tufa blocks taken from the hill underneath. Beyond this, towards the Arch of Titus, are the paving stones of an ancient road which was probably the approach to the palace, and to the left of this road stand the relics of one of the most ancient gates, the Porta Mugionia. This is described by Vacca as having been discovered at the

---

[1] The name Basilica Jovis, placed here by Rosa, probably refers to a temple and not to this tribunal.
Plin. Panegyr., 47.

end of the sixteenth century, when it was still decorated
with marble. The substructions alone now remain, and close
to them may still be traced the foundations of an ancient
temple which can be no other than the temple of Jupiter
Stator. Solinus says that the house of Tarquinius Priscus
was near the Porta Mugionia, and Livy states that he lived
near the Porta Mugionia. The statue of Cloelia is also said
by Livy to have stood at the top of the Sacra Via which was
near the Arch of Titus, and this statue is further placed by
Pliny near the Porta Mugionia.[1] The remains of the temple
show that it was arranged according to the cardinal points of
the heavens, looking north and south. On the foundation
stones are the names of Philocrates and Diocles, masons
employed in building. Three old inscriptions referring to
the worship of Jove were found here, and are to be seen in
the Palatine Museum. *Jupiter Stator.*

Near the ruins of this Temple of Jupiter Stator we find
vast blocks of substruction which belong to the complicated
ranges of buildings occupying the north-eastern end of the
hill, and generally believed to have been erected by Caligula.
They extend along the side of the hill over the Forum, and
along the Clivus Victoriae by which we entered, to the point
which overlooks the Velabrum. The modifications and
enlargements of this structure during the ages succeeding
Caligula have rendered it a confused mass of ruins, and the
walls and chambers now left have served chiefly as substructions for the lofty mansions erected upon them in the course
of ages. From the corner of these ruins, next to the Temple
of Jupiter Stator, runs a long arched cryptoporticus or
covered passage, which can be entered from the ruins of
this temple or from below nearer to the modern entrance
gateway. It is supposed that this may have been the
cryptoporticus in which, as we learn from Josephus,
Caligula was assassinated on his return from the ludi palatini
given in front of the palace. He is said to have turned off
from the direct line of entrance, and to have passed into this
covered way in order to hear and see some youths from Asia
performing. The assassins, after accomplishing their end, *Crypto- porticus.*

[1] 'Rome and the Campagna,' p. 34.

were afraid to venture through the front of the palace, and took refuge by hiding in the house of Germanicus.[1]

House of Tiberius.

At the western end of the cryptoporticus a house has been disinterred by the late excavations, and it has been inferred that this must have been the one called by Josephus the house of Germanicus. Whatever name may now be assigned to it, the house appears to have been preserved for some reason from destruction, and it seems reasonable to conclude that some connection with the earlier history of the imperial Cæsars rendered it an object of veneration and care. The space between the cryptoporticus, along which we have passed, and the so-called basilica of the palace, is supposed to have been called the Area Palatina, where those who came to call upon the emperor had to wait.[2] The long cryptoporticus was connected with the Flavian public buildings, and perhaps also previously with the house of Augustus, by a branch passage which runs off from the long cryptoporticus at right angles, towards the back of the atrium and lararium. By this means the emperor could pass from his private palace to the public audience and banqueting chambers without encountering the crowd of those who were waiting for audience in the area. In this area was found, in 1868, the pedestal bearing the name of Domitius Calvinus, now placed on the site of the ruined temple which lies farther to the west, and which we shall presently mention.

In the angle of the cryptoporticus near the house of Germanicus, are some beautiful remains of decorative work, consisting of paintings of birds and winged genii. These have been much injured by the damp exuding from a piscina which was constructed here in the second or third century for the keeping of fish, and which can be entered at the angle of the cryptoporticus. Near this piscina is the entrance to the building called the house of Tiberius or Germanicus. The construction of this house belongs to the period of Roman architecture, when reticulated work formed of the harder tufa, with small diamond-shaped stones, and with corners and connecting parts of the same stone, but without brickwork, was generally used. It was therefore

[1] Josephus, Ant. Jud. xix. 1, 15. [2] Gell. N. A. xx. 1, 2.

probably built during the later republican times, and this agrees with the supposition that it was the works of Tiberius's father or grandfather. Suetonius says that Tiberius was born on the Palatine.[1] The leaden pipes which have been found here, bear the names of Julia, the daughter of Titus, of one of Domitian's, and one of Septimius Severus's freedmen.

The house is divided into two main parts, one of larger dimensions for receiving guests and showing hospitality, and the other of smaller sized rooms, for the family. The vestibule is an arched passage adorned with paintings on the walls, and mosaic pavement. From this the atrium is entered which had no impluvium, but was covered entirely with a roof. On the left are the remains of an altar of the Lares, and at the further side of the atrium are three large rooms, the decorative paintings of which are well preserved.

In the central chamber, the walls are divided into large compartments by columns of the Composite order, adorned with vine leaves. One of the large scenes represented here is that of Polyphemus, who, after having crushed his rival Acis with an enormous rock, turns towards Galatea, who is riding on a hippocampus. Another, placed above the frieze, is a picture of a domestic initiation ceremony, as the sacred tænia which is being presented seems to prove. A third picture, also above the frieze, shows the preparations for a sacrifice. On the right sits a female figure, with a mantle, and a faun standing before some utensils for ablution, which are being lifted by a second female figure, while the sacrificial kid is being brought by a young slave. The next picture represents a row of houses along the side of a street or road, at the door of one of which a lady with her maid is knocking, while four or five figures present themselves above on the balconies. The last picture is one of Io hidden in the wood of Juno at Mycenæ, and watched by Argos, with a figure of Hermes descending by Jove's command to rescue Io. The names of Io, Argos, and Hermes are legible here.

The room on the left hand of this one is also divided by Composite columns adorned with vine leaves, and by a

[1] Suet. Tib. 5.

beautiful frieze of giallo antico. The lower compartments have no figures, but the upper are ornamented with designs of genii and fantastic flowers.

The room on the right hand is decorated with beautifully-designed paintings of flowers and fruit, hanging from one column to the next. From these festoons hang the emblems of various divinities, the lyre of Apollo, the timbrel of Cybele, and the mystic sieve and mask of Bacchus. These seem to indicate that this was the lararium of the house. The frieze contains a number of landscape and marine views, with many figures of men and animals painted on a yellow ground.

At the north-western corner of the atrium opens a fourth chamber, which may perhaps have been the dining-room, or triclinium, decorated with trophies of sacred emblems of Diana and Apollo. The atrium communicates with the rooms at the back of the house and with a small courtyard by means of a corridor. Some of these rooms were used as baths, others seem to have opened towards the street, the pavement of which still remains along the side of the house.

Palatine temples.

On the other side of this street is an entrance to the subterranean caves which have been cut in this part of the hill. These hollows were mainly stone quarries and wells. A puteal, or well-cover, has been placed over one of these in front of the house which we have described. On this side of the street also stand the foundations which have been supposed to have belonged to the priests of the Temple of Jupiter Propugnator on the Palatine, some portions of the fasti of whose college have been found near the Basilica Julia and the Marforio.[1] There is also the foundation of a temple, called by Rosa the Temple of Jupiter Victor, to be seen extending from this street towards the viridarium of the aedes publicae of Domitian before mentioned, and towards the edge of the hill which looks over the Circus Maximus. These ruins consist of masses of tufa work mixed with later brickwork of the Antonine times. The pedestal with the name of Gnaeus Domitius Calvinus which is placed here came, as we have said, from the spot called the Area Palatina before men-

[1] Orelli, Inser. 6057, 6058.

tioned. The Notitia also places the Temple of Jupiter Victor in the Area Palatina, and for these two reasons the name seems to be wrongly applied to this ruin. We can trace in it the remains of a building raised on a basement with lofty flights of steps, alternating with terraces in front, towards the Circus Maximus, just as we find at Tibur and at Tusculum temples, placed on the side of a hill with high flights of steps ascending to them.[1]

The remainder of the upper level of this north-western corner of the hill is occupied by numerous ruins of squared tufa stone, which evidently belonged to some of the most ancient and venerated relics of Rome. This was, no doubt, the part of the Palatine to which the name Germalus was given, in memory of the Germani, or twin-brothers, Romulus and Remus, who were cast ashore at its foot from the flooded waters of the Tiber. Two distinct edifices have been disclosed here, from the first of which, a rectangular foundation of tufa stones, a passage bearing marks of great antiquity descends towards the church of Anastasia and the gas works. This rectangular ruin has been called by many various names, such as the Temple of Jupiter Feretrius, the Tugurium Faustuli, the Temple of the Magna Mater Cybele, or of the Lares Præstites. The descending passage to the Vallis Murcia has been supposed to be the Scala Caci mentioned by Solinus,[2] and it is possible that the legend of Cacus refers to this point of the Palatine next to the Aventine. The marks on the stones of this descent are probably only quarry marks. No brickwork is found here in the lower ruins, nor any marbles. But in the mass of fragments there are remains of the republican and of the imperial restorations of the many venerated buildings and altars which must have stood upon this corner of the hill. On the right hand of this descent a small rectangular court was discovered in 1872, with a staircase and a channel for water running through it. This is thought by Lanciani to have been possibly the fifth Argean Chapel, which was somewhere on the Germalus. A statue found here bears some marks of having represented the goddess Cybele.

Germalus and Scala Caci.

[1] See 'Rome and the Campagna,' p. 178.   [2] Solinus, i. 18.

Auguratorium.

The most conspicuous ruin at this end of the hill is a mass of concrete and tufa blocks, apparently of the republican era, in the shape of a rectangular basement. This has the form of a temple in antis, *i.e.* with projecting wings, and faces the south, commanding a view over the Aventine and Tiber valley. Cav. Rosa has conjectured that this is the ruin of the auguratorium mentioned by the Notitia as situated near the other most ancient sacred spots on the Palatine. But an inscription which records the restoration of the auguratorium by Hadrian does not support this view, as the work now remaining is mostly republican.[1] Lanciani thinks that this may have been the Ædes Matris Deum, to which the statue found as before mentioned in front of it belonged.

At the back of the so-called auguratorium we find a long series of rooms running in a line across the hill from north-west to south-east, which have vaulted roofs and are similar to those found below in the domus Gelotiana, before described. Cav. Rosa has inferred with reason from this and from the graffiti in these rooms that they formed a part of the offices and guard-rooms attached to that large portion of the palace which lay on the site now occupied by the gardens and the vast masses of brickwork at the northern corner of the hill. The graffiti to be seen here are chiefly the scribblings of soldiers' names, rude sketches of ships and animals, and combats of gladiators.

Tiberiana domus.

Several passages of the Roman historians lead us to conclude that the suite of rooms occupied by Tiberius were situated here. It was from the Tiberiana Domus, as Tacitus relates, that Vitellius surveyed the conflagration of the Temple of Jupiter on the Capitol, and the engagement between his adherents and the Flavian party under Sabinus. The Tiberian part of the palace was also that through which, as Tacitus also tells us, Otho descended into the Velabrum, after joining Galba at the sacrifice in the Temple of Apollo on the Palatine.[2] Afterwards, the Tiberiana Domus became the favourite residence of Antoninus Pius and Marcus Aurelius,

---

[1] Orelli, 2286.   [2] Tac. Hist. i. 27.

and it was probably during their reigns that the library which we find mentioned by Gellius was established here.¹

We now pass through the garden grounds which lie over the remains of the Domus Tiberiana, and descend on the side which looks over the Forum, by a long staircase through the immense masses of brickwork and concrete which are said to have been part of the insane additions of Caligula to the imperial palace. He is declared to have made a passage from this wing of the palace to the back of the Temple of Castor below in the Forum, in order that he might appear in that sacred shrine as an equal of the twin gods and an object of worship when the Senate met there. He also joined this corner of the palace with the Capitoline Temple of Jupiter by a huge viaduct, which passed over the Basilica Julia, in order that he might thus make himself the contubernalis of Jupiter.² Some of the substructions of this viaduct are to be seen near the back of the church of S. Maria Liberatrice. We now leave the Palatine by the Clivus Victoriæ, along which we entered, and turn to the arch of Titus and the ruins which stand near it.

THE VELIA.

Near the arch of Titus the Palatine Hill runs out in a gradually sloping ridge north-eastwards towards the Esquiline Hill. On one side of this ridge the ground sinks towards the Forum Romanum, and on the other towards the Meta Sudans and the Coliseum. The level of the pavement under the arch of Titus is fifty-three feet above the ancient pavement of the Forum. It seems probable that this outlying part of the Palatine was that which bore the name of Velia.³ *The Velia.*

On the summit of the ridge above described stands the arch of Titus, the most complete of all the monuments of imperial Rome. The central part of the original building remains, and is easily distinguished from the subsequent travertine restorations by being constructed of Pentelic marble. The height of the arch is forty-nine feet and its breadth forty-two feet. *Arch of Titus.*

¹ Hist. Aug. Ant. Pius, 10; Ant. Phil. 6; Gell. xiii. 20.
² See 'Rome and the Campagna,' p. 160, Note 1.
³ See 'Rome and the Campagna,' p. 162.

Originally there were two fluted Corinthian columns on each side of both faces of the arch, the two inner of which are now left, while the two outer are modern. Over the arch are two bas-reliefs of Victory which, though much injured, are still remarkable for the beauty of their outlines. On the keystone of the side towards the Coliseum is a figure of Rome, and on the other side Fortune with a cornucopia.

The most interesting parts of the arch have fortunately been preserved by their protected position in the interior. On each side is a magnificent alto-relievo, representing the triumphal procession of Titus after the capture of Jerusalem. The relievo on the south side shows a number of persons carrying the spoils of the Jewish Temple. The golden candlestick, the golden table for showbread, and the trumpets are clearly recognizable. These, according to Josephus,[1] among other utensils of the Jewish temple, were deposited in Vespasian's Temple of Peace. The procession is moving towards a triumphal arch.

In the northern relief the emperor is represented in his triumphal car, drawn by four horses, and surrounded by his guards and suite. Victory is holding a crown over his head, and the goddess Roma guiding the reins. The interior of the arch is ornamented with richly-carved rosettes and coffers, and upon the crown is a rather undignified representation of the apotheosis of the emperor astride upon an eagle's back.

On the Coliseum side a small portion of the entablature is left. The frieze had a bas-relief, which partially remains, of a sacrificial procession. The attica is modern, with the exception of the inscription. That the arch was erected after the emperor's death is shown by the title Divus, and also by the figure of his apotheosis under the archway. Another arch had been erected in the Circus previously in the year 80, when the Coliseum was completed, and Titus gave a great festival. The date of the extant arch is, therefore, the year 82 or 83.

Temple of Venus and Rome. Almost the whole of the southern slope of the Velia towards the Coliseum is occupied by the ruin of a vast foundation which extends under the church and convent of

[1] Josephus, Bell. Jud. vii. 5, 7.

S. Francesca Romana. The substructions, of which the inner core only, consisting of rubble-work, is left, were originally cased with travertine blocks. They form an enormous quadrilateral terrace, round which a portico of granite columns ran. Upon this was raised a basement some

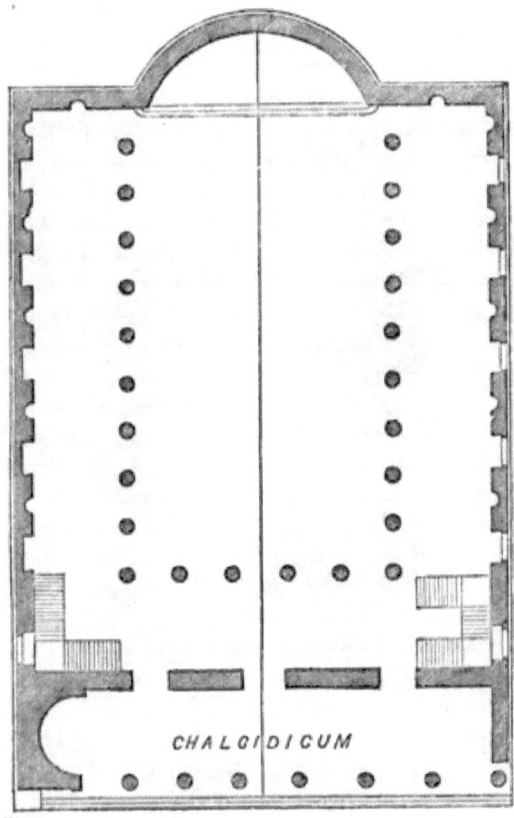

Fig. 9.

four or five feet higher, and a building with two apses back to back, similar to the tribunes of a basilica. These are ornamented with large square coffers and niches for statues. It has been generally inferred from the statements of Dion Cassius and Spartianus that this building was the Temple of Venus and Rome built by Hadrian and dedicated by the

Antonines, but burnt down in the time of Constantine and restored by him.[1] Pope Honorius I. stripped the bronze tiles from the roof, and they were placed on the Basilica of S. Peter, whence they were taken by the Saracens in A.D. 846. In the fifteenth and sixteenth centuries, limekilns were set up near the arch of Titus by the Romans and the marbles of this spot were burnt into lime.[2] The two tribunes which stand back to back and the buildings near them have not the appearance of a temple, but rather of a legal court or basilica. For this reason, and also because a large portico of this shape is represented in the marble plan of the city, the fragments of which are now in the Capitoline Museum, as having belonged to the Porticus Liviæ, Mr. Parker, in his 'Archæology of Rome,' has maintained that this was the Porticus Liviæ, built by Augustus and afterwards used by Hadrian for the Temple of the Sun and Moon. Jordan has also shown that the Porticus Liviæ was near this spot, but he places it farther to the north-east, behind the Basilica of Constantine.[3] Since Dion Cassius speaks of the Temple of Venus and Rome as having been close to the Coliseum and also near the Sacra Via, and Spartianus says that it stood in the vestibule of the Domus Aurea of Nero, we are almost compelled to assign this position to that temple.[4]

Domus Transitoria. Nero's enormous extension of the Palatine buildings must have occupied a great part of the Velia, reaching across it from the Palatine to the Esquiline. But his great Domus Aurea and its surrounding porticoes and halls, which were called Domus Transitoria, and occupied not only the slope of the Velia but also the site of the Coliseum, were destroyed by the Flavian emperors who succeeded him, and we can only point to one fragment of the Domus Transitoria which stands near the corner of the Basilica of Constantine at the side of the path which leads between that ruin and the buildings of S. Francesca Romana.

Basilica of Constantine. The vast arches of the ruin called the Basilica of Constan-

[1] See 'Rome and the Campagna,' p. 170.
[2] See 'Rome and the Campagna,' p. 171.
[3] Parker's 'Archæology of Rome,' vol. ii. p. 98. Jordan, 'Forma urbis Romæ'; Berlin, 1874, p. 37.
[4] 'Rome and the Campagna,' p. 169.

tine form, next to the Coliseum, the most conspicuous object in the neighbourhood of the Forum, and they were long supposed to have belonged to the Temple of Peace, Vespasian's great temple. But the decision of modern archæology has assigned them to Constantine, on the ground that the brickwork is of much later date than the time of Vespasian, and also that the few remains of decoration which are extant bear indications of a great decline of ornamentative art when they were constructed. Further evidence has been derived from a coin of Maxentius, the rival of Constantine, having been found in 1828 sticking in the mortar of one of the fragments. Aurelius Victor says that the basilica called by the name of Constantine was begun by Maxentius.[1] The three gigantic arches now standing formed the roof of the eastern aisle of the basilica, which consisted, as the foundation clearly shows, of a central hall and two side aisles. The arches are sixty-eight feet in span and eighty feet high. They are ornamented by octagonal caissons or coffers, containing central rosettes and the interspaces are relieved by rhomboidal panel work. The two side arches have their backs walled up, and there are six arched windows in each wall. At the back of the central arch is a semicircular tribune, with niches for statues and a central pedestal. Some of the marble ornaments of this tribune are still left, and show in their rude execution evidence of the Constantinian style of art. A screen seems to have separated the tribune from the interior of the hall. In front of the three great arches can be plainly seen the spring of the enormous roof which covered the central hall of the basilica. This central hall must have been at least 80 feet in width and 115 feet in height.

The southern aisle was of the same construction and size as the northern, and in place of the tribune had a grand entrance on the side towards the arch of Titus. A flight of steps and a portico with porphyry columns, two of which are now in the Conservatori Museum on the Capitol, formed the approach to the entrance. A white column from the central hall is to be seen erected in front of S. Maria

---

[1] Aur. Vict. Cæs. xl. 26. See 'Rome and the Campagna,' p. 166.

Maggiore, where it was placed in the seventeenth century by Paul V.

At the western end of the central hall was a tribune, the ruins of which are now occupied by a warehouse, and at the eastern end an entrance in three divisions opened into the road between the basilica and the portico of the so-called Temple of Venus and Rome. This entrance had a vestibule or verandah similar to those found at S. Giovanni in Laterano and at S. Maria Maggiore, and answering to the building called a chalcidicum by Vitruvius.[1] (Fig. 9, p. 33.)

SS. Cosma and Damiano.

The church of SS. Cosma and Damiano which now stands at the north-western end of the Basilica of Constantine is, like many other churches in Rome, constructed on the ruins of some ancient temple. A most careful account has been given of its various stages of construction by Mr. Parker.[2] This may possibly have been the site of the original Temple of the Penates, and some archæologists have thought that the round temple which has been converted into the vestibule of the church was that of the Penates. The doorway of this temple with its columns, frieze and bronze doors, has been raised from the lower level of the old temple, on which the crypt of the church now stands beneath the floor. At the back of this the nave of the church was built on the ruins of some unknown temple, and behind the apse of the nave is said by Mr. Parker to have been the wall on which the celebrated Capitoline marble plan of Rome was hung. The fragments of this plan, which was shaken down, he thinks, by the fall of a great mass from the Basilica of Constantine, were found here. The chapel of the Penates was on the road from the summa Sacra Via to the Carinæ, which would place it near this spot.[3] The name "Temple of Romulus" given to the ruins by mediæval writers may have been derived from some restoration by Romulus, son of Maxentius.

Lavacrum of Heliogabalus.

We now pass through the arch of Titus along the ancient road towards the Coliseum, and on the slope of the

---

[1] Vitruv. v. 1. [2] 'Archæology of Rome,' vol. ii. p. 75.
[3] See 'Rome and the Campagna,' p. 163.

Palatine to our right stand the ruins of a mediæval church which was excavated in 1873 by Cav. Rosa. This is said to have been called the church of S. Maria Antiqua, and to have been placed upon the ruins of the lavacrum of Heliogabalus.[1] The chambers now disclosed seem to have been used as a bath. Along the side of the hill near this are numerous ruins similar to those on the other side of the Palatine, which were apparently guard rooms.

[1] Lampridius, Hist. Aug. Ant. Hel. 8, 17, in ædibus aulicis. Parker, 'Archæology of Rome,' vol. ii. p. 92.

CHAPTER II.

THE FORUM ROMANUM.

Temple of Castor. AT a short distance from the entrance to the Palatine we can enter the Forum near the ruins of an ancient temple, three columns of which are still standing. These three columns are among the most conspicuous and beautiful remains of ancient Rome. No doubt can now be felt that they belonged to the Temple of Castor and Pollux. The situation agrees with that which is pointed out by the Ancyræan inscription, and by the fact that Caligula made a passage from the Palatine Palace to this temple.

The substructions of this building have been cleared, and the length and breadth of the basement and of the steps forming the approach can now be clearly seen. The three columns belonged to the central part of the south-eastern side. They are of most elegant proportions, and their capitals, architrave and frieze are ornamented with decorative work of the very best period of Græco-Roman architecture. The designs on the entablature are most delicate and perfect, and well repay a minute examination. Besides the usual ornaments upon the cornice and corbels there is along the upper edge a row of beautiful lions' heads, through which the rain-water ran off.

The temple had evidently eight columns in front, and eleven side columns, reckoning in the corner column. The approach was raised high above the forum level, and has three steps projecting beyond the line of the next building, the Basilica Julia. The lines of the front steps are preserved, and also those of the side towards the Capitol, while the other side has been destroyed. The pavement in front of this has been miserably altered and mended at a late date, probably after the fourth century.

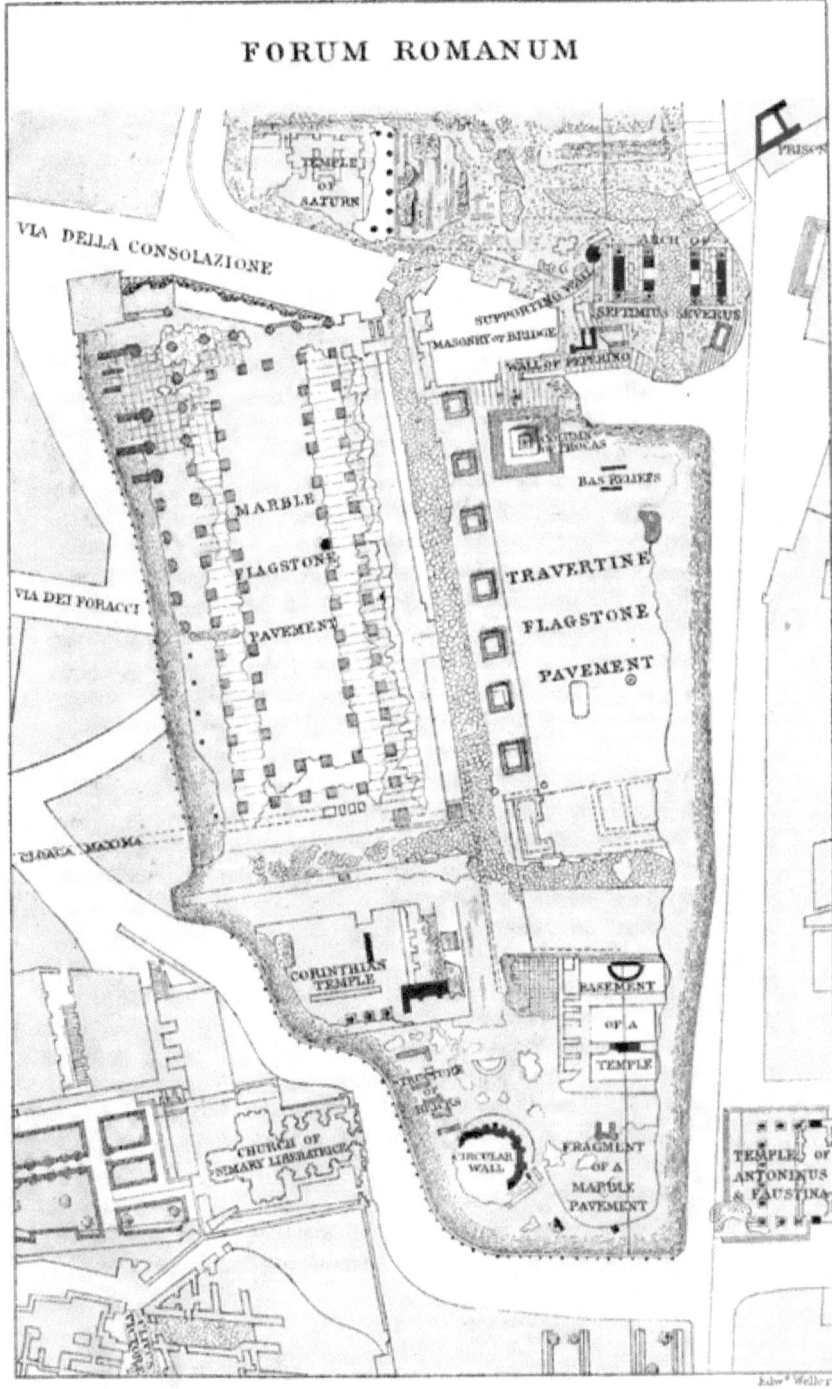

The capitals when compared with the earlier Corinthian capitals of the Pantheon, show a longer and narrower type which is also found at the Temple of Vespasian and the peristyle of Nerva's Forum, the Colonacce. The lower foundations of the basement are of old tufa rubble construction, and possibly belong to the date of the original foundations in B.C. 494 by the dictator Aulus Postumius, who vowed to build it at the battle of the Lake Regillus in the Latin war. It was afterwards dedicated by his son in B.C. 484. Two restorations are mentioned, the first executed by L. Metellus Dalmaticus, consul in B.C. 119, and the second by Drusus and Tiberius in A.D. 6. The temple was used for meetings of the senate, for harangues from its steps to the people in the forum, and for holding courts of law. A register of changes in the value of money was kept in the tabularium of the temple, and deposits were made here as in many other temples.[1] Standing as the old temple did near the veteres tabernæ of the forum, and the newer restorations of them near the Basilica Julia, it was convenient for business transactions. On the north-west side a street pavement leading to the Velabrum has been laid bare, which may be that of the Vicus Tuscus.

Descending from the Temple of Castor to the ancient pavement of the Forum Romanum, we find at the north-eastern corner of the ruin the remains of a puteal or well-house which has naturally been supposed to be the fountain of Juturna from its neighbourhood to the Temple of the Twin Brethren, who are said to have given their horses drink there after the battle of Regillus. *Puteal.*

A little farther to the south the basement of a round building is to be seen, which may very probably have been the ancient Temple of Vesta. This was a round building, as we conclude from Ovid and Plutarch's notices, and was intended by Numa, the first founder, to denote the spherical shape of the earth which Vesta personified, or the original family hearth.[2] *Temple of Vesta.*

In front of the Temple of Castor a large block of substructions has been cleared, which is with great probability *Chapel of Julius Cæsar.*

---

[1] See 'Rome and the Campagna,' p. 100. [2] Ibid. p. 103.

assigned to the chapel built in honour of Julius Cæsar, and called the Heroon of Cæsar. Ovid's lines, in one of his letters from Pontus—

> "Like the twin brethren whom in their abode
> Julius, the god, beholds from his high shrine,"

seem to prove that the heroon was in front of that temple. The body of Cæsar was burnt in front of the regia and Temple of Vesta, which were at this end of the Forum, and the heroon was placed on the spot where it was burnt. The remains of two small staircases were found at the sides of the heroon, and a wider staircase in front. The epithet "high," given by Ovid to its position, seems to be in accordance with the raised basement. The semicircle of masonry on the north side has not been satisfactorily explained. It is usually supposed to have belonged to the Julian rostra, but its shape is not such as to support this idea.

Temple of Antoninus and Faustina.

To the north-east of the heroon of Julius Cæsar, we find the ancient pavement of the road which ran along the north-eastern side of the Forum, and to this road descend the steps of a temple with a conspicuous row of six cipollino columns, and with two columns and a pilaster besides the corner column on each side. These columns have Attic bases and Corinthian capitals of white marble. The inscription upon the plain architrave in front shows that the temple was first dedicated to Faustina alone, and that the first three words, including the emperor's name, were added after his death. The Faustina here commemorated was probably the elder Faustina, wife of Antoninus Pius, as a representation at this temple is given on one of the medals struck in her honour.[1] She died in A.D. 141, and Antoninus Pius in 161. The frieze of the temple is ornamented at the sides with a bold and finely-executed relief representing griffins with upraised wings, between which are carved elaborately-designed candelabra and vases. A considerable part of the side walls of grey peperino blocks anciently faced with marble is still

---

[1] Eckhel, vii. 37. On the mistaken appropriation of the temple to M. Aurelius, see 'Rome and the Campagna,' p. 114.

standing. A church was built here at a very early time, but the present building which forms a strange contrast in the meanness of its style and proportions to the massive grandeur of the grey old ruin which embraces it, was built in 1602 by the guild of the Roman apothecaries.[1]

We now pass along the ancient stone pavement towards the Capitol, and observe how small the space occupied by the ancient Forum Romanum was. The temple we have just left stood in the north-eastern corner, and the columns of the two temples opposite to us on the slope of the Capitol mark the other end of the Forum. The central pavement now laid bare is of travertine flags, while the roads are marked by basaltic blocks. On the side of the central space runs a row of seven large masses of brickwork, which seem to be the bases of pedestals which supported dedicatory columns, or statues similar to the one still standing at the end, which has become known to English travellers as "the nameless column with the buried base" of Byron. Since Byron's time the base of this has been unburied, and bears the name of Smaragdus, proclaimed exarch of Italy for the eleventh time,[2] who erected it in honour of the Emperor Phocas. The date is given by the words INDICT. UND., which show that Smaragdus was in his eleventh year as exarch, and we know that he was exarch under Mauricius for five years, A.D. 583–588, and six years under Phocas, A.D. 602–608. His eleventh year would thus be in 608, and this was the fifth year of Phocas' reign, so that the last words of the inscription confirm the explanation given of the previous words INDICT. UND.[3] "P. C." in the inscription probably mean, as Clinton explains, post consulatum, which was the way of reckoning in the later years of the Eastern Empire.

Extent of the Forum.

Seven brick pedestals.

Column of Phocas.

In the centre of the Forum traces of the base of a large pedestal can be discerned, and this is supposed to have been

Pedestal of equestrian statue.

---

[1] See Reber's 'Ruinen Roms,' p. 132.

[2] Corp. Inscr. Lat. vol. vi. pt. 1, No. 1200. "Indictionis undecimo Post Consulatum pietatis ejus anno quinto" are the last words of the inscription. "In the eleventh year of his appointment and the fifth year of his reverence the emperor." See Nibby, 'Roma antica,' p. 152; Zell. Epigr. 1226. A D = A Deo.

[3] See Clinton, Fast. Rom. A.D. 608.

the position of the equestrian statue of Domitian described at length by Statius, who says in the first poem of his 'Silvae' that an equestrian statue of Domitian stood at the north-western end of the Forum, looking towards the other end. It was a triumphal statue erected in honour of Domitian's campaigns against the Catti and Daci. The poet describes its position very accurately, mentioning the Heroon of Julius Caesar which faced it, the Basilica Julia on the right, the Basilica Paulli on the left, and the temples of Concord and Vespasian behind. The Temple of Saturn is omitted for some unknown reason. Statius also alludes to some other principal objects in the Forum, the Temple of Vesta, the Temple of Castor, and the statue of Curtius. He concludes with prophesying that the statue will outlast the eternal city.[1] It seems, however, probable, as Mr. Nichols in his admirable book on the Forum has said, that the statue was removed after Domitian's death, when his memory was execrated, or was dedicated to a succeeding emperor, and that the statement of Herodian about the dream of Severus, who imagined that he saw an equestrian statue in the Forum, a colossal representation of which remained there in the historian's time, may refer to this pedestal.[2]

Trajan's bas-reliefs. Two of the most interesting monuments which have been brought to light by the recent excavations in Rome were discovered in 1872, near the base of the column of Phocas, where they have been re-erected. They consist of marble slabs, sculptured with bas-reliefs and forming low screens. Each screen is constructed of slabs of unequal size, and some of these have been unfortunately lost. Their original position has been restored as nearly as possible, and they stand parallel to each other in a line crossing the area of the Forum. On the inner sides of both of these sculptured screens, the sacrificial animals, the boar, sheep and bull, always offered up at the Suovetaurilia, are represented.

The other sides, which are turned outwards, represent scenes in the Forum, and are commemorative of some public

---

[1] Stat. Silv. i. 1. Mr. Parker thinks that this was the pedestal of a statue of Constantine. Archæol. vol. ii. pl. xix.
[2] Nichols, 'The Roman Forum,' p. 78.

benefaction of one of the emperors, probably Trajan or Hadrian. On one of them Italia is represented thanking the emperor for establishing some "alimenta publica," public relief institutions, and for apportioning lands to encourage needy parents to rear their children. Such relief funds and lands intended to supply the defective population of Italy were first established by the Emperor Nerva, and afterwards by Trajan, Hadrian, and the Antonines, and are frequently commemorated on medals, and mentioned by the historians Dion Cassius and Aurelius Victor, and the authors of the Augustan history.[1] The emperor is represented in a sitting posture, and stretching out his hand towards a child presented by a woman in the character of Italia, who apparently holds another child ready for presentation. Behind the emperor's seat is the fig-tree called Navia or Ruminalis, which is said to have grown near the rostra, and also the figure of Marsyas which stood in the same place. At the other end of this sculptured scene stands a speaker with a roll in his hand, addressing a crowd of citizens from a rostrum, which may perhaps represent the publication of the edict establishing alimenta.

The other bas-relief scene shows a rostrum at one end, from which a sitting figure is superintending the burning of large bundles of books, carried and placed in front of him in a heap. The outline of a figure applying a torch can be traced, and also of several attendants. At the opposite end to the sitting figure the fig-tree and Marsyas are placed as in the other relief.

The style of art in which the reliefs are executed cannot, in Professor Henzen's opinion, belong to an earlier period than Trajan's reign. The treatment corresponds to that on those reliefs taken from Trajan's arch, and set up on Constantine's arch. After Trajan's time the style of bas-relief was so much altered that we cannot suppose them to have been sculptured later than the first year of Hadrian.

As Trajan gained great popularity in the early years of his reign by an abolition of the arrears of certain debts due to the imperial treasury, amounting to a large sum,

---

[1] See 'Rome and the Campagna,' Appendix, p. 452.

and as he also established alimenta, these reliefs have been generally supposed to commemorate his public benefactions, in founding relief institutions and cancelling public debts.

The backgrounds of both the sculptures are occupied by representations of some public buildings, but it does not seem possible to identify these with any certainty. That they roughly represent some of the temples and Basilicas in the Forum in a sketch is all we can say. One of the temples shown in the relief which depicts the foundation of alimenta has only five columns in its portico, showing a want of accuracy in the drawing which throws great doubt upon its topographical value. The archæologists who have endeavoured to name the buildings have agreed in calling the Ionic and the Corinthian portico in the relief where the account books are being burnt those of the Temples of Saturn and Vespasian, with an arch of the tabularium between them, and the long row of arches the Basilica Julia, but they differ as to the buildings shown in the other relief, for while Mr. Nichols thinks that the Basilica Julia is here again represented with the Heroon of Julius Cæsar and the arch of Augustus, Signor Brizio is of opinion that we have here the north-western side of the Forum with the Basilica Æmilia.[1] The rostra are probably meant to represent temporary wooden constructions.

The most reasonable conjecture which has yet been made as to the purpose which these sculptured screens served is that they formed a pons or passage along which voters passed at a time of election from the Forum to the office where the votes were taken. A great part of the structures used at such times was probably temporary, and made of wood for the occasion. Another explanation suggested by Mr. Nichols is that they formed a passage leading to an altar and statue of the Emperor. It may be that the sculptures never reached their destined site, but were left here, as many of the marbles on the Tiber banks were, and gradually buried in rubbish.

Basilica Julia.

We now pass to the rows of restored bases of columns,

[1] Gardhausen, 'Hermes,' viii. 129. Nichols, 'Roman Forum,' p. 67. Ann. dell. Inst. 1872. Mr. Nichols's explanation does not account for the position of the fig-tree and Marsyas satisfactorily.

which occupy the long space on the south-western side of the seven pedestals above mentioned. Here we find the ground plan of the great Basilica Julia marked out by a treble row of columns at each of the larger sides, and a double row at each end. One pier of the outer row towards the Forum has been restored by Rosa so as to show the original height.

The proof that these ruins belong to the Basilica Julia which was planned by Julius Cæsar, and begun by him but completed by Augustus, who dedicated it to his grandsons Caius and Lucius, is the statement in the monumentum Ancyranum, in which it is placed between the temples of Saturn and Castor.

A second proof is derived from two inscriptions found during the process of clearing the site, one of which records the repair of the Basilica Julia, and the erection in it of a statue by Gabinius Vettius Probianus, prefect of the city in A.D. 377, and the other the rebuilding of the Basilica Julia under Maximian after the fire which destroyed it in the time of Carinus and Numerian. This site is also assigned to the Basilica on the Capitoline plan which may be seen on the staircase of the Capitoline Museum. The outline given there, and marked by the name Basilica Julia, agrees in proportion, and in the rows of columns with the extant remains, and this shows that the present ruin is the same in its main points with that which stood in the time of Severus, when the Capitoline plan was made.[1] Seven steps lead up to the level of the floor from the Forum level.

A great deal of legal business was transacted here, as may be seen from the frequent mention of it in Pliny's Epistles. There were four tribunals, of which Quintilian speaks, at which four trials could be carried on at the same time; but these tribunals were probably wooden and temporary erections, and there is no trace of any semicircular apses, such as those in the Basilica of Constantine. One of Caligula's amusements, as we are told by Suetonius, was to stand upon the roof of this basilica, and throw money to

[1] Jordan, 'Forma urbis Romæ,' pp. 4, 25. The proportion of the length to the breadth is nearly that given by Vitruvius as proper for a basilica.

the mob in the Forum to scramble for. Whether the basilica was covered over in the centre is not certain, but it probably was so, with two aisles open to the Forum. The row of arches standing at the north-west corner is partly a restoration of the basilica by Canina, and partly consists of some piers and a wall standing behind, which has not yet been satisfactorily identified with any ancient building. The most probable supposition is that they belonged to the Porticus Julia mentioned by Dion Cassius, and were parts of an earlier edifice, in front of which and upon which the basilica was placed by Augustus.

Cloaca. Under the southern end of the floor of the Julian Basilica, an opening has been made in which the arch of the main cloaca of the Forum valley can be seen passing across the Forum towards the Subura. This is the drain of which Juvenal speaks, when he says that the fish taken from the Crypta Suburæ is the climax of indignity offered to the unhappy parasite Trebius at his patron's table.[1] The course of the drain runs from here under the Via dei Fenili down to the Janus Quadrifrons in the Velabrum, where it meets other branches and passes down to the Tiber. Between the eastern end of the Basilica Julia and the temple of Castor ran the Vicus Tuscus, of which the paving-stones may still be traced. At the western end the Vicus Jugarius led towards the Velabrum, but this is buried under the present Via della Consolazione, and cannot be seen.

Arch of Tiberius. The Arch of Tiberius, which stood at the corner of the Basilica Julia, where the Vicus Jugarius and the Clivus Capitolinus diverged, cannot be clearly traced, though some of its ruins have been thought to exist among those uncovered at the edge of and under the modern road. This arch has been with great probability supposed to be that alluded to by Tacitus in speaking of the recovery of the Roman standards lost by Varus, and retaken by Germanicus under the auspices of Tiberius.[2] The triumphal arch represented on the Arch of Constantine is also thought to be that of Tiberius placed here.

Temple of Saturn. We now pass under the modern road to the foot of the

[1] Juv. Sat. v. 104.   [2] Tac. Ann. ii. 41.

Capitoline Hill, and proceed to examine the most prominent ruin at the western end of the Forum. This consists of eight columns, six of red granite forming a front, and two

Temple of Saturn.   Temple of Antoninus and Faustina.   Coliseum and Arch of Titus.   Temple of Castor.

side columns of grey granite. The capitals of these and the decoration of the entablature, architrave and friezo surmounting them are of a late and debased Ionic order with volutes in the later style, and they have been pieced together in the last restoration of the temple with extraordinary negligence. Unequal spaces are left between the columns, and some are set upon plinths while others are without them. One of the side columns has been so badly re-erected that the stones are misplaced, and consequently the diameter of the upper portion is of the same size as that of the lower. The restored carving on the inner frieze is of the roughest description, and the barbarous negligence of the whole restoration shows that it cannot have been done earlier than the fourth or fifth century. A comparison of the ruins now remaining with the plan as given on the fragments of the Capitoline map, bearing the name SAT VRNI has been made by Jordan, who shows that the remains of a prominent and peculiar flight of steps in front of the six columns correspond to the rough sketch on the plan, and that this flight of steps facing north must be taken to be the front of the temple.[1] The pavement stones of the road which led from the forum past the front of the temple may still be traced curving round this projecting flight of steps. Little doubt now remains that the ruin of the eight columns, the name of which has been so much discussed, belonged to the Temple of Saturn.

The inscription now upon the front was placed there at its latest restoration which, as we have seen, was in Christian times, and the name of the divinity is therefore omitted.

This temple was one of the most revered and ancient in the city, and its foundation is traced back in legendary myth to the Hellenic Kronos. The earliest date given for the dedication is B.C. 498. Many restorations must have taken place. An inscription recording one in the time of Augustus by Munatius Plancus has been found. This temple long retained the name of the Mint, from the fact that the state treasures were deposited under the care of the god Saturnus, as one of the most venerated of Roman deities.

Area of the Dii Consentes. The ancient road leading up to the Capitol made a turn behind the Temple of Saturn, and a portico with semi-Corinthian or Composite columns has been restored from some columns and capitals found here in 1835. At the back

[1] Jordan, 'Forma urbis Romæ,' p. 26.

of this portico were twelve recessed chambers occupied by chapels of the twelve deities called the Dii Consentes. Four of these still remain under the modern Via del Campidoglio. The walls are chiefly of brickwork, apparently of the second or third century, but the back wall against the ascent to the Capitol is of hard tufa. The interiors were faced with marble, of which traces are left. From the inscription found in 1835 upon the architecture it appears that Vettius Prætextatus, a prefect of the city in A.D. 367, restored the statues of the Dii Consentes, which had stood here from ancient times. Varro mentions gilded statues of the gods of the council as near the Forum, and also speaks of their temple. This portico and chambers cannot, however, have been a temple, but were evidently clerks' offices connected with the state depositories near the Temple of Saturn. Cicero speaks of the clerks of the Capitoline ascent.[1] Vettius Prætextatus, who restored the building in 367, was notorious for his opposition to the Christian religion and for his zeal in supporting the ancient cultus. He held several offices, and was pro-consul of Achaia under Julian, and probably recommended himself to that emperor by his attachment to the old Roman religion.

Below the portico and its chambers stands another row of lower chambers, three of which are said by Marliani to have been found entire in the sixteenth century. Inscriptions found here give the name of Schola to the chambers, and hence they have been called Schola Xanthi, from the name of Xanthus, which occurs in the inscription as a restorer. They were undoubtedly clerks' offices, similar to those behind the portico of the Dii Consentes above them. *Schola Xanthi.*

We now turn from the portico of the Dii Consentes to the three Corinthian columns which stand under the large building called the Tabularium. These three columns have now been proved to belong to the ruin of a temple dedicated to Vespasian by his son Domitian. This position of Vespasian's temple agrees with the statements of the Notitia and Curiosum and of Statius. The inscription, of which only the letters ESTITUER now remain, was seen and the whole of it tran- *Temple of Vespasian.*

[1] Cic. Phil. ii. 7.

scribed by a writer of the ninth century, whose MS. is preserved at Einsiedlen.¹ It recorded the restoration of this temple by Severus and Caracalla. The letters ISTITUER stand at the lower edge of the frieze, showing that there was another line above. This upper line was DIVO. VESP. AUG. S.P.Q.R., and referred to the original building of the temple, while the lower line recorded its restoration. The temple was approached by a flight of steps from the road between it and the Temple of Saturn, the uppermost of which were placed between the columns and have been partially restored. The three columns which now remain are the three corner columns of the portico. They have fluted shafts and Corinthian capitals. The letters of the inscription were of metal, and the holes of the rivets which fastened them are still visible. The architrave and cornice are ornamented very richly with the usual mouldings, and there are some most interesting reliefs upon the frieze representing sacrificial implements and the skulls of oxen. A horsetail for sprinkling, and a sacrificial knife with a vase, a patera, an axe, and a high priest's mitre are plainly distinguishable. Another portion of the entablature was pieced together by Canina and is still kept in the rooms of the Tabularium. The walls of the cella were built of travertine faced with marble. Against the back wall stands a large pedestal which supported the statue of the deified Emperor.

Temple of Concord.

Next to the temple of Vespasian, we are told by Statius, stood the Temple of Concord. The site is also determined by passages in Plutarch and in Dion Cassius, and by the plan given in the Capitoline map. Excavations were carried out here in 1817, 1830, and 1835 which resulted in disclosing the foundations of the temple, and in finding some inscriptions which attest the dedication of this spot to the goddess Concord. The temple of Concord was founded according to Livy, Ovid, and Plutarch by Camillus in B.C. 367, on the memorable occasion when the senate after a long and anxious debate, wisely determined to make peace with the Commons by throwing open the office of Consul to the plebeian order.²

¹ See 'Rome and the Campagna,' p. 58.
² See 'Rome and the Campagna,' p. 91.

It was placed near the old meeting-place (Comitium) of the privileged families (gentes), as if constantly to remind them that the newly established concord of the community was under the special sanction of the gods. When the Temple of Camillus was first restored we do not learn. The earliest notice of a new Temple to Concord is the statement that the Consul Opimius was ordered by the senate on the death of C. Gracchus to build a new temple to Concord. The temple seems to have been a kind of Pantheon or museum, for it was filled with a great number of statues of various gods, and with curiosities. On the left-hand side of the remaining foundations of the cella are two large pedestals which probably supported two of the principal statues.

Tiberius rebuilt it after his German campaign in A.D. 6 and 7, and dedicated it in honour of himself and his brother. The form of the latest restoration, which seems to have been carried out after the building behind it, the so-called Tabularium, was built, as it is placed so close to that building and must have rendered the decorations on its walls invisible, can be traced by the present relics of foundation walls, and presents a singular deviation from the normal plan of a Roman temple. The pronaos, or front chamber, is narrower than the cella or shrine behind it, and forms a sort of porch to it. This is an instance of the form of temple called prostylos by Vitruvius, and consisting of a broad Tuscan cella with a narrow Greek portico.[1]

The cella has greater breadth than depth. The basement is of considerable height in front, and some of the steps, Cicero's Gradus Concordiae[2] can be traced, while the enormous threshold of African marble still remains. A coin of Tiberius shows us that the temple had a portico of six columns in the Corinthian style, and a group of three figures embracing, as a symbol of Concord, at the top. One of the bases of the columns is still preserved in the Capitoline Museum, and a portion of the frieze was restored by Canina, showing that the decorative work was of great beauty. The inscription is given in the Einsiedlen MS. of the ninth century, and the

[1] See 'Rome and the Campagna,' p xxix.
[2] Cic. Phil. vii. ch. 8. The third Catilinarian oration was delivered here.

temple was still standing in the twelfth century, as we learn from the Ordo Romanus, a procession route book. The stones were probably carried away for building purposes in the thirteenth century. Between the ruins of the Temple of Concord and those of Vespasian's Temple, the foundations of a little chapel of Faustina may be seen. The name has been given to it from an inscription discovered here.

Arch of Severus. Close to the ruins of the Temple of Concord stands the triumphal arch of Septimius Severus, composed of three archways of Pentelic marble. The side archways are connected with the central archway by small openings in the intervening walls, and the arched interiors of all three are decorated by square coffers with rosette ornaments. On each side stand four columns of Proconnesian marble with Composite capitals, on the pedestals of which are bas-reliefs representing figures of barbarian captives clothed in breeches and wearing the chlamys and Phrygian cap, and conducted by Roman soldiers wearing the lacerna. The spandrils of the arches are ornamented with the usual figures of Victory and symbols of captivity, in the outlines of the river gods of the Euphrates and Tigris. Between each pair of outer and inner pillars there are large bas-relief sculptured scenes executed in a very confused and tasteless style. The four lower and narrow compartments show the goddess Roma receiving the homage of the East, which is personified by a woman wearing a tiara. Behind her, in a long train of carts and carriages, come the spoils of the various nations conquered by Severus. Above this narrow line of figures which runs round below the four compartments above the side arches, are four larger bas-reliefs representing the sieges and victories of Severus in Parthia, Adiabene, and Arabia. On the side towards the Forum is represented on the left hand the raising of the Parthian siege of Nisibis in northern Mesopotamia by Severus after he had crushed his rivals Æmilianus and Pescennius Niger in Pontus and Syria. The taking of the town of Carræ west of Nisibis, and the march of the Roman army thence against the Adiabenians are also here portrayed. The compartment on the right hand, looking from the Forum, contains a bas-relief representation of the surrender of

Abgarus, king of Osroene,[1] and the siege of the town of Hatra on the Tigris.

On the other side towards the Capitol and so-called

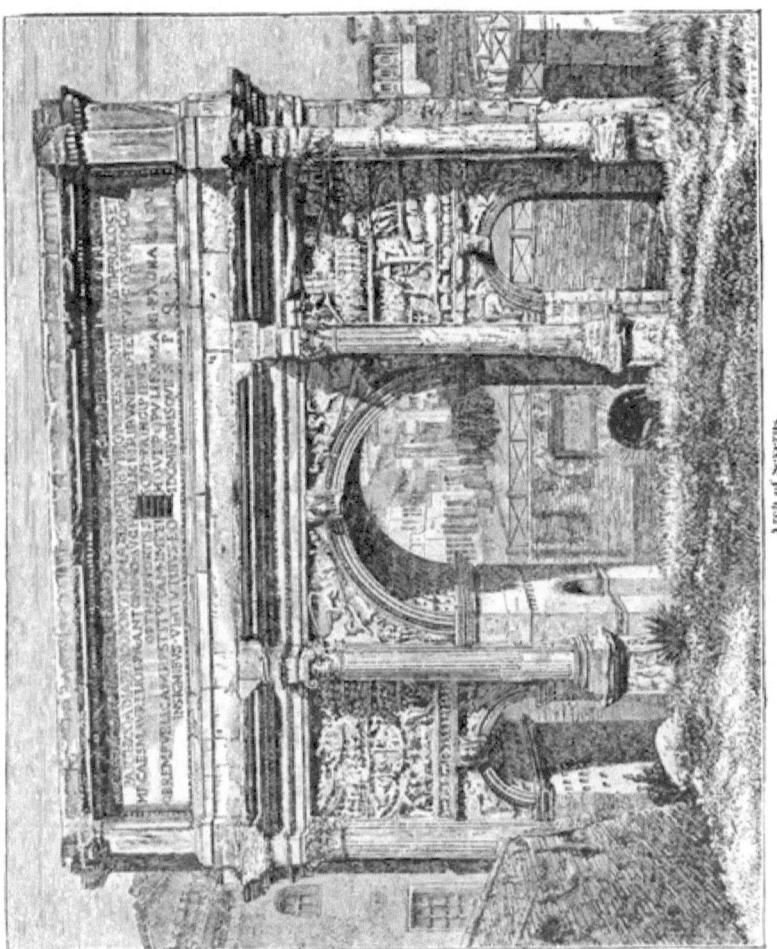

Arch of Severus.

Tabularium, the second campaign of Severus in the East is portrayed. On the right hand the flight of the Parthians from Babylon, the entry of the Romans into that city and

[1] Dion. Cass. lxxvii. 12.

the second siege of Hatra are represented. On the left is the wresting of the towns of Seleucia and Ctesiphon from the Parthians, the flight of their king Artobanus and the surrender of the Arabians who had joined the Parthian side.[1]

The entablature which surmounts these arches is badly designed and executed, the projections over the columns being far too heavy. Upon the attica above the entablature there are the traces of nails on the corner pilasters which seem to have borne some military ensigns. The whole central space of the attica is occupied by a long inscription formerly inlaid, as appears from the rivets, with metal. Upon a coin of Severus giving a representation of the arch, a chariot with six horses is shown standing over the attica, and on the four corners were equestrian statues.

From the inscription it appears that the arch was built in the year A.D. 203. The repetition of the title Parthicus, points to the Parthian campaigns of Severus. In the fourth line the name of Geta and his titles have been erased, as in other ruins of the same date, and the words OPTIMIS FORTISSIMISQUE PRINCIPIBUS inserted in their place. In the middle ages the tower of a church called SS. Sergio e Bacco was built upon the top of this arch, but was removed in 1536 on the entry of Charles V. by command of Pope Paul III.

Ruins under the road across the end of the Forum. Near the Arch of Severus, and also between the temple of Saturn and the corner of the Basilica Julia, the modern road runs over archways. Under the archways some substructions of large peperino stones and other forms of building have been disclosed. These may have belonged to pedestals upon which statues were placed, or in the case of those near the arch of Severus to the later Rostra and Graecostasis, and in the case of those near the corner of the Basilica Julia to the Arch of Tiberius. The round pedestal which stands near the Arch of Severus was possibly the pedestal of the Miliarium Aureum, as it is not strong enough to bear the weight of a heavy statue.[2]

A representation of the Rostra of the Empire which may have stood here is given in the relief on the face of the Arch of Constantine, which looks towards the Coliseum, where three

---
[1] Herodian iii. 9, 10, 11. Hist. Aug. Vit. Sev. 9, 16, 17.
[2] See Parker's Archaeol. vol. ii. pl. xi.

arches are seen, corresponding to the Arch of Severus on the right, and one arch corresponding to that of Tiberius on the left. Constantine is shown in this bas-relief addressing the people from the rostra.

Under the church of S. Giuseppe dei Falegnami, which stands near the Arch of Severus, are two chambers, which are always shown as the ancient prison of Rome, said to have been first built by the King Ancus Martius, and then rebuilt or enlarged by Servius Tullius. The upper of these two chambers is of an irregular shape, but the lower is constructed in a conical form by the gradual projection of the stones forming the sides. This mode of building an arch is of very early date, before the introduction of the principle of the round arch, and is found in the oldest tombs of Etruria, and in well-houses at Tusculum and Cære.[1]

The Carcer.

There can be no doubt that this part of the building is of great antiquity. But the proofs that it ever formed a prison are not so clear. This has been inferred from the striking account of the imprisonment of Jugurtha by Sallust, who states that Jugurtha was placed in a cell with water at the bottom, and exclaimed, "Hercules, how cold your bath is!" Hence it has been thought that the prison must have had water in it, as this chamber has on the floor.

Another proof that this is the ancient prison, called in the middle ages the Mamertine prison, from a statue of Mars or Mamers, or from the Forum Martis near it, has been derived from the statements of many Roman authors, who place the prison on the slope of the Capitol, near the Forum, and speak of an inferior as well as a superior chamber. The prison was probably in this neighbourhood, but the shape of the conical vault is rather that of a well-house. Mommsen has therefore suggested that this was the original purpose of the lower chamber, and that it was used as a cistern for collecting the water from the surrounding slopes. The top of the ancient conical vault is truncated and closed, with the exception of a round hole, by slabs of stone fastened together with iron cramps.

A communication with the arched sewers which run down

---

[1] See 'Rome and the Campagna,' p. 351, Appendix.

to the Forum, and also with an archway which reaches up the slope to some large chambers on the north-west under the Vicolo del Ghettarello, has been opened by Mr. Parker, and these longer vaulted chambers which are of great antiquity, have been taken to be extensions of the original regal prison. But there is no sufficient evidence to show that these arched passages were used for any purpose of transit, and they were more probably channels for draining off the water, which would otherwise have accumulated in the chambers or on the slopes.[1]

An inscription is fixed in the outer wall, recording a restoration of the building by the Consuls C. Vibius Rufinus and M. Cocceius Nerva, as ordered by a decree of the Senate. These two men were consules suffecti before A.D. 24, probably in A.D. 22, the ninth year of Tiberius. But the name of the building is not mentioned in this inscription, and it seems uncertain whether it has not been removed from elsewhere.

There was another and larger prison in this district, and this larger prison was called the Lautumiae. Forty-three Ætolian prisoners are said by Livy to have been crucified in the Lautumiae, which must therefore have been certainly much more extensive than the cell which is called the Career Mamertinus. Seneca also mentions the request of a prisoner, Julius Sabinus, that he might be removed from the Career to the Lautumiae.[2] There seems, therefore, to be no distinct proof that the conical cell was ever anything more than a water tank, and the name of prison which has been attached to it is probably a mediaeval legend invented to indicate a spot which might be venerated as the prison of St. Peter.

Tabularium.

On the side of the Capitoline Hill towards the Forum, a very high and wide mass of building, now called the Palace of the Senator, and used for the transaction of urban business, stands. This is founded upon an ancient range of masonry of which a considerable part still remains, measuring about 220 feet in length, and 50 feet in height. An entrance has been made from the Via del Campidoglio, and as the wall was cut through for this purpose, the structure of the building may

---

[1] See Jordan, Top. Rom. p. 13, Note 20.
[2] Liv. xxxvii. 3. Seneca, Contr. ix. 4, 21.

be best observed here. On the inner side red tufa has been used, and on the outer grey peperino, and the blocks are laid alternately lengthwise and crosswise, as in the Servian wall building. A great mass of masonry of this sort without cement, forms the main substructions of the building. Along the front run the traces of an arcaded passage, which anciently led across from one side to the other of the building. The arches were walled up by Nicolas V., in order to bear modern buildings above them. One has now been opened to show the architecture. A pavement of basaltic lava, such as was used in the streets of ancient Rome, has been found in the arcade, showing that it was a public passage. The architecture of the building is Doric, which points to an early date, and the capitals and cornice are of travertine. It is probable that another arcade ran above the one now traceable. A high flight of steps leads up into the chambers from the archway now walled up at the back of the Temple of Vespasian. From the architecture it may be concluded that these remains of a large ancient building date from the republican times of Rome, and are almost the only relics of that era. This ruin is generally called the Tabularium, but it has been shown by Mommsen that there is no ground for supposing that the name was ever applied to it in any ancient writings, and that the name is more properly Ærarium Populi Romani, or Ærarium Saturni, and that it was attached to the Temple of Saturn. Many of the temples in Rome had æraria attached to them, and it does not appear that any central place of deposit ever had the name of Tabularium alone, without further title, especially applied to it. The inscription which has been placed at the entrance, and records the construction of some building, or part of, a building by Q. Lutatius Catulus, when consul, was placed where it now stands by Canina. It is supposed by Mommsen to refer to the repairs and alterations of the vaults under the Capitol, which were carried out in pursuance of Sulla's plan of improvements on the Capitol, and after Sulla's death were continued for many years by Q. Catulus.[1]

---

[1] Corp. Inscr. Lat. i. 591, 592. Mommsen, Ann. Inst. 1858, p. 211. Canina, Rom. Ant. p. 290. Virgil's use of the plural tabularia is not, therefore, merely poetical: Georg. ii. 502.

CHAPTER III.

THE COLISEUM AND ESQUILINE.

Meta Sudans.

ON the road from the Forum Romanum to the Coliseum, after passing through the Arch of Titus, we descend between the platform and ruins of the Temple of Venus and Rome, and the remains called the lavacrum of Heliogabalus, mentioned previously, and, close to the south-western corner of the mass of substruction on the left, we find a conical column of brick-work about thirty feet high. A large breach on the side towards the Coliseum shows that the centre was pierced with a perpendicular pipe, and the eastern exhibits traces of having been divided into three ledges or stages. This conical building stood in the centre of a circular basin, the ruin of which has been traced out and restored. The shape would of itself point to the purpose which this building served, even if this were not rendered clear by the remains of a water-course which descended to it from the Esquiline. The name Meta Sudans by which the ruin is known comes from the mediæval list of buildings known as the Curiosum Urbis, but the earliest authentic authority to which we can appeal for its date is a coin of Alexander Severus, A.D. 222. The passage of Seneca in which he gives the name Meta Sudans as being a spot at which the flute-players and trumpeters made a din by their practice, does not give us any information as to its position, and therefore we are not justified in assuming that the fountain was erected in Nero's time.[2] The coins of Titus which represent the Coliseum do

---

[2] Seneca's letter was written from Baiæ, which seems to place the building he speaks of there and not at Rome. The word "meta" was used by the Latin classical writers in speaking of haystacks or cream-cheeses made in a conical shape. Columella, ii. 19; Mart. i. 44.

not show it. Cassiodorus and other chronologists place the date of the Meta Sudans in Domitian's reign, and this agrees with the coins of Titus and also with the nature of the brickwork, which is of the Flavian era.

Near the Meta Sudans at the entrance of the Via di S. Gregorio stands the Arch of Constantine, which is the most completely preserved of all ancient Roman buildings. The name of Constantine, revered by subsequent ages, seems to have defended the archway from the barbarous spoliation which attacked most of the great monuments of Rome. The most interesting feature of this arch in the history of art is the proof which it gives of the decline of art in the fourth century. Some of the reliefs with which it is ornamented were taken from an older arch, probably that which formed the entrance to Trajan's Forum, and those which are of Constantine's time show a coarse and harsh style of execution in lamentable contrast to the flowing and delicate lines of the more ancient work by their side.

Arch of Constantine.

Among the sculptures which belong to the earlier and better period are the large reliefs under the central arch and those which are placed on either end of the attica. These four were originally parts of a larger relief which has been sawn into four equal pieces for the purpose of adorning Constantine's arch. The order in which they stood in the original design has been pointed out by Bellori. The first part is that now placed on the inside of the middle archway towards the Coliseum, the second stands on the side of the attica over the arch towards the Cælian, the third on the inside of the middle archway towards the Palatine, and the fourth upon the attica on the same side. When united they represented Trajan crowned by Victory, with the goddess Roma standing near, a battle between Dacians and Romans, ending in the defeat and submission of the barbarian army. The dress of the Roman soldiers and of the Dacians is similar to that represented on Trajan's column, and quite different from the Roman military habit in the age of Constantine. Beside these four rectangular reliefs the eight circular sculptures which stand over the smaller archways belong to the time of Trajan. They represent hunting scenes and sacrificial ceremonies. One of them, the second from the left, upon the side towards the Coliseum, has a remarkable figure of the Emperor with a nimbus or cloud encircling his head, exactly similar to those represented round the heads of modern saints. The eight large reliefs upon the attica over the side archways are also of the workmanship of Trajan's time, and commemorate some of the exploits of that emperor, among which may be mentioned the construction of a road through the Pontine marshes represented upon the second relief from the left on the side of the attica towards the Coliseum. The reclining figure with a wheel represents the road, and the other figures the surveyors, one of which is perhaps Apollodorus, the famous Greek architect of Damascus. The other reliefs upon the sides of the attica represent interviews of Trajan with barbarian princes, and the common sacrifice of the Suovetaurilia, so frequently depicted on the reliefs of the columns of that emperor, and also on the large marble screens now standing in the Forum Romanum. The remainder of the sculptures belong to the Constantinian era, and contain, viewed as works of art, nothing worth attention. One of them on the side next to the Coliseum is, however, of great interest to the antiquarian, as it represents the rostra of the later Empire and the northern end of the Forum, with the arches of Severus and Tiberius, and the end of the Basilica Julia, and another, on the side towards the Via di S. Gregorio representing the victory of Constantine over Maxentius at the Milvian bridge, is historically valuable.

The figures which stand in front of the attica have the Dacian costume, and have been removed from some one of Trajan's buildings. Upon the side of the central archway can be still seen the traces of nails which fastened some Roman ensigns to the stones. Similar traces of nails are to be seen upon the arch of Severus as before mentioned.

The inscriptions over the smaller arches refer to the decennalia or vicennalia, a festival celebrated after the time of Augustus every ten years of an emperor's reign when he was supposed to have the imperium conferred upon him afresh. The meaning of the expression VOTIS X. VOTIS XX. seems to be that these inscriptions were put up on the "vota" or day when vows were made for the emperor's safety at the beginning of the tenth and twentieth years of his reign. This is not an uncommon signification of the word "vota" in later Latin. The day which was usually called vota was either the first or third of January, and the custom of offering these vows was retained long after Christianity had been nominally made the state religion, so that it is not surprising to find it alluded to on Constantine's arch.[1] The words on the other side of the arch sic. x. sic. xx. may be interpreted as the form of words used in making vows to the emperor. "Sic x. annos regnet; sic xx. annos regnet." "May his reign last ten years more or twenty years."

The larger inscription which is cut upon the attica on both sides shows that the arch was erected in honour of the victory of Constantine over Maxentius, and the union of the empire under one sovereign. It is not, however, certain that the arch was built in the first year of Constantine's sole reign, for not only do the words INSTINCTU DIVINITATIS "by inspiration of the Deity," seem to indicate a more decided leaning to Christianity than Constantine showed at the beginning of his reign, but the title of Maximus, which is found in the inscription, does not occur in the coins of Constantine before the tenth year of his reign.

The solid contents of this arch, as may be seen by ascending the staircase which is entered by a door at some height from the ground at the end nearest the Palatine Hill, are mainly composed of pieces of marble taken from other buildings, and it has even been suspected that the plan itself, which in beauty of proportion surpasses the Arch of Severus, was borrowed, together with the materials, from Trajan's Arch or some older building now destroyed.

We now pass from the Arch of Constantine, with its borrowed ornamentation, to the great ruin of Rome, the Coliseum, or Flavian Amphitheatre. Although two-thirds of the original building have disappeared under the shameful treatment to which the barbarous nobles of the middle ages

The Coliseum.

[1] See Casaubon's note on Spartian, Hist. Aug. p. 40; n.c. Tac. Ann. vi. 17; xvi. 22.

subjected it, enough still remains to show the arrangement of the entrances, passages, and seats of this wonderful con-

The Colosseum, from the Palatine Hill.

struction. The plan of the whole may be best described as consisting of three principal massive concentric elliptical arcades. The intervals between each of these are filled in with other arched work containing corridors and staircases, and between the innermost of these three arcades and the wall which surrounded the arena was a triple system of substruction supporting the lower parts of the rows of seats in the amphitheatre. The stone used throughout is travertine, with the exception of some interior work of brick and concrete, and some pumice-stone in the arches. The elliptical shape was probably chosen instead of the circular in imitation of the amphitheatre of Curio, which was composed of two semi-circular theatres with their stages between them. The name Coliseum was possibly derived from the great colossal statue of Nero which for a long time stood close to the Flavian Amphitheatre, and when the real history of the amphitheatre was lost, would naturally become the most prominent mark by which it could be designated. This colossal statue was placed originally in the vestibule of Nero's Golden Palace, and was 120 feet high, according to Suetonius. The material was bronze and the artist was Zenodorus. It appears that Vespasian, and afterwards Hadrian, moved the colossus to make room for their new buildings, and that it was finally placed upon the massive pedestal of brickwork which still remains on the north of the Coliseum. That it actually stood upon this pedestal is shown by a coin of Alexander Severus, which represents the Coliseum with the colossus close to it. It is said by Gibbon that the name Coliseum was also given to the amphitheatre at Capua without reference to a colossal statue. The Capuan title may, however, have been taken from the Roman.

The major axis of this huge amphitheatre, from one outside wall to the other, measures 602 feet, the minor 507. The principal outer wall is 157 feet in height, and is divided into four stories.[1] Of these the lowest stands on a substruction of two steps, and originally consisted of a row of eighty arches, between which stood half columns of the Doric order.

---

[1] The great amphitheatre at El Djemm in Tunis is 480 feet by 420 and 102 feet in height, that at Pola in Istria 437 by 346 feet and 97 feet in height. Shaw's 'Travels,' i. p. 220. Ann. dell' Inst. 1852. Allason's Pola.

These outer arches, with the exception of thirty-three archways, have disappeared. Upon these rests a very simple entablature without any of the usual peculiarities of the Doric style, and rather belonging to the Ionic, a mixture of styles not very rare in Rome.[1] The arches are all numbered. These numbers were probably intended to correspond to those upon the entrance tickets and rows of seats, in order that the spectators might find their proper seats with ease. There is a staircase and a vomitorium corresponding to every four arches, and the vomitoria as well as the entrance arches were all numbered to prevent confusion. A ticket for the amphitheatre at Frosinone has been found. It bears an inscription CAN. VI. IN. X. VIII., thus giving the position and number of the seat. The arches which stood at the extremities of the minor axis were the approaches to the imperial pavilions. They were ornamented with marble columns and carved work on the exterior, and led in the interior to a large withdrawing-room, from which there was a separate passage to the emperor's throne (pulvinar) on the podium. On the Esquiline side the imperial entrance may still be recognised by a slight projection in the substructions, and by the pillars of white marble lying near it, which originally stood on each side. The same arrangement was doubtless made on the Caelian side, where the Emperor Commodus made himself an underground approach. The other two principal entrances at the extremities of the major axis lead directly into the arena, and were probably used for the entry of processions or marching bodies of gladiators, or machines of various kinds.

The entablature of the first story is surmounted by an attica, with projections corresponding to the columns below. Above these stand the arches of the second story, between which half-columns of the Ionic order are placed. The details of the architecture here are in a very meagre style, for the spiral lines on the volutes are omitted, and also the usual toothed ornaments of the entablature. The same remark applies to the third story, the half-columns of which have Corinthian capitals with the acanthus foliage very

---

[1] The tomb of Scipio Barbatus in the Vatican is another curious instance of this mixture of Doric and Ionic decorative forms.

roughly worked. The fourth story has no arches, but consists of a wall, pierced with larger and smaller square windows placed alternately, and is decorated with pilasters of the Composite order. Between each pair of pilasters three consoles project from the wall, and above these are corresponding niches in the entablature. The purpose of these was to support the masts upon which the awnings were stretched.

The second and third of the principal concentric walls contain arches corresponding to those in the outer wall. Corridors run between these concentric walls, and on the first and second floors of the outer ring, and the first floor of the inner ring, these circles afford a completely unobstructed passage all round. The other corridors are blocked up in parts by various staircases, leading to the upper rows of seats.

Within the third principal concentric arcade the supports of the building take the form of massive walls, radiating from the centre of the ellipse, and divided by elliptical corridors into three ranges. Between these massive walls and in the corridors are the steps and passages leading to the lower seats of the amphitheatre. The actual seats which were of marble have been all pilfered for the benefit of the Roman palaces and churches of the feudal ages, but we can still make out with tolerable certainty the five principal divisions into which they were separated. The lowest of these, called the podium, was a platform raised twelve or fifteen feet above the arena, upon which were placed the chairs of the higher magistrates and dignitaries. This was protected by railings and nets full of spikes, and sometimes also by trenches, called euripi, and horizontal bars of wood or iron which turned freely round, and thus afforded no hold to the paws of a wild animal.

Above the podium were four different orders of seats, divided by belts of upright masonry from each other. The first of these consisted of about twenty rows of seats, and was appropriated to the knights and tribunes, and other state officers. The upper row of this set was probably at a height of about ten feet above the top of the arches of the lowest story. The next ranges of seats between the second and third belt were appropriated to Roman citizens in general, and held the greatest number of spectators.

The wall dividing these seats from the next set was very high, and contained, besides the vomitoria or entrance doors, a number of windows for the purpose of lighting the corridors and passages. A considerable part of this wall is still extant upon the side towards the Esquiline Hill. Above it ran the third set of seats, occupied by the lower classes of the people, and above this again, and separated from it by a very low wall without vomitoria, was the fourth group of seats, immediately under the windows of the uppermost story, and covered by a portico which ran round the whole top of the building.[1] The traces of this uppermost row of seats and of the colonnade which supported the portico may still be seen on the side towards the Esquiline Hill.

The seats in this part seem to have been partly appropriated to women, partly to the lower classes. On the roof of the portico stood the workmen whose business it was to manage the awnings, and to move them as the sun or rain required. The number of seats in the whole amphitheatre is said to have been 87,000, and a considerable number, in addition to these, could stand in the passages between the seats at the entrances of the vomitoria, and in other vacant places, so that the whole number which the building, when filled from top to bottom, could hold, was probably not less than 90,000.

The exterior arcade of the building diminishes in thickness towards the top, in order to render it more stable, and while the Doric and Ionic columns of the first and second stories stand out from the wall by nearly three-quarters of their circumference, the third row of Corinthian columns projects less, and the uppermost row are merely pilasters.

Much discussion has been raised on the question of the awnings or *velaria* required for so large a space. It is impossible of course, in the absence of any distinct con-

---

[1] This portico is shown in the medals of Titus and Alexander Severus. The remains of a similar portico exist in the amphitheatre at Thysdrus (El Djemm) in Tunis. See Canina in the Ann. dell' Inst. 1852, tav. d'Agg. U.

temporaneous description, to discover the exact mode of suspension adopted. Venuti supposes that a net of cords constructed like a spider's web, with both radiating and concentric ropes, was suspended over the amphitheatre, and that by pulleys arranged over this the vela were drawn across any part which happened to be exposed to the sun. By means of pulleys attached to this network of rope, the little boys mentioned by Juvenal as caught up to the awnings may have been drawn up. The ropes and pulleys, we are told by Lampridius, were managed by sailors. In rough and windy weather the awnings could not always be drawn, and umbrellas coloured according to the favourite's colours, or large broad-brimmed hats called causiæ or birri, were then used. Martial has written some amusing epigrams, showing how jealously the seats appropriated to any particular privileged order were reserved. He gives the names of Lectius and Oceanus to the boxkeepers of his time, who chased intruders from the seats to which they were not entitled. And he describes with great humour the attempts of a certain Nanneius to smuggle himself into a better place than he was entitled to. The pickpockets of Martial's time also frequented the amphitheatre.

The anxiety of the public to attend the shows was so great that they occupied the free seats in the amphitheatre before dawn in the morning, and gave fees to the officials to keep places for them, when any favourite gladiator or bestiarius was announced to perform. The shows lasted whole days, and hence various contrivances for keeping the spectators in good humour, and filling up the intervals between the combats. Seneca tells us of the meridiani, a class of slaves who were kept on purpose to fill up the midday leisure hours with sham fights, and ludicrous pranks played upon the bodies of those killed or half killed in the previous fights. The air was cooled with immense jets of water projected from the centre of the arena, or from holes in the statues, and scented with fragrant essences, among which extract of saffron mixed with wine seems to have been the most popular.

The *arena* of the Coliseum was originally about 250 feet

in length, and 150 feet in breadth. It seems now much larger on account of the removal of the wall of the podium. The attention which has been drawn to the arena during the last few years by the re-opening of the hypogæa, or subterranean passages, renders it necessary to allude to the subject of these hypogæa, and to estimate how far the recent excavations have thrown new light upon the history and construction of the great amphitheatre. When the French occupied Rome, and it was incorporated into their empire in the four years preceding the Battle of Waterloo, the French Government carried out considerable excavations in the arena of the Coliseum, and besides clearing the podium and the chambers annexed to it, they opened the cryptoporticus which runs underground towards the Cælian Hill, and also discovered the passages beneath the arena which have been now excavated again.

A great controversy was raised at that time as to the real level of the original arena between several of the archæological professors and antiquarians of Rome. The same controversy has now been again revived, and the same questions as to the probable date of the underground constructions have been again raised, but with as little hope as ever of arriving at a satisfactory solution. The truth seems to be that, as in most amphitheatres, these hypogæa were constructed at the very first erection of the Coliseum, but have been altered, neglected, filled up, and again cleared out many times during the eventful history of the building, and that it has now become impossible to trace the various stages of such destructions and restorations. As often as the drains which were intended to carry off the water became choked and failed to act, these lower chambers and passages were filled with water and rendered useless.

The French excavations conducted till the early part of this century, 1810-1814, showed the general character of the chambers and passages under the arena. They consist of one central passage which extends under the arena from end to end in the line of the major axis of the ellipse. Parallel to this there are four narrower rectilineal passages on each side connected with each other by archways and surrounding these are three curved passages following the elliptical curves of the sides of the amphitheatre. The material of which these walls were originally built was great blocks of travertine similar to those in the surrounding construction of the amphitheatre, but they have been patched and propped in many places with tufa stones and brick, and now present a strange miscellaneous mass of masonry. These underground passages are similar to those found under the arena at Pozzuoli and Capua. It would seem that they must have been necessary, in addition to the chambers under the staircases of the building, for keeping wild beasts in large numbers, or for marshalling and arranging the long processions which were sometimes exhibited in the arena, or for other unusual exhibitions requiring more room for preparation than could be otherwise afforded. In the amphitheatre at Verona the passages under the arena seem to have served the purpose of drains, as they are much less extensive than those under the Coliseum, and are apparently connected with the channels which conducted the rain-water from the upper part. The same is the case with those at Pola in Istria, but at Pozzuoli and at Capua the hypogæa are of a similar character to those in the Coliseum, and were evidently used in connection with the exhibitions on the arena.

The excavations of 1810-14 do not seem to have been carried deep enough to show the floor of the hypogæa, and among the principal new objects of antiquarian interest discovered by the recent operations have been some large blocks of travertine sunk in the floor of the passages, and pierced in their centre with large round holes. These holes have evidently been the sockets into which upright posts of some kind were fixed. In some of these sockets a metal lining still remains, and in one of them the remains of a wooden post are said to have been found. Many conjectures as to the purpose of these sockets have been hazarded. They have been imagined to be the points on which revolving doors turned, or the holes into which posts for chaining wild beasts were fixed, or the capstans for the purpose of winding the ropes attached to stage machines. The explanation which appears to me to be the most probable is that they were used for the erection of temporary wooden posts in the same way in which at the present time such movable posts are used in some of the doorways of large houses in Rome, to divide the doorway temporarily into two distinct passages, by attaching a rope to the posts. When long processions had to be marched across the arena it would be necessary, if they were marshalled below, to have the course of the entering processionists and of those returning kept apart by some such device as that of a rope stretched between posts of this kind.

A large wooden framework has been found in the central passage, blackened by long exposure to the water. This seems to have been a contrivance for making an inclined plane on which heavy machines could be dragged up from below.

Another discovery which has been made is that of two cryptoportici, one of which extends towards the Esquiline and the Thermæ of Titus, and the other opens out from under the eastern end of the longer axis of the Coliseum. A few graffiti of interest representing gladiatorial figures, and some fragments of inscriptions relating to restorations of the building, or to the munificence of those who indulged the public with amphitheatrical exhibitions, have also been found.

The mode in which the naval contests mentioned by Dion as having been exhibited in the Coliseum were conducted, cannot be stated with any certainty. They were given by Titus at the dedication of the building and probably before its completion, so that the space now occupied by the hypogæa may then have been filled with water previously to the construction of the dividing walls.

Perhaps no building of ancient Rome is so strikingly characteristic of the builder, and the age in which he lived as the Flavian amphitheatre. Vespasian is described by historians, and represented on coins, and in extant sculptures, as a thick-set, square-shouldered man, with a short neck, small eyes, strongly marked but coarse features wearing an expression of effort. He cared little for the elegancies of life, and was plebeian in his tastes, and regardless of appearances, but set a high value on manliness and obstinate, unflinching endurance.

During his reign the prevalent feeling in the Roman nation was that of a worn-out and repentant prodigal. Sick of the frivolity and wanton debauchery of the Neronian age, yet unable to return to the ascetic simplicity of primitive times, men adored, for want of a better idol, the blunt honesty and coarse strength of the Flavians. What if their emperor wished that his courtiers should smell of garlic rather than of perfumery, if in his contempt for speculative genius he dubbed the agitating philosophers of his day "barking curs."[1] Yet he stood before them as a proof that the stern old vigour of the national character was not yet extinct, and that the profligate effeminacy of the previous generation had not yet rotted the Roman character to its core. The same massive power of endurance, yet ponderous and vulgar character, belongs to the architecture of the Coliseum. It exhibits a neglect, almost a contempt for elegance of proportion. The upper tiers are as heavy and solid as the lower. Its arcades are massive, practical, built to last for ages; the full, elaborate details of the Ionic and Corinthian orders, in which an artistic eye usually finds so much pleasure, are merely hinted at as superfluous.

Doubtless as we now see it, the ruin is far more effective than the complete building can ever have been. For when complete the appearance of the Coliseum must have been heavy and oppressive. The enormous unrelieved, flat surface of the upper wall must have seemed ready to topple over or to crush the arcade below. But now that earthquakes and barbarous hands have made such ghastly rents in its sides, the outline has become more varied, and the base more proportioned to the superstructure, so that although we can still recognise the flavour of a somewhat vulgar and material age, yet all that would have offended the eye has been removed, and the historical memories which cluster around its walls, of mighty emperors and bloodthirsty mobs, of screams of death or triumph, of gorgeous pageants and heroic martyrdoms, combine to render the

[1] Suet. Vesp. viii. 13.

Coliseum in its decay the most imposing ruin in the whole world.

Two architectural merits have been pointed out in the Coliseum, the impression of height and size conveyed by the tiers of arches rising one above another, and the graceful curves produced by the continuous lines of the entablatures as they cross the building. But what the Roman emperor under whose auspices this great building was raised would doubtless have valued more than any elegancies of design which could have been pointed out to him, is the perfect adaptation of the structure to its purposes. After the great catastrophe at Fidenæ where 20,000 persons were injured or killed by the breaking down of a wooden amphitheatre, solidity and safety were the principal requisites. Free ingress and egress for crowds of spectators, as well as for any great personages who might attend, was indispensable. A glance at the plan of the Coliseum will show how admirably each of these objects was attained. The extraordinary solidity of the building removed all possibility of the failure of any part to bear whatever weight might be heaped upon it, and the entrances, galleries and vomitoria were by the oval form of the building rendered so numerous that each seat in the whole cavea was accessible at once and without difficulty. A system of carefully arranged barriers in the passages would effectually prevent confusion and excessive crowding.

In endeavouring to adorn the great amphitheatre of the metropolis more richly than those of the provinces its architect defeated his own object. Some of the provincial amphitheatres, as that of Capua, though in other respects like the Coliseum, show a simpler and therefore more natural exterior. When the Doric order is retained in all the tiers, it harmonises far better with the rude strength of such an edifice than the Corinthian and Ionic orders of the Coliseum. At Verona and Pola a still further improvement is made by the rustication of the exterior. At Nismes, on the other hand, the faults of the Coliseum are aggravated by breaking the entablatures, and introducing pediments over each front; and in the small Amphitheatrum Castrense at Rome, where the

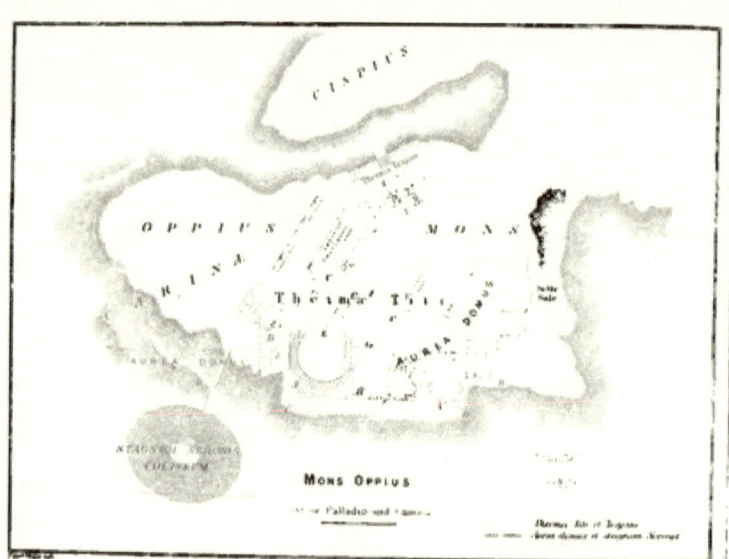

Corinthian order is executed in brick, a lamentable illustration of Roman want of taste is exhibited.

The holes which are now so conspicuous in the travertine blocks of the exterior wall of the Coliseum were probably made in the middle ages to extract the iron clamps by which the stones were fastened together. Some antiquarians have however held that they are the holes in which the beams of the buildings which clustered round the Coliseum in mediæval times were fixed. At the end of the fifteenth and at the beginning of the sixteenth century, the travertine blocks of the amphitheatre were used as a quarry from which to build palaces, and it is said that the Palazzo di Venezia, the Palazzo Farnese, and the Palazzo della Cancelleria were constructed of the stone robbed from hence. During part of the eleventh and twelfth centuries a castle of the powerful family of the Frangipani, which afterwards belonged to the Annibaldi stood in the walls of the Coliseum. Later generations of nobles and popes since the beginning of the nineteenth century have propped the building by buttresses of brickwork, and have endeavoured to postpone the date foretold by two Anglo-Saxon pilgrims as that of the fall of Rome. "When the Coliseum falls, Rome will fall."[1]

Aurea Domus of Nero. Baths of Titus. The Coliseum was built by Vespasian in a depression between the Cælian and Esquiline Hills, which had been occupied by a large lake of ornamental water, called the Stagnum Neronis, used by Nero for aquarian entertainments and exhibitions. The vast palace known as the Domus Aurea Neronis extended along the side of the Esquiline on the north of the Coliseum. The Flavian emperors destroyed this palace, and Titus built a new group of courts and chambers over the ruins. The relics of these buildings of Titus are now remaining mingled with the substructures and lower parts of the Domus Aurea which they superseded. They are entered by a gateway on the road leading from the Coliseum to S. Pietro in Vincoli.

So far as we can draw any conclusion from the fragmentary and confused piles of ruins now left, and from the plan which Palladio sketched at a time when the remains of the palace

---

[1] Gibbon, 'Decline and Fall,' ch. lxxi.

had not so completely disappeared, it seems that this part of Nero's palace consisted of a long straight façade of buildings extending along the slope of the Esquiline from east to west in the direction marked on the plan (A—B). In front of this there seems to have been a projecting court surrounded by small chambers (C—D). A few of these still remain at the western end, and are used as a dwelling-house for the custode. Behind the above-mentioned façade were numerous rooms of various kinds, and courts surrounded with colonnades. One of these courts with its adjacent corridors and apartments is now partly accessible (E, F), but the greater part were filled in with rubbish when the baths of Titus were built over them, and have never been entirely cleared. In the centre of this court the remains of a fountain-basin and a pedestal may be seen. The area is now traversed by parallel walls built by Titus to serve as substructions to his Thermæ. These are indicated on the plan by the dotted lines in black.

All the rooms in this part which are now accessible have arched roofs, and are covered with decorative paintings. Fortunately a great number of these have been preserved to us by artists who copied them before they were destroyed by damp and the soot of the cicerone's torch. At the present time scarcely enough remains to show the beauty and delicacy of the designs. The best preserved paintings are in the long north corridor, where is also an inscription illustrating Persius, Sat. i. 113 :

> "Pinge duos angues: pueri, sacer est locus, extra
> Mejite."

The two snakes were symbolic of the Lares Compitales, and are common at Pompeii. Raphael adopted the same style of ornamentation as that preserved here in the Loggie of the Vatican. The rooms now shown, which contain a bath and other household apparatus, apparently belonged to a private house, and may either have formed a part of the Aurea Domus, or of some house built on its site at the time immediately following Nero's death. The eleven rooms (F) which occupied the north side of the court (E) contain traces of wooden staircases leading to an upper story. The decorations and fittings of these appear to have been so inferior to those of the other rooms, that we must suppose them to have been occupied by the imperial slaves, or by the household troops. At the northern end of this row of chambers is a room with mosaic pavement at a considerably lower level than those surrounding it, and which must therefore have belonged to some building earlier in date than the Domus Aurea. It is sometimes called a part of the House of Mæcenas, but there is no authority for this, and it is more probable that the House of Mæcenas stood nearer to the Agger of Servius.

Another portion of the Domus Aurea is still visible at the SETTE SALE, a large brick building lying in a vineyard to the left of the Via delle Sette Sale. The purpose of this was plainly to serve as a reservoir for water, and it is shown to have belonged to the Domus Aurea, and not to the Thermæ of Titus, by the correspondence of its position with the ground-plan of the former. It may have been afterwards used in connection with the Thermæ, and was possibly preserved with that view, while the rest of the palace was destroyed or buried. The peculiar construction of the interior, which is divided into nine compartments, communicating with each other by openings—not placed opposite to each other, but in a slanting direction across the building—is said to have been so arranged in order to prevent the heavy mass of water from bursting open the sides of the building. The group of the Laocöon was found near the Sette Sale, and it is supposed that the state-rooms of Titus may have contained that group of statues. *Sette Sale.*

Returning to the ruins of the Baths of Titus near the Coliseum it may be observed that these Thermæ were connected with the Coliseum by a portico, traces of which can still be seen on the north side of the amphitheatre. The arrangement of the building corresponded in some degree to that of the Baths of Caracalla, consisting apparently of a large square court surrounded by various offices and places for recreation, in the centre of which stood a vast mass of building containing the bath-rooms. The sides of this court were not parallel to any lines of *Thermæ or Baths of Titus.*

building in the Domus Aurea, and, therefore, in order to form a level area many new substructions had to be erected. This is plainly the case with the theatre (A), which occupied the centre of the side towards the Coliseum. In order to raise this to the level of the rest of the area, the nine huge arched chambers, which are now a most conspicuous part of the ruins, were erected, and one of the courtyards of the Domus Aurea was filled, as we have seen, with parallel walls of brickwork. On each side of the theatre there were probably gymnasia, libraries, or ball courts (B B). The central building was occupied with the frigidarium and tepidarium, and the other usual adjuncts of a large Roman bath (C C C).

The catalogue called the 'Curiosum urbis Romæ' places not only the Baths of Titus but also those of Trajan in the third region. The anonymous MS. of Einsiedlen places Trajani Thermæ near the Church of S. Pietro in Vincoli; and Anastasius in his 'Life of Symmachus,' mentions them as near the Church of S. Martino. It is, therefore, abundantly proved that the Thermæ of Trajan stood at the back of the Baths of Titus, and it is here that we find them placed in the plan of Palladio. That they were distinct buildings seems clear from an inscription in which they are separately mentioned. A satisfactory explanation of the apparently strange fact that Trajan erected new and smaller Thermæ near those of Titus is given by one of the chronologers of the period, who speaks of the Baths of Trajan as intended for women, for whom there was no separate accommodation provided in those of Titus. The scattered ruins to the north of the Baths of Titus may have belonged to Trajan's Baths.

On the Esquiline Hill, besides the Baths of Titus, the Domus Aurea, and the Sette Sale, we find four remarkable ruins, which are called the Trophies of Marius, the Arch of Gallienus, the Minerva Medica, and the Auditorium of Mæcenas.

Trophies of Marius. The ruin called the Trophies of Marius stands at the corner of the Via di S. Bibiana. It consists in the lower part of a number of small and curiously shaped compartments of brickwork, with openings at seven or eight different points. Underneath these, and now hidden under the level of the ground, is a large basin or tank, and above them the upper part of the building is formed by the remains of three niches, in which stood the marble trophies now placed upon the balustrade of the steps of the Capitol. They were removed to the Capitol by Sixtus V. in the year 1585. The name Trophies of Marius is an attempt to explain the more ancient name of Cimbrum, which we find attached to the ruin in the middle ages, by identifying the trophies with the Tropæa Marii mentioned by Suetonius as having been pulled down by Sulla and restored by Julius Cæsar.[1] But although we must allow that there is some probability in the supposition that the Marian trophies may have occupied these niches, yet it is certain that the building itself was intended to serve another purpose, that of the castellum or principal reservoir of an aqueduct, with a public fountain in the form of a cascade in front. The basin which has been discovered under the building, and the peculiar shape of the complicated interior structure, can be best explained thus, and the remains of some part of the aqueduct itself may be seen at the back. It was at one time supposed that the Aqua Julia ended here but it is now generally acknowledged that the ruin belonged to the Aqua Alexandrina, and that the name Nymphæum Alexandri, found in the catalogues of the fifth region, must be assigned to it. The Alexandrine Aqueduct was built by Alexander Severus in the year A.D. 225. Water was brought to Rome by means of it from a spot near the Lake Regillus, and a portion is still visible on the left hand of the Via Labicana about two miles from Rome. The level of this aqueduct corresponds exactly with the building in question, and the style of brickwork and architecture are such as might belong to the third century. It is possible, as Reber remarks, that Alexander Severus may have found the exact spot where the Trophies of Marius had been placed by Julius Cæsar convenient for the castellum of his aqueduct, and have used the trophies to ornament the new building which he erected.

Close to the Church of S. Vito, and spanning the Via di S. Vito, stands the Arch of Gallienus, erected by M. Aurelius

Arch of Gallienus.

---

[1] Suet. Jul. ii. Propert. iv. ii. 46.

Victor, prefect of Rome in A.D. 262, in honour of the Emperor Gallienus and Empress Salonina. It is constructed of travertine, and the ornamental work upon it is extremely simple, consisting only of pilasters crowned by roughly worked Corinthian capitals, and surmounted by an entablature of the commonest kind. Part of the basement is buried under the present level of the soil, and from a sketch by San Gallo of its state in the fifteenth century there appears to have been a pediment above the entablature, and two smaller archways on each side. The inscription, which is now hardly legible, is cut upon the architrave and contains a flattering description of one of the most singularly accomplished and incapable emperors of Rome, of whom Gibbon says, "Gallienus was a master of several curious but useless sciences, a ready orator and elegant poet, a skilful gardener, an excellent cook, and most contemptible prince."[1]

Minerva Medica.

In the grounds of the Villa Magnani, which are reached from the Via di S. Bibiana, are two small Columbaria, one of which formerly contained inscriptions relating to the family of the Arruntii, and also one which belonged to Statilius Taurus, a nobleman mentioned by Tacitus. This was decorated with scenes from the Æneid of Virgil, but these are nearly destroyed. In the same gardens, not far to the north-west of the Porta Maggiore, stands a lofty and picturesque ruin, comprising a central decagonal hall surrounded by four other apartments, the ground-plan of which has been preserved by San Gallo. The central hall contained nine deep niches, and the entrance passes through the tenth side. Over the niches and the entrance archway are round-headed windows, and the roof was of vaulted brickwork. Traces still remain of stucco work and cement on the inner walls, from which it appears that they were covered with ornamental work and in some parts with marble.

Parts of the pavement, which was of porphyry, have also been found, and in the neighbourhood of the ruin a number of sculptures have been at various times discovered, among which are statues of Pomona, Æsculapius, Adonis, Venus, Hercules, Antinous, some Luperci, and a Faun. The old

---

[1] Gibbon, 'Decline and Fall,' ch. x.

topographers, Blondus Flavius and Lucius Faunus, give the name of Terme di Galuccio or Galuzze to the ruin, and this name has been ingeniously explained as referring to the Thermæ or Basilica of Caius and Lucius. But there is no good foundation for this conjecture, or for the identification of the building with the Temple of Minerva Medica, mentioned in the Notitia. The latter name was derived from the supposed discovery here of the Pallas Giustiniani, now in the Braccio Nuovo of the Vatican. But another and more ancient account asserts that the statue of Pallas was found near S. Maria sopra Minerva, and therefore the name of Minerva Medica cannot with any certainty be applied here.

Canina has proposed another explanation of the name Galuzze. He thinks that the ruins belonged to the Palatium Licinianum, which is mentioned by Anastasius, in his 'Life of Simplicius,' as near the Church of S. Bibiana. This palace, he thinks, is identical with the Pleasure Gardens of Gallienus, who bore the name of Licinius, in which, according to Trebellius Pollio, he used to bathe and banquet with his courtiers. The name Galuzze is, therefore, according to Canina, derived from Gallieni Liciniaria, and the building may be supposed to have formed a part of the baths in Gallienus's pleasure grounds, resembling as it does in its construction the great rotunda of the Baths of Caracalla. The proximity of the Arch of Gallienus adds probability to this conjecture. The basin now standing in the ruin is not ancient, and therefore cannot be held to support this conjecture, but the brickwork and style of architecture are said by competent judges to be such as might have been erected at the time of the later Empire. The building called Minerva Medica by the Notitia may have been near this spot, as some inscriptions here discovered show, but it most probably consisted only of a chapel of no great extent standing near the Via Prænestina.

The extensive alterations which have been carried on at Rome during the last few years in the district at the back of the Viminal and Esquiline Hills, where a new quarter of the city is being laid out, have disclosed a number of fragments of sculptures and inscriptions, a detailed account of which has been given from time to time in the *Bullettino della*

Commissione Archeologica Municipale, and in the letters of Mr. Hemans to the *Academy*. The most interesting relics bearing upon topographical questions are the inscription relating to the Macellum Liviæ and Forum Esquilinum found near the Arch of Gallienus, and the supposed foundations of the Villa of Mæcenas.

Most of the antiquarian and artistic relics lately discovered here have been deposited in the Capitoline Museum.

Unfortunately the necessary extension of the buildings attached to the railway station has resulted in the destruction of a large portion of the Servian Agger. Some large fragments of the huge blocks belonging to the Servian wall may be seen at the back of the station. Traces of a road and a gate were found which have been supposed to belong to the Via and Porta Viminalis, and many confused heaps of ruins, the relics of private houses built up against the side of the agger. In one of these the bricks bore the date of the third consulship of Servianus, A.D. 134, and of that of Niger and Camerinus, A.D. 138.

A Hermeracles in marble was found near the station, which is figured in the *Bullettino della Commissione* for March 1873, and numerous mosaic pavements, one of which is laid on the floor of the waiting-room at the station.

Auditorium.

One of the buildings attached to an ancient house in this neighbourhood has been carefully preserved and walled in for protection. It stands near the ruin called the Trophies of Marius, and not far from the Arch of Gallienus, and consists of a semicircular recess with ledges rising one above another in the form of a miniature theatre. A more correct description of the site is given by stating that it stands where the former gardens of the convent of the Redentoristi were situated. This building has, on account of its resemblance to a theatre, and of its position on a spot over which the famous Gardens of Mæcenas probably extended, been called the Auditorium of Mæcenas, and romantic ideas have been connected with it as having been the actual auditorium where Virgil and Horace may have recited their poetry to their great patron. This view, however, has been shown to be untenable by Signor Mau, who thinks with more probability that the ruin in question is an ornamental recess for decorative works of art and flowers or a fountain. Such recesses may be seen in some of the houses at Pompeii. The paintings on the walls are of a style similar to those in the Villa of Livia at Prima Porta, and the building may therefore possibly belong to the Augustan age.

The inscriptions on the Porta S. Lorenzo at the eastern side of the Esquiline Hill tell the history of the several gateways here built by Augustus and other emperors down to Honorius. The aqueducts run along the walls from this gate to the Porta Maggiore. *Porta S. Lorenzo.*

The Gateway of Honorius was removed from the Porta Maggiore by Gregory XVI. as the inscription on the present gate records. The removal of the old gateway disclosed the Tomb of Eurysaces, a bread contractor, which is a very fantastic monument, constructed of stone mortars used for kneading dough, and ornamented with some curious bas-reliefs of a good period of art, representing the operations of baking. The inscriptions upon it are as follows: "EST HOC MONIMENTUM MARCEI VERGILEI EURYSACIS PISTORIS AC REDEMPTORIS APPARETORUM. FUIT ATISTIA UXOR MIHEI FEMINA OPTIMA VEIXSIT QUOJUS CORPORIS RELIQUIE QUOD SUPERANT SUNT IN HOC PANARIO." The latter of these inscriptions, however, probably belongs to some other tomb, the remains of several having been found here, which lead to the supposition that this was a spot especially devoted to the burial of bakers. *Porta Maggiore. Tomb of Eurysaces.*

The present gateway is formed by two arches of the Claudian Aqueduct, which runs along the course of the walls from this point to the corner near the Amphitheatrum Castrense. The arches are built of rusticated travertine blocks, and each of the piers is pierced with a smaller arch, decorated with Corinthian half-columns of rustic work and pediments in the usual Græco-Roman style of a triumphal arch. This gateway is one of the most characteristic creations of Roman architecture. It conveys more than any other building I know, except, perhaps, the rusticated archways of the amphitheatre at Verona, the impression of rough force and solidity. Over the arches are three atticas, upon which the following inscriptions are cut, recording the erection and renewal of the Claudian aqueduct by Claudius, Vespasian, and Titus:

TI. CLAUDIUS DRUSI F. CAISAR AUGUSTUS GERMANICUS PONTIF. MAXIM. TRIBUNICIA POTESTATE XII. COS V. IMPERATOR XXVII. PATER PATRIE AQUAS CLAUDIAM EX FONTIBUS QUI VOCABANTUR CÆRULEUS ET CURTIUS A MILLIARIO XXXXV. ITEM AMERIEM NOVAM A MILLIARIO LXVII. SUA INPENSA IN URBEM PERDUCENDAS CURAVIT. IMP. CÆSAR VESPASIANUS AUGUST. PONTIF. MAX. TRIB. POT. II. IMP. VI. COS. III. DESIG. III. P. P. AQUAS CURTIAM ET CÆRULEAM PERDUCTAS A DIVO CLAUDIO ET POSTEA INTERMISSAS DILAPSASQUE PER ANNOS NOVEM SUA IMPENSA URBI RESTITUIT.

IMP. T. CÆSAR DIVI F. VESPASIANUS AUGUSTUS PONT. MAX. TRIBUNIC. POTEST. X. IMP. XVII. P. P. CENS. COS. VIII. AQUAS CURTIAM ET CÆRULEAM PERDUCTAS A DIVO CLAUDIO ET POSTEA A DIVO VESPASIANO PATRE SUO URBI RESTITUTAS CUM A CAPITE AQUARUM A SOLO VETUSTATE DILAPSÆ ESSENT NOVA FORMA REDUCENDAS SUA IMPENSA CURAVIT.

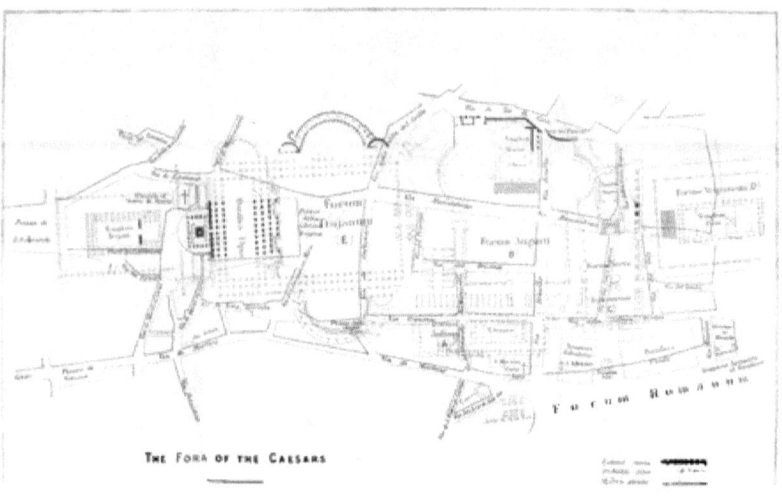

THE FORA OF THE CAESARS

CHAPTER IV.

THE IMPERIAL FORA AND THE CAPITOLIUM.

The whole space between the Quirinal and the Capitoline Hills *Trajan's* was occupied by the immense Forum and public buildings *Forum.* which Trajan constructed. The Column of Trajan, with its wonderful spiral reliefs, still marks the site of this great mass of masonry; but the remainder, which included a basilica, two libraries, a temple, and two extensive porticoes, has disappeared with the exception of a fragmentary ruin in the Via della Salita del Grillo under the Quirinal. This ruin is the remains of *Ruin in* a part of the great semicircular side of Trajan's Forum *the Salita del Grillo.* under the Quirinal Hill. It consists of a brick building of two stories high, containing in the lower story small rooms measuring about ten feet square, probably shops or offices for notaries and lawyers' clerks. The interior of three of the rooms is covered with plaster, and painted roughly. The floors were covered with mosaic pavement of a common kind, of which much still remains in situ. Above these rooms runs a corridor with arched windows, at the back of which a row of large and high chambers opens, resting upon the natural rock of the Quirinal Hill. The front is faced with brick pilasters on travertine basements, in a mixed Doric and Ionic style, and there were formerly pediments over the windows.

It will be seen by reference to the plan that a small portion of the Forum of Trajan can be now seen in the Piazza della Colonna Trajana. The arch from which the beautiful bas-reliefs on Constantine's Arch were robbed, probably stood in the Via del Priorato at some distance from the Piazza.

The two double rows of bases now to be seen in the Piazza formed a part of the great Basilica Ulpia, part of the ground-plan of which is still preserved on two fragments of the Capitoline map. Many fragments are to be seen here of the columns which supported the roof of the basilica, among which those of grey granite, probably belonging to the outer rows of columns, are most conspicuous.

Column of Trajan.

The great PILLAR with its well-known spiral bas-reliefs, perhaps the most interesting and instructive monument of antiquity in Rome, was surrounded when the buildings round it were complete with a narrow court not more than forty feet square. The south side of this was formed by the Basilica Ulpia, the eastern and western by the libraries, and on the north there was probably an open colonnade, the line of which can be traced leading to the structures beyond, where stood the temple dedicated to Trajan. Thus we discover a fact which seems at first somewhat surprising, that the pillar could not be viewed in its full height from any side, and that the upper part of it alone was visible from the Forum over the roof of the basilica. That it was intentionally thus enclosed is evident, for had the Greek architect Apollodorus of Damascus, who designed the Forum, wished it to be where the full colossal proportions could be seen, the open space of the Forum was close at hand, in the centre of which it might have been placed. But it is not unlikely that the sight of a column was almost inseparable in the Greek architectural ideas from an entablature and pediment. The Greeks did not place their statues on the top of columns, and probably had this reason for it, that a single column cannot form a whole by itself, and wears a forsaken and deserted aspect when viewed from any distance. An obelisk conveys a different meaning, and the use of a single column cannot be justified by it. The obelisk tapers upwards and completes itself, but a column instantly brings the idea of support with it. Obelisks, moreover, were never used singly by the Egyptians, but always placed in pairs. The intention of the architect was not that the column should be viewed as we now view it, as a whole, but that the colossal statue of the emperor might be raised on high above his splendid group of buildings, and also that the bas-reliefs should be conveniently viewed from the surrounding galleries.

The height of the column is 124 feet from the pavement to the foot of the statue. It stands upon a pedestal of marble

The Column of Trajan.

eighteen feet high, ornamented on three sides with highly interesting bas-reliefs representing trophies of Roman and Dacian armour of various kinds, the Roman labarum and the Dacian dragon, coats of mail made of scale or chain armour, helmets, curved and straight swords, axes, clubs, bows, quivers, arrows, lances, trumpets, and several kinds of military tools. On the fourth side two genii bear the tablet on which is the inscription: SENATUS POPULUSQUE ROMANUS IMP. CAESARI DIVI NERVAE F. NERVAE TRAJANO AUG. GERM. DACICO PONTIF. MAXIMO TRIB. POT. XII. IMP. VI. PP. AD DECLARANDUM QUANTAE ALTITUDINIS MONS ET LOCUS TANT[is operi]BUS SIT EGESTUS.

The last words of this inscription are illustrated by a passage of Dion Cassius, who says that Trajan placed a colossal pillar in his Forum to be his own tomb, and also to show the amount of labour expended upon the Forum, the slope of the hill which previously occupied the site having been dug away so as to afford a level space for the Forum. There is no need to interpret this, as some writers have done, to mean that the ground on the spot where the column stands had previously been as high as the top of the column. Such an interpretation seems highly improbable. The view taken by Becker and Brocchi is more tenable, that the words allude to the cutting away of the Quirinal Hill, which was steep and inaccessible before but was sloped away to a point on the side of the hill as high as the top of the column. Brocchi's geological observations have made it almost certain that the ground has not been cut away to any great depth between the two hills.

The top of the column is only six feet lower than the level of the Villa Aldobrandini on the top of the Quirinal, and two feet higher than the Piazza di Ara Cœli. If, therefore, at any time the ground on the site of Trajan's Forum was as high as the column, it must have formed a ridge between the Capitoline and Quirinal Hills, higher than the Capitoline and very nearly as high as the Quirinal.

In the base of the column the ashes of Trajan were deposited in a golden urn. Sixtus V. had the chamber in which the urn was placed opened, but found it empty, and it has now been walled up.

Above the pedestal are two flat stones ornamented with garlands of oak leaves, and upon them rests a round base carved in the shape of a laurel wreath. The shaft which stands immediately upon this is composed of nineteen cylindrical blocks of marble, on the outside of which a spiral band of beautifully executed bas-reliefs winds from bottom to top, covering the whole shaft. The capital is a single ring of egg-shaped ornaments with arrowheads between them, and a simple border below. On a pedestal above it stood originally the colossal bronze-gilt statue of Trajan. This statue and pedestal were probably carried off during the robberies committed at Rome by the Byzantine emperors, A.D. 663. Sixtus V. replaced it by a modern cylindrical pedestal and statue of S. Peter. The ancient winding staircase hewn in the solid blocks of marble, and lighted by narrow openings, still leads to the top. From thence it may be seen how difficult it is to suppose that the ground ever rose to such a height between the Capitoline and Quirinal as has been imagined by many historians and topographers.

The magnificent wreath of bas-reliefs which winds round the shaft may be best studied by means of the model to be seen in the French Academy on the Pincian Hill, or that in the Kensington Museum. It contains the history of two campaigns against the Dacians, and has been ingeniously and minutely interpreted by several writers. A complete account of this marble history of the Dacian wars, with a discussion of all the historical and antiquarian points connected with it, would occupy several volumes, and we must, therefore, content ourselves with noticing the general character of the work and some few of the more interesting portions. *Bas-reliefs representing scenes in the Dacian wars.*

Two campaigns are represented. The first of these took place in the year 101, and during it Trajan's army passed down the river Save and crossed the Danube in two divisions at Kastolatz and at the confluence of the Tjerna. The two divisions effected a junction at the pass of the Bistra, called the Iron Gate, which they forced, and then attacked and took the royal city Zermizegethusa. Trajan was not satisfied with this success, but pushed on into the heart of the enemy's *Trajan's first campaign in Dacia.*

country, and gained a great victory at Tapæ, after which Decebalus, the Dacian king, sued for peace.

The bas-relief begins at the base by a representation of the banks of the Save, down which the Roman army passed, and shows military storehouses, piles of wood, stacks of hay, and wooden huts. Then follow forts with soldiers on guard, and boats carrying barrels of provisions.

The river god Danube then appears and looks on with astonishment at the bridge of boats over which the Roman army is passing. The baggage of the soldiers on the march, tied to the top of the vallum or palisade which they carry, and the different military standards, are very distinctly shown. Many of the men are without covering on their heads, but some wear lions' skins. The emperor and his staff are then introduced. He is sitting upon a suggestus or platform, and Lucius, the Prætorian prefect, sits beside him. The snovetaurilia, a grand sacrificial celebration, is the next scene, with priests in the Cinctus Gabinus and trumpeters. After this the emperor is seen making a speech to the army, and a little farther on the building of a stone encampment enclosing huts is being carried on with great vigour, and bridges are being thrown across a river, over which cavalry are passing.

A battle seems then to take place, and the heads of two enemies are being brought to the emperor. The Dacian army with the dragon ensign and the Dacian cap, the symbol of superior rank, seen upon the statues of the Dacian prisoners on the Arch of Constantine, appears. Jupiter gives the victory to the Romans, the Dacian camp is burnt, and the Dacians fly.

Numerous representations of forts, boats, different kinds of troops, skirmishes, and sieges follow, ending with the surrender of Decebalus and the return of Trajan to Rome, where a great festival is celebrated. The arrival at Rome, and the crowd of Romans going to meet the great conqueror, are very vividly drawn. An immense number of bulls for sacrifice, altars, camilli, and half-naked popæ are introduced into the triumphal rejoicings, and the first campaign ends with the figure of Trajan offering incense on the altar of Jupiter Capitolinus.

A somewhat similar series of scenes are represented in the sculptures which depict the second campaign. Perhaps the most interesting is that of the great bridge over the Danube, made of wood supported on stone piers, the foundations of which may still be seen in the bed of the river. Apollodorus, the architect of the Forum, designed this immense work, which crossed the Danube at a spot where it is not less than 1300 yards wide, near the village of Gieli. A permanent road into Dacia and secure communications with his basis of operations having thus been secured, Trajan gradually advanced from post to post, driving the Dacians into the mountainous parts of the country. The sculptures represent a number of skirmishes and assaults upon fortified places, but no regular pitched battle. At last the ghastly spectacle of the head and hands of Decebalus is exhibited on a board by two soldiers in front of the Prætorium. This disgusting scene is followed by a representation of the storming of the last strongholds of the enemy in the mountains, and a mournful procession of fugitives carrying away their goods and driving their cattle into exile forms the close of the sculptured history of the Dacian campaigns of Trajan.[1]

In these curious bas-reliefs we have a treasury of information on the religion, the military science, the habits and dress of the Romans of the Empire far more valuable than ten thousand pages of descriptive writing. The lover of Roman antiquities will learn more by studying Fabretti's engravings of these reliefs, or the casts at the French Academy at Rome, and at the Kensington Museum, than by much book-labour. The descriptions of Livy and Polybius, Cæsar and Tacitus, receive life, and movement, and interest as we look at the actual figures (oculis subjecta fidelibus) of the general and his staff; the Prætorian guards marked by their belts over the left shoulder; the fierce-looking standard-bearers and centurions with their heads covered by lions' skins, the shaggy manes of which stream down their backs; the rank and file carrying enormous stakes; the master masons, sappers, and pioneers, with their axes and crowbars; the lancers, heavy and light cavalry, and royal chargers; the Sarmatian horse-

[1] See Dion Cassius, lxviii. 9-13.

men, clothed, both riders and steeds, in complete scale armour, and the Moorish cavalry, riding without reins.

Bridges are constructed, Roman causeways laid, forts attacked with all kinds of military engines; the charge of cavalry, the rout and confusion of a defeated army, are all most vividly depicted. Trajan in person traverses the ranks on foot, or mounts the suggestus and harangues his men, or receives with simple dignity the submission of the enemy, or marches with all the pomp of a Roman procession under the triumphal arch. The soldierlike simplicity of the great military emperor is strikingly portrayed. There is no silken tent, or richly decorated chariot, or throne, or canopy of state to be seen. His colonel of the guards sits beside him, as an equal, on the suggestus. In the midst of a battle the emperor tears up his robe to bind the wounds of his soldiers; he is present everywhere, wearing a sword and fighting in person. Nothing could be more illustrative of the state of Roman affairs in that iron age when again, as in the olden times, a rough and unlettered warrior, fresh from the camp, swayed the destinies of the empire.

In this vast spiral relief there are said to be above 2500 figures of men sculptured, and the higher they are placed on the column the larger are their dimensions, showing the care that was taken to counteract the effects of the increased distance from the eye. The whole of the carving from base to summit is executed with equally minute care, though the upper part can never have been easily visible, except from the windows or roofs of the basilica and the libraries which, as we have seen, were placed very near. The opinion which prevailed for some time, that the figures had been coloured, is incorrect, as the more minute examination since made has proved that the colours imagined to be artificial are the natural results of the decay of the stone and oxidisation of the metallic parts of the structure, under the effects of the rain, sun, and dust.

Remains found on the site. A vast number of fragments of columns, of inscriptions, and of architectural ornaments have been dug up at various times on the site of Trajan's Forum. The great granite columns which now lie near the base of the pillar were found in laying the foundations of the Church of S. Maria in Loreto, by the architect, the elder San Gallo, and are mentioned as lying near that church in the middle of the sixteenth century. The equestrian statue of Marcus Aurelius, in the Piazza del Campidoglio, stands upon a pedestal made by Michael Angelo out of an immense fragment of entablature found on the site of Trajan's Forum.

An inscription, which is now built into the wall on the north of the pillar, commemorates the remission of all debts to the emperor's private purse (fiscus) by Hadrian, a fact which we find also mentioned in Dion Cassius and Spartianus. The latter writer adds that it was in the Forum of Trajan that Hadrian publicly burnt the list of his debtors, and the inscription was no doubt intended to mark the spot of this act of liberality or bribery.

The ruins of two portions only of the Forum Julium, which Ruins of adjoined that of Trajan, have been discovered in modern the Forum Julium. times. The first is a considerable part of the outer wall of the Forum, standing in the court of the house No. 18 in the Via del Ghetarello, a small street which opens out of the Via di Marforio, near the Carcer and the Church of SS. Martina e Luca. This ruined wall consists of three arches composed of large blocks of peperino and travertine skilfully cut and joined without mortar and under-built by another arch, as if in order to enable the wall to bear a great weight. The length of the fragment of wall is about 50 feet and the highest point about 30 feet.

The other relic of Cæsar's Forum is now no longer visible. We obtain our information about it from Palladio, the architect, about the middle of the sixteenth century, who relates that while he was at Rome the ground-plan of a temple was uncovered in digging the foundations of a house between the Salita di Marforio and the temple of Mars Ultor, a description which points plainly to the block of houses behind SS. Martina e Luca. There was a peculiarity in the intercolumniations of this temple, which Palladio particularly remarked. The distance between the columns, he says, was the eleventh part of the diameter of a column less than a diameter and a half.

<small>Forum of Augustus. Temple of Mars Ultor.</small> The almost universal opinion of Roman topographers now is that the three Corinthian columns on the left-hand side of the Via Bonella and the massive arch which leads from it into the Via di Tor di Conti are the remains of the Temple of Mars Ultor, which Augustus built in his Forum, and of the north-eastern portion of the enclosing wall.

This opinion was already held by Palladio in the sixteenth century, but the Italian antiquaries since his time have adopted the most various hypotheses on the subject. There is, it is true, no actual proof that this was the temple of Mars Ultor, but there is strong presumptive evidence that it was so. The 'Catalogue of the Curiosum' places it next to the Forum Julium in the eighth region. Now the eighth region was bounded on the east, in this neighbourhood, by the Quirinal Hill and the Via del Sole, or a street a little to the east of it, and we are tolerably sure that the forum transitorium filled up a great part of the space between the temple in question and the above-mentioned street, and that the Forum Julium intervened between it and the Forum Romanum, while the Forum Trajani limits the space to the westward within which we can suppose the Forum Augusti to have been. Thus the only space left in the eighth region within which the Forum of Augustus can be supposed to have been contained, is that bounded by the Via della Croce Bianca, the Via del Priorato, and the Via di Tor di Conti.

The ruins of the temple consist of three lofty fluted Corinthian columns, a pilaster of white Carrara marble, a part of the surmounting architrave, and the corresponding wall of the cella of the temple. Antiquarians are of opinion that the purity of style and elegance of these columns, and their ornamentation, forms a strong proof that they were designed and executed in the best times of Roman architectural art, and cannot belong to a period later than that of Augustus. The richest decorative work is to be seen under the roof of the portico, between the columns and the wall of the cella.

<small>Exterior wall. Arco dei Pantani.</small> These three columns stood at the side of the temple which abutted on the exterior wall of the Forum, as the ruins show. A large portion of this wall is still standing on each side of

the arch called the Arco dei Pantani. The arch itself is built of travertine, the wall of blocks of peperino laid alternately with the longer and shorter sides outwards as in the masonry of the tabularium. In the middle ages a door was fitted on to this archway, and a portion of the stone was cut away on the west side. This has injured its architectural beauty very much. It has also been stripped of the marble facing with which it was probably covered originally, and being now half buried in the rubbish of ages, it presents a somewhat mean and rough appearance.

This archway formed one of the entrances to the Forum Augusti from the east. The wall of the enclosure can be traced for a considerable distance on each side of it, but there are no other archways now open. The monotonous appearance of so high a wall is relieved by having the edges of the stones cut so that each block stands out separately, and the lower part of the wall is divided into two, and its upper into three stages by projecting ruins of travertine.

It is said that the blocks of stone in this masonry are fastened with wooden bolts made in the shape of double swallow tails, and that some of these have been found completely petrified. When the Forum was first designed Augustus encountered great opposition from owners of private house property; and through fear of the unpopularity which wholesale evictions might have caused, he accommodated the shape of the external walls to that of the ground he could occupy. Hence arose the irregular line of the exterior, which was, however, reduced to a symmetrical plan inside by secondary walls. The general shape of the interior area of the enclosure was that of a broad oblong piazza with two large semicircular side extensions or wings (somewhat like those in the Piazza S. Pietro) opposite to and corresponding to each other. The area was large, for the horse races, and games in honour of Mars were held here once when the Tiber had overflowed the circus.[1] The temple stood at the northern end between these two side extensions, and occupied about one-sixth of the whole space. Tribunals were placed in the hemicycles and courts of law held there.

[1] Dion Cass. lvi. 27.

Some portions of the semicircular recesses are still extant by which their plan may be traced, but the outer wall is in no part preserved entire except at the back and sides of the temple. Its height at the back of the temple is 120 feet, and over the Arco dei Pantani 100 feet, which we must suppose to have been the normal height of the rest of the enclosure. These enormous walls served as a defence against fire, no less than to exclude the traffic and noise of the streets.

Although it is possible that Augustus may have entertained the design of erecting a new group of public buildings as a means of gaining distinction and popularity before the battle of Philippi which established his power, yet so far as we know, the temple of Mars Ultor and the Forum Augusti owed their existence to a vow made by the emperor immediately before the decisive battle of Philippi, B.C. 42, to build if victorious a temple to Mars as the avenger of his adopted father. The dedication of the temple took place in B.C. 2, accompanied with most magnificent shows of gladiators and splendid sham sea-fights.

Forum of Nerva.

The Colonnacce.

The Forum of Nerva was in the district through which the Via della Croce Bianca passes, and was connected with the ruin commonly called the Temple of Minerva, still standing on the right-hand side of that street where it is crossed by the Via Alessandrina. Two columns are there to be seen now called the Colonnacce, half buried in the earth, surmounted by an entablature and an attica. The wall behind the columns is built of blocks of peperino of unequal size, and is in a style of masonry inferior to the walls of the Forum of Augustus. In it may be seen the traces of an arch which has been filled up with the same stone as that of which the wall is built. The columns, which are of fluted marble, stand out in front of the wall; but, as in the Arch of Severus, the entablature does not lie between them, but projects from the wall over the capitals, and unites them with the wall. The edges of the architrave are richly decorated, and the frieze contains an elaborately carved bas-relief, which, though unfortunately much disfigured, can be partially understood by the help of old engravings taken before it was reduced to its present lamentable state.

From these it appears that the figures represent various attributes of Minerva as the patroness of household management. Some of them are drawing water, others weaving or

Forum of Nerva as it stood in 1606. From Du Perac, 'Vestigj di Roma.'

spinning, and others dyeing, washing, holding scales and purses as if bargaining. The remaining portion of the design is incomplete, and was probably carried round the rest of the frieze of the enclosure.[1] On the cornices, both upper and lower, the ornamentation is very rich, but not so chaste as work of the Augustan period. In the centre of the attica stands a figure of Minerva in alto-relievo, with spear, helmet, and shield.

That this beautiful ruin, which is one of the most picturesque in Rome, belonged to the wall of Nerva's Forum is rendered certain by the old views of the sixteenth century, which represent it as part of the inner side of the wall enclosing a splendid temple which stood to the north-west of it. Seven of the columns of this temple were still standing in the fifteenth century, belonging to the left-hand side of the portico, and a considerable part also of the walls of the cella with the pilasters of the portico. The cella of the temple adjoined the semicircular part of Augustus's Forum on one side, and, as will be seen by the plan, the wall of the enclosure met it on the other, so that only the portico of the temple projected into the open space of the Forum.

On the front were the words, probably the last line of a longer inscription, IMP. NERVA CÆSAR AUG. PONT. MAXIM. TRIB. POT. II. IMP. II. PROCOS, showing that the temple was dedicated by Nerva.

There can be but little doubt that this was the temple of Minerva begun together with the Forum by Domitian, and finished by Nerva. It is true that there is no actual mention in any of the ancient writers of a temple of Minerva here, but the assertion of Dion Cassius that Domitian had a particular reverence for Minerva and Janus, and the character of the designs and statues of Minerva found upon the ruined part of the enclosure already described, leave little doubt on the subject. The name of Palladium given to the Forum by Martial also agrees with this supposition.

The fate of the Temple of Minerva is better known than that of most of the ancient temples in Rome.

In the time of Pope Pius V. (1566–1572) the building of a new quarter of the city was begun in this district. The streets Via Alessandrina and Via Bonella were laid out, and

---

[1] The frieze is described and representations of it are given in the Annali and Monumenti dell' Inst. 1877.

as the new quarter grew, the ruins of the old temple became an impediment to their progress, which Paul V. in the beginning of the seventeenth century ordered to be removed, and to be applied to the construction of the Chapel of S. Paul in the church of S. Maria Maggiore and that of the Fontana Paolo upon the Janiculum. The great gateway which stood at the end of the Via della Croce Bianca was suffered to remain for a century longer, but is now quite gone.

We now return to the Piazza Trajana. Between it and the Piazza del Campidoglio, in a street called the Via di Marforio, are two of the more ancient ruins in Rome consisting of tombs now built into the walls of houses. These tombs are monuments of imperial Rome, and were probably outside the ancient Servian Wall not far from the Porta Ratumena. Tomb of Bibulus.

The more prominent of the two, the Tomb of Bibulus, stands close by the junction of the modern streets of Macel de' Corvi and Marforio. The front of it only can be seen, as the rest is built into the wall of a house. The inscription is as follows,

C . POPLICIO . L . F . BIBULO   AED . PL . HONORIS .
VIRTUTISQUE . CAUSSA . SENATUS .
CONSULTO . POPULI . QUE . JUSSU . LOCUS .
MONUMENTO . QUO . IPSE . POSTEREIQUE .
EIUS . INFERRENTUR . PUBLICE . DATUS . EST .

The inscription was also placed on the side of the tomb, where the beginning of it may still be seen. It must not be inferred that the privilege of being buried within the walls was granted to Bibulus contrary to the regulations of the twelve tables, which forbade any corpse to be buried or burnt within the city walls. Had this been the case the exemption would have been expressly mentioned in the inscription, and besides this the course of the Servian Wall, which crossed the depression between the Quirinal and Capitoline, would naturally run so as to exclude the tomb. The inscription only records the gift of the burial place to Bibulus by the Senate, and is intended to prevent the burial of any other person there, except the family of Bibulus.

An Ædile of the name C. Bibulus is mentioned in the 'Annals' of Tacitus in the reign of Tiberius, A.D. 22, and the style of the tomb agrees tolerably well with this date. The whole is built of travertine, and the basement is of the simplest description possible. Four Doric pilasters with Attic bases surmounted by an Ionic entablature, ornamented with wreaths of fruit and ox-skulls, form the whole decoration of the front. Bergau, however, thinks that the architecture is Italian, and should not be called by these Greek names.[1]

The other ruin of a tomb is in the wall of a house nearly opposite to that of Bibulus, and is reduced to a shapeless mass of remains.

Capitolium. Temple of Jupiter.

Passing from the Tomb of Bibulus to the Piazza del Campidoglio, and thence to the Caffarelli or southern end of the Capitoline Hill, we find in the gardens of the German Embassy an excavation which shows a number of tufa blocks fitted together without mortar, and in an irregular manner.[2]

The area of the great temple and the wall surrounding it have been traced out by Lanciani and Jordan among the fragments which are found in this garden, and on the north side of the Caffarelli palace, and between the garden and the rotunda of the museum. Jordan thinks that the measurements of the area indicated by these fragments correspond to the size of the environs of the temple as given by Dionysius, and that they afford a conclusive proof that the great temple of Jupiter was on the Caffarelli and not on the Ara Cœli height. The north-eastern corner of the excavation in the Caffarelli garden shows a part of these constructions, and a fragment may be seen in the wall of the Montanara Garden in the Vicolo di Monte Caprino.

The natural features of the Capitoline Hill could hardly have been more completely concealed than they are by the present situation of the buildings upon it, even if those buildings had been erected with the express purpose of changing the appearance of the hill. For the convent of Ara Cœli and the Palazzo Caffarelli, which occupy respectively the north-eastern and south-western summits of the hill, are

---

[1] See 'Rome and the Campagna,' p. xlii.
[2] See the Annali and Monumenti of the Inst. di Corr. arch. 1876.

comparatively low and unconspicuous, while the so-called Tabularium and above it the Palace of the Senator compose a lofty pile which nearly fills up the depression between these two heights. To the spectator looking at the Capitol from the Forum, the higher part of the hill appears to lie nearly in the centre, whereas in reality the shape is that of a double hill rising at each end. The north-eastern end is somewhat curved round towards the north, while the south-western approaches within 300 paces of the river. The whole core of the hill is formed of the harder volcanic tufa, a section of which may be plainly seen, composing the face of the low precipice now shown as the Tarpeian rock, and also in a courtyard surrounded by cottages, near the spot called Palazzaccio. This tufa was, as has been frequently mentioned, used as a building stone in the early ages of Rome before the lapis Gabinus, or Albanus (peperino) or the lapis Tiburtinus had been introduced.

The Tarpeian Rock whence criminals were hurled, was, according to the older Italian topographers down to the time of Nardini, placed at the western edge of the hill towards the Tiber, where the Piazza Montanara now is. But Dureau de la Malle in the Mémoires de l'Académie for 1809, pointed out that this was inconsistent with the statements of Dionysius, who says that it was over the Forum, and that the executions took place in full view of all the people. This would seem to place it on the S.E. side towards the Palatine near S. Maria della Consolazione. Becker's objection that the hill is less steep there than at the western edge, may be met by the fact that several large masses of rock are recorded to have fallen down from this spot, and therefore the face of the cliff is entirely changed. The further objection that the criminals would have fallen into the Vicus Jugarius, instead of which they ought, according to custom, to have been cast over the city walls, seems to rest on the assumption that criminals were always thrown over the walls, no proof of which has been adduced. Tradition is equally divided between the two localities, and therefore the passages of Dionysius above quoted must be held at present decisive in favour of the side towards the Palatine and Forum.

Tarpeian Rock.

Thermæ of Constantine.

It has been conclusively proved by Becker, that Aurelian's Temple of the Sun which was commonly supposed to have occupied the Colonna Gardens, and to which the huge fragments near the Capitol which lie there were thought to have belonged, was not here but in the Campus Agrippæ on the Campus Martius. For the Notitia and the Chronologers both place it in the seventh region or Via Lata, which occupied the eastern side of the Campus, and mention castra as attached to it. Further, Vopiscus when describing a drive in which he accompanied Junius Tiberianus, the prefect of the city, seems to place the Temple of the Sun at a much greater distance from the Palatine than the Colonna Gardens are.

The ruin with which it was identified, formerly called turris Mæcenatis, or Frontispicium Neronis, has now been pulled down, but a part of it, and especially one huge mass of carved marble, remains in the Colonna Gardens. Representations of the Frontispicium Neronis as it was before its destruction, may be seen in Donatus and the older topographers. The fragments of stonework are now thought to have belonged to the entrance of the Thermæ of Constantine.

The site of the building erected upon the Quirinal by the mad emperor Heliogabalus, and called Senaculum Mulierum in which he assembled the Roman matrons for consultation about the laws of fashion in dress and manners, is not known.

The site of the Thermæ of Constantine, which are placed by the Notitia next to the Capitolium antiquum, is tolerably well defined by the notices of the Anonymous MS. of Einsiedlen, and by an inscription found near the Quirinal Palace, recording their restoration by Petronius Perpenna probably in the year 443. Both of these indicate the Palazzo Rospigliosi as standing upon the ground once occupied by the central building of the Thermæ. The Anonymous MS. mentions the Thermæ on the road between the Church of S. Agata and that of S. Vitale. Pozzio, Albertini, Fulvius, Q. Fauno, and Gamucci, all agree in confirming this evidence. Large portions of the ruins were still standing in their time, and in Du Perac's views, published in the seventeenth century, the central part of the buildings is represented. Another part of the ruins of these baths was found in the construction of the Quirinal Palace in the time of Paul V.

There can be no doubt that these Thermæ, which were of great extent, reached nearly across the Quirinal Hill, occupying the sites of the present Palazzo Rospigliosi, part of the Colonna Gardens and the Quirinal Palace. Three statues were found in the ruins, representing Constantine and two of his sons. These are supposed to have stood near the grand entrance of the Thermæ. The first is now in the Portico of the Lateran Basilica, the two others were placed by Paul III. on the balustrade of the Piazza Capitolina. The famous pair of the Dioscuri and their horses, which now ornament the Piazza di Monte Cavallo, were also discovered on this site. The history of these well-known sculptures cannot be traced farther back than the time of Constantine, whose Thermæ they adorned. The old tradition which states that they were a present from Tiridates to Nero is in some degree supported by the mention of the equi Tiridatis in the Notitia, but is not confirmed by any other evidence. That they are not rightly supposed to represent the Dioscuri can hardly be doubted, and the inscriptions which ascribe them to the chisels of Phidias and Praxiteles respectively are erroneous. For not to mention that the exact reproduction of nature in its highest type of symmetry, peculiar to the style of the highest Greek art is absent, and that we find instead the conventional mode of representation characteristic of the revival of art under the emperors, it seems hardly possible that Praxiteles, who lived more than half a century after Phidias, should have occupied himself in imitating and completing a group begun by his predecessor.

Statues found in the Thermæ of Constantine.

These colossal figures and the statues of Constantine mentioned above, probably stood in the grand court of the Thermæ. There are now no traces left of the outer enclosure of this court, but the plan of the central blocks of buildings has been preserved by Palladio, in whose time there was doubtless a sufficient portion left to enable him to reconstruct the whole. It is somewhat different from the plan of most of the other Thermæ, having a large semicircular court on one side surrounded with arcades, the purpose of which has not been discovered. The other halls and apartments are of the usual size and shape, with the exception of the exedræ, which are rectangular. At one side of the enclosing court, apparently the north side, there was a large theatre similar to that at the baths of Titus.

Some of the older topographers had conjectured that the ruins in the Colonna Gardens, wrongly, as has been shown, ascribed to Aurelian's Temple of the Sun, and also the massive substructions and stairs which have been found behind the stables of the Quirinal Palace on the west slope of the hill, belonged to the Thermæ of Constantine. This conjecture has been revived and ingeniously supported by Professor Reber, who remarks that the outer court of the Thermæ, to judge by the extent of that of the baths of Diocletian or of Caracalla, may very well have reached across the whole breadth of the hill from east to west, and further that the approach to the Thermæ would naturally be placed on the west side, where the Imperial fora lay. If so, the building called the tower of Mæcenas stood exactly in the position at the summit of the colossal flight of stairs now hidden under the Papal stables which would answer to the entrance portico of the Thermæ. The fragments of the so-called Tower of Mæcenas are very similar to those of the portico of Octavia, which was also the entrance to a grand enclosure. They consist of two huge blocks of marble, the largest of which is seventeen feet in length, ornamented with mouldings of the usual Corinthian character, and with a frieze beautifully decorated with festoons of foliage enclosing birds and genii. The style is of a late epoch, and might very probably belong to the Constantinian age.

CHAPTER V.

THE VELABRUM AND THE CIRCUS FLAMINIUS.

THE church of S. Giorgio in Velabro, which stands between the Palatine Hill and the river near the Piazza Bocca della Verità, retains the ancient name of this district, formerly a swamp called the Velabrum. This is perhaps the best point from which to begin our survey of the ruins of the Velabrum. The most conspicuous ruin near the church is the archway called Janus Quadrifrons, from its quadrilateral shape. It is a massive square building of white marble, with four piers supporting as many arches which are united in the centre, by a vaulted roof. Each pier has on the exterior twelve niches in two rows, with semicircular shell-shaped crowns. These two rows of niches were formerly separated by a projecting cornice which is now nearly destroyed except in the interior. The niches nearest to the corners on the north and south sides are not hollowed out, but only traced on the exterior surface, in order not to endanger the solidity of the angles. The present height of the building is thirty-eight feet, but it probably had an attica originally upon the top to which the staircase still extant led, and in which were some small rooms for the transaction of business. Upon the key-stones of the arches two figures can be still recognized, one of Rome and the other of the patroness of trade, Minerva. The exterior surface was doubtless decorated with rows of Corinthian columns between the niches, a large quantity of remains of such columns having been found in clearing the base, and in the niches themselves statues of various deities probably stood. *Janus Quadrifrons.*

The purpose of this arch was probably solely ornamental, and it stood by itself in some part of the Forum Boarium. The rooms in the attica may have been used for the accommodation of some of the officials of the cattle market. The builder and date are alike unknown. From the style of its architecture and sculptures, it has been pronounced decidedly later than the age of Domitian, to whom from his fondness for building Jani, it might be attributed. Platner and Becker suggest that it is identical with an archway called the Arcus Constantini—in the catalogue of the eleventh region—but a comparison of the style of the remnants of sculptures upon it with those on the existing arch of Constantine, does not confirm this conjecture.

<small>Arcus Argentinorum.</small>
Close to the Janus Quadrifrons stands a stone ornamental doorway now partly built into the wall of the church of S. Giorgio in Velabro. It is constructed of brickwork with marble facings, and consists of two square piers decorated with pilasters of the Composite or Roman order at the corners and surmounted by a horizontal entablature of rich carved work. There is no trace of an attica above. The inscription, still well preserved, shows that it was erected by the money-changers or bankers, and other merchants of the Forum Boarium, in honour of Septimius Severus, his wife Julia, and his son Antoninus (Caracalla). As in the case of the Arch of Septimius in the Forum, so here the words III. PP. PROCOS. FORTISSIMO FELICISSIMOQUE PRINCIPI and PARTHICI MAXIMI BRITANNICI MAXIMI were inserted by Caracalla in place of the name and titles of his murdered brother Geta.

Not only in the inscriptions of the time of Septimius Severus, but even in the reliefs we everywhere find Geta's figure erased.

On the shafts of the pilasters are representations of military ensigns, which bear upon their circular tablets and above the eagles likenesses in relief of two Cæsars, Severus and Caracalla. The third likeness, that of Geta, has been erased in every instance. In each of the spaces between the pilasters are four panels with sculptures in relief. The lowest of these represents the merchants of the Forum Boarium bringing cattle as victims to the altar. The compartment above these exhibits various instruments used in sacrifice, similar to those found upon the Temple of Vespasian. Upon the larger central panel are the figures of the imperial family engaged in sacrificing, and it can easily be seen that from some of these the figure of Geta has been carefully chiselled away.

In one of these large panels is the figure of a barbarian captive with the Phrygian cap so common upon the sculptures of the triumphal arches. The upper compartments contain festooned ornamental work and a few figures of men. The front of the architrave and frieze is almost entirely occupied by the inscriptions, and is not highly ornamented, but the cornice, which is divided into seven ledges, is overladen with various decorative patterns without purity of design or excellence of execution. The date of the erection of this monument is stated in the inscription to be the twelfth year of the tribunitia potestas of Severus and the seventh of Caracalla, which corresponds to the year A.D. 204. Reber thinks it possible that the merchants of the Forum Boarium intended it as a testimonial of gratitude to Severus for having built the neighbouring Janus Quadrifrons to ornament their quarter of the city.

The oldest monument of Roman masonry is the remaining portion of a cloaca in this district, commonly identified with the Cloaca Maxima of Livy, which reaches from a spot near the church of S. Giorgio in Velabro and the Janus Quadrifrons to the Tiber bank near the Ponte Rotto. The ancient archway has been broken open here, and can be reached by descending into a hollow near the Janus Quadrifrons. Near the Janus Quadrifrons, at the above-mentioned spot, seven cloacae unite and pour their waters into the still extant portion of the Cloaca Maxima, so that a large stream is constantly flowing through it. These branch sewers are built with solid brick arches, but the main archway, though fronted with modern brickwork, consists of massive blocks of tufa, and at short intervals of every few yards has an arch of travertine introduced, to add to its solidity and strength. The original size of the archway, one-third of which is now choked up with mud, was twelve feet four inches high, and ten feet eight inches wide. Strabo and Pliny say that a cart loaded with hay could pass through some of the Roman sewers, and certainly in the case of this

Cloaca Maxima.

cloaca, it would not be impossible to do so were it cleared of mud.

M. Agrippa, the Haussmann of Rome, is said, when ædile, to have traversed the main sewer in a boat. The whole length of this remaining portion is at least three hundred and forty yards, and it makes several bends, following probably the direction of the ancient streets. The mouth is still visible, when the Tiber is not high, at a spot called the Pulchrum Litus, near the round temple usually called the Temple of Vesta. The immense size is due to the fact that it was not only a sewer for refuse, but a drain for the lake of the Velabrum, and the many land springs of the Forum, and must be classed with the emissarium of the Alban Lake and other gigantic undertakings of the kind, such as the cuniculus at Veii, executed about B.C. 539. For a distance of about forty feet from the mouth the cloaca is constructed of a triple arch of peperino, mixed with some blocks of tufa, but throughout the rest of its course it consists of a single arch of tufa with occasional bands of travertine. The masonry along the embankment of the shore on each side, is partly of peperino and partly of tufa and travertine blocks laid along and across alternately.

Livy gives the early history of this extraordinary work in his first Book. In the thirty-eighth chapter he ascribes the commencement of the undertaking of draining the Velabrum and Forum to Tarquinius Priscus, and in the fifty-sixth he says that Tarquinius Superbus completed the Cloaca Maxima as a receptacle for the refuse of the whole city. Dionysius agrees in giving the same account of the origin of the system of cloacæ, and Pliny enumerates the cloacæ among the wonders of the great metropolis, and expressly mentions Tarquinius Priscus as entitled to the credit of having first originated this great work of public utility. His words are—" Seven streams, after traversing the city, are united and their water so compressed into one channel as to sweep everything along with it like a torrent, and when a great body of rain-water is added to this the very walls are shaken by the agitated waters; and sometimes the Tiber rises and beats back into them, and vast opposing masses of water meet and struggle, yet the solidity of their masonry resists and stands firm. Huge weights are carried over them, whole buildings undermined by fire or by some accident fall upon them, earthquakes shake the very ground around them, yet they have lasted for seven hundred years from the time of Tarquinius Priscus almost uninjured, a monument of antiquity which ought to be the more carefully observed since it has been passed over in silence by some of our most celebrated historians."

The Tarquins are said to have compelled the Roman people to work at these huge structures, just as the kings of Egypt and Assyria exacted task-work from their subjects; but in palliation of the cruelties alleged against them by the historians it must be noted that in the one case buildings of permanent public service were built, while in the other, only the vanity of a despot was flattered.

Not far from the Janus Quadrifrons, and close to the Pons Æmilius, or Ponte Rotto, stands a small temple, now converted into the church of S. Maria Egiziaca, which presents an unsolved problem in Roman topography. The substruction of this temple, which has been laid bare, consists of tufa cased with travertine. The form of the temple is that called tetrastylos by Vitruvius, having four Ionic columns in front and seven at the sides. The four front columns and two on each side, forming the pronaos, originally stood clear, but are now enclosed within the wall of the church. The remaining five on each side with those at the back were half columns set against the wall of the cella. The shafts of the half columns are of tufa, but the bases and capitals, with the entablature and the columns of the pronaos, are of travertine. On the frieze and cornice are the remains of ornamental work, which is now rendered almost invisible by the stucco with which the walls have been covered. The Ionic volutes on the corner capitals of this temple are in the later style, while the side capitals are in the usual style.

Fortuna Virilis.

This building has usually been supposed to be the temple dedicated by Servius Tullius to Fortuna Virilis, and situated on the bank of the Tiber. The passage of Dionysius upon which this supposition rests is as follows: "Servius Tullius built two temples to Fortune, one in the Forum Boarium, and the other upon the bank of the Tiber." [1]

It is most probable, as Reber suggests, that we have here the Temple of Servius dedicated to Fortune without any special title. Dionysius, as we have seen, places this in the Forum Boarium, and Livy describes it as intra portam Carmentalem, and mentions it in tracing the course of a conflagration between the Salinae near the Porta Trigemina and the Porta Carmentalis. But there was another temple, that of Mater Matuta which stood close to the Temple of Fortune, and there is no evidence showing to which of the two the ruin in question belonged. Both were founded by Servius, and reckoned among the most venerable relics of ancient Rome. Becker urges the claims of the Temple of Pudicitia Patricia, which Livy places in the Forum Boarium near the round Temple of Hercules, to this site. But this was merely a small shrine, containing a statue and not a templum. So far as an opinion can be formed of the date of the temple from the materials and style of architecture, it seems to belong to the later republic.

So-called Temple of Vesta.

On the Piazza della Bocca della Verità, at a short distance from the temple we have just been considering, stand the remains of a small round temple commonly called the Temple of Vesta. Perhaps of all the ruins of Rome this is the most familiar to the eye of the tourist. A considerable part of the cella is still standing, ornamented with a simple and elegant cornice. Round this stand nineteen graceful Corinthian columns of white marble. The entablature is unfortunately destroyed, and the rude modern tiled roof with which the building has been capped completely spoils the picturesque effect of the ruin.

The name now given to it rests on no other evidence than its circular shape, and as we have no mention of a Temple of Vesta in the Forum Boarium it must be at once condemned as a misnomer. It has also been called the Temple of the Sibyl or the Temple of Cybele without better reason. The most probable conjecture as to its name is that first suggested by Piale, that it is the round Temple of Hercules in

[1] Dionys. iv. 27.

the Forum Boarium mentioned in the tenth Book of Livy, and alluded to by Festus as the Æmilian Temple of Hercules.

Palatine Hill. Æmilian Temple of Hercules, and mouth of Cloaca Maxima. Bell tower of S. Maria in Cosmedin.

The appellation Æmiliana certainly seems to point to the neighbourhood of the Æmilian bridge. The style of its architecture may be attributed to a restoration in the latter half of the first century A.D. Formerly, it was called the Church of Madonna del Sole, from a favourite image of the Virgin in it, and at an earlier period S. Stefano delle Carozze, from the discovery of a marble model of a chariot in its neighbourhood, but in 1810 it was cleared out and restored, and since then it has not been used as a church, but contains a small collection of marble fragments.

Temple of Ceres.

At the entrance of the valley of the Circus Maximus, and on the south side of the Piazza della Bocca della Verità stands the church of S. Maria in Cosmedin which is built upon the ruins of an ancient temple. Ten columns still remain in their original places, seven of which stand in a line parallel to the entrance, and three others in the left-hand side wall of the church. Some of the columns are built into the walls of the Sacristies on the right of the entrance, and reach through the roofs to the upper story. The material of which they are made is white marble, and the order to which they belong the Composite. Parts of the wall of the cella may still be seen in the sacristy, built of tufa which was originally faced with marble. The design of the capitals and chiselling of the ornamental work upon them is of the best period of art, and one of them may conveniently be examined in the room over the sacraria, and in the organ loft. Behind the apse of the church are some large chambers built of massive blocks of travertine, which were probably attached to the Carceres of the Circus as stables or offices of some kind, and the position of these compels us to assume that the front of the temple faced towards the Velabrum, and that the seven columns parallel to the façade of the present church belonged to the side of the temple, while the three in the left-hand wall formed a part of the front. Otherwise the travertine chambers at the back must have formed some part of the temple, and it is difficult to see how this could have been the case, as they are evidently not the walls of the cella, and cannot be brought into any symmetrical position with the rows of columns.

The Temples of Pudicitia Patricia, of Mater Matuta, and of Fortune have been severally identified with these ruins by the writers of Roman topography. But it has been shown already that the first of these was probably a mere chapel, and that the other two must be placed nearer to the Carmental gate, and therefore the conjecture of Canina that the church of S. Maria in Cosmedin was the Temple of Ceres, Liber, and Libera appears much more likely to be true. For that temple is included in the eleventh region by the Curiosum and Notitia, and is placed by Vitruvius, Tacitus, and Pliny close to the Circus Maximus, while Dionysius expressly says that it stood just over the barriers of the Circus Maximus. The account of Vitruvius answers to the ruins which still remain. For he says that the temple was of the description called aræostyle, i.e. with wide intercolumnar intervals, and it will be found that the intervals between the columns now standing are nearly four times their diameter. Vitruvius also says that it was of the Tuscan order of architecture, and in this seems to contradict Pliny who, quoting Varro's authority, speaks of it as the first temple at Rome which had Greek ornamental work. Their statements may be reconciled by observing that Pliny is speaking of the decorations of the temple by Damophilus and Gorgasis, and not of the style of architecture. The aræostyle arrangement of the columns was probably preserved even after the complete restoration by Tiberius, at which time, as Pliny relates, the old Greek frescoes were cut out and framed, and the terra cotta statues removed from the roof. The temple was first vowed by A. Postumius, the dictator in the Latin war of B.C. 497, on account of the great scarcity of provisions which then prevailed. It was dedicated three years afterwards by the Consul Spurius Cassius, a statesman who showed a disposition to imitate the great architectural works of the regal period, contrary to the generally frugal spirit of the early republican fathers. In the year B.C. 31, a destructive fire, which raged between the Circus and the Forum Olitorium, destroyed the Temple, and with it some of the most valuable treasures of Greek art which it contained. Among these, besides the frescoes of Damophilus and Gorgasis above mentioned, was the famous pictures of Dionysius by Aristides, for which Attalus bid sixteen talents, a price which excited the attention of Mummius, and induced him, although unable himself to appreciate the merits of such works of art, to suspect its value, and carry it to Rome in spite of the remonstrances of Attalus.

The restoration was undertaken by Augustus, and finished by Tiberius in A.D. 17. This temple was to the Plebeian Ædiles what the Temple of Saturn was to the quæstors, and it was enacted that the decrees of the Senate should be delivered over to the Ædiles there, an enactment which seems never to have been carried out.[1]

The medieval names of this church, in Cosmedin, and in Schola Græca, seem to point to the possession of the church by Greek monks after the division of the empire, and the piazza in which it stands is called Bocca della Verità from the strange figure of a head under the modern portico of the church, in the mouth of which it is said that persons whose veracity lay under suspicion, were required to place their hands while making oath, in the belief that the mouth would close upon their hands if the oath taken was a false one.

Carceres of the Circus Maximus. Immediately behind the church are the arched buildings of travertine blocks which have already been mentioned as belonging to the Carceres of the Circus. The largest of these is now used as a store-room for articles of church furniture, and stands on the right side of the tribune of the church. They are perhaps situated too far towards the river to be portions of the actual Carceres from which the chariots started, but they may have formed one side of a courtyard behind the Carceres, in which the harnessing and preparation for the races took place.

Theatre of Marcellus. The ruins of the Theatre of Marcellus which are still standing in the Piazza Montanara afford us a fixed point from which to begin our survey of the region of the Circus Flaminius, which lies to the north-west of the Velabrum. For it appears certain that the ancient half columns, arches, and other ruins evidently belonging to a semicircular theatre, which are now covered by the Palazzo Orsini Savelli, belonged to the theatre of Marcellus. Suetonius distinctly places this theatre under the Tarpeian hill, and of the other two stone

---

[1] Tac. Ann. ii. 49. Dionys. vi. 7, 94. Vitruv. iii. 3, 5. Plin. N. H. xxxv. 4, 24. 10, 99. 12, 151.

Theatre of Marcellus.

theatres at Rome we know that the Pompeian lay further to the north-west, and that the theatre of Balbus was near the Ponte Sisto. The masonry and architectural details of this building, though corresponding in many respects with the Coliseum are more carefully worked, and show an earlier and better period of art.

There had previously been a stone scena built near this spot by Æmilius Lepidus, which was perhaps used by Julius Cæsar who first began to build this theatre. It was not finished until the year B.C. 11 when Augustus opened it, and named it after his nephew Marcellus, son of Octavia. In the time of the Flavii the scena was restored, having perhaps suffered from the fire which burnt the Porticus Octaviæ, and it seems to have again required repairs in the time of Alexander Severus, who is said to have wished to restore it.[1]

The Curiosum mentions it as if still in use, and gives the number of spectators it would contain as 20,000. In the Middle Ages it was, like all the other great buildings of Rome, turned into a castle by Pietro Leone, a nobleman of great power in the time of Urban II. and Pascal II., and celebrated for his factious violence. The shape of the building was thus completely altered. The great family of the Savelli came into possession of it in the twelfth century, following Pietro Leone, and after them the Orsini. The lower stories are now occupied by workshops, small wine vaults, and rag and bone warehouses, frequented by the rustics of the Campagna, who are usually to be seen in considerable numbers in the Piazza Montanara in front of it.

From the piazza two rows of the exterior arcades are visible, each containing twelve arches and thirteen columns of travertine. The lower arcade is now buried to the depth of one third of its surface below the level of the present ground. Its half columns are of the Doric order, with a Doric entablature and triglyphs, and are surmounted by a low attica with projecting bases for the half columns of the upper arcade. The height of this upper arcade was originally somewhat less than that of the lower. It has half

---

[1] Auson. Sept. Sap. prol. 22. Mon. Ancyr. tib. iv. Hist. Aug. Alex. Sev. 44.

columns of the Ionic order, carrying a simple entablature with an architrave of three projecting ledges, a plain frieze, and a cornice with toothed mouldings. No actual remains of a third arcade above these two are now to be found, but it can hardly be doubted that one existed originally, and that it was of the Corinthian order. Some parts of the substructions of the seats are said to be still extant in the cellars of the Savelli residence, consisting of diverging walls similar to those still to be seen in the Coliseum. By means of these, the ground plan of the cavea of the theatre can be completely restored. There are no remains of the scena. Upon one of the fragments of the Capitoline plan, partly restored, the name Theatrum Marcelli is legible. There seems, however, to be some doubt as to the genuineness of this fragment.

The bridge near the theatre of Marcellus is now called the Ponte Rotto from its broken condition. The two remaining arches are not ancient, but probably stand upon the site of an ancient bridge which was called the Pons Æmilius. Livy mentions this bridge as the first stone bridge built over the Tiber, and states that it was begun in B.C. 179 by M. Fulvius Nobilior, and M. Æmilius Lepidus the censor, whose name was given to the Basilica Æmilia, and that it was finished in B.C. 142 by the Censors Publius Scipio Africanus, and L. Mummius. The bridge was named after M. Æmilius Lepidus as Pontifex Maximus, and as a more popular statesman than Fulvius. The bridge afterwards bore the name pons lapideus, from being the first stone bridge built over the Tiber, and in contradistinction to the pons sublicius. *The Ponte Rotto.*

There is abundant evidence as to the position of this bridge, for the Fasti Capranici place it ad Theatrum Marcelli, and the Cosmographia of Æthicus ad Forum Boarium, both of which indications point to the Ponte Rotto.

A short distance above the Æmilian bridge is the island of the Tiber. According to the legend, this island was formed by the corn belonging to the Tarquins grown on the Campus Martius, which after their expulsion was consecrated to Mars. After consecration the corn could not be used for food, and was therefore cut and thrown into the Tiber, and *Island of the Tiber.*

from this corn, when collected into heaps by the stream, the island was formed. Until the fifth century of the city, the island remained consecrated and uninhabited, but in B.C. 292 a Temple of Æsculapius was built upon it in consequence, as the story went, of the holy snake brought from Epidaurus having swum to shore there. The island was probably at this time also protected with stone embankments, and the two bridges were built, whence the name inter duos pontes was given to it. A fragment of this ancient stone embankment, which was in the shape of a ship, may still be seen in the garden of the Franciscan Monks of S. Bartolommeo, representing part of the prow of a ship, with a snake and the head of an ox carved in relief upon it.

The two bridges uniting the island to either bank were probably, as has been said, first erected in or about the fifth century of the city, but the existing bridges, though ancient, must be considered as restorations of the older fabrics.

The bridge on the side towards the Campus Martius was built by L. Fabricius in B.C. 62, as the inscription still extant on the bridge shows. In accordance with this we find Dion Cassius giving it the name of Pons Fabricius, and a coin with the title L. Fabricius gives on the other side a bridge with a snake, plainly pointing to the island of the Tiber.

Another inscription, also still remaining upon the bridge, states that it was examined and found in good repair by Q. Lepidus and M. Lollius, consuls in B.C. 21.

This bridge is the oldest now standing on the Tiber, and the masonry is of admirable solidity and workmanship. It was called, in the Middle Ages Pons Judaeus, from its proximity to the Jews' quarter of the city, and now bears the name Quattro Capi from the jani quadrifrontes which stand upon it.[1] These jani were formerly the posts which supported the railings of the bridge, as may be seen by the holes bored in them for the ancient bronze bars.

The twin bridge on the right-hand side of the river, dates from the imperial era, and probably, like the Pons Fabricius, replaced a much older bridge of the same age as the Temple of Æsculapius.

[1] See Reber, Ruinen Roms, p. 316. Eckhel, Num. Vet. tom. v. p. 210.

Two inscriptions are still legible on this bridge, from which we learn that it was finished in the year A.D. 370, and dedicated to the use of the Roman people in the name of the Emperor Gratianus, by Valentinian, Valens and Gratianus. These inscriptions must be understood as referring to the rebuilding of the bridge, though they are so worded as to claim the credit of its first erection. That there was an older bridge is clear, not only from the fact that the island was called inter duos pontes before the time of Gratian, but also from the name pons Cestius, which occurs in the Notitia, and undoubtedly belongs to that bridge. It is not clear who Cestius was, but it is generally supposed that a præfectus urbi of that name in B.C. 48 is the person after whom the bridge was named, and this agrees with the statement of Dion Cassius about the building of the Fabrician bridge.

The church of S. Nicola in Carcere, which stands in the Via della Bocca della Verità close to the Piazza Montanara, contains the remains of two or perhaps of three temples.

These ruins consist first of three fluted columns of travertine with Ionic capitals, which stand in the façade of the church of S. Nicola. Above them is a part of the ancient entablature, and in the room to the left of the portico of the church are two more columns built into the wall. In the nave of the church on the left hand are remains of the cella of the temple, to the pronaos of which the five columns belonged. The walls of the cella were, as has been discovered by excavations, constructed of travertine blocks. At the end of this left-hand wall of the cella, there stood before the last restoration of the church, the remains of a pilaster of the Doric order with an Attic base, and opposite to this pilaster another column. The position of the six columns shows that the temple was of the form called peripteros, i.e., surrounded by a continuous colonnade. *S. Nicola in Carcere.*

On the right-hand side aisle of the church are five other columns built into the wall, and a pilaster which evidently belonged to a second temple standing side by side with the first. These columns are not so high as those of the first temple described, and their style and the intervals between them are different. A portion of the entablature, which is of a simple character, still surmounts them. Two more columns of this temple are to be seen in the wall of the house which stands to the right of the church. It was surrounded with colonnades on three sides, but the back of the cella was ornamented with pilasters only.

On the left-hand side of the church are six more half-exposed columns, and some remains of an entablature which may have either belonged to a third and smaller temple standing by the side of the first, or may have been merely the portico of some other building.

The materials of which these buildings consist are chiefly travertine and peperino, and their difference of style shows them to have been erected at different times, probably during the Age of the Republic. It is commonly assumed, from their position near the theatre of Marcellus, that they are to be identified with the Temples of Spes and Juno Sospita. As the Temple of Pietas was removed to make room for the theatre, we cannot suppose that we have here any part of it, and the Temple of Janus would probably have assumed a different form.

It is recorded by Livy that M. Acilius Glabrio erected an equestrian statue near the Temple of Pietas. During some excavations made in 1808 by the architect Valadier, the pedestal of an equestrian statue was found in the small piazza opposite to the church of S. Nicola. It appears possible that when the Temple of Pietas was removed to make way for the theatre, this statue may have been preserved and set up here as near as possible to the original site.[1]

Portico of Octavia. In the street called the Via di Pescaria, which runs north-westwards from the Theatre of Marcellus, stand four fluted Corinthian columns, two on each side of the street. These formed part of the principal entrance to a colonnade or portico, some of the other columns of which can be traced at intervals in the walls of the houses further on in the Via di Pescaria along which the line of the colonnade ran. The entrance or gateway faced towards the south-west, and over the arch looking into the little Piazza di Pescaria will be seen an inscription recording its restoration after a fire, by Septimius

---

[1] Ann. dell' Inst. 1850. p. 347. Monum. v. xxiv.

Severus and Caracalla (M. Aurelius Antoninus) in the year
A.D. 203, the eleventh year of the tribunitian power of
Severus. No traces can be found of the erasure of Geta's
name, which Caracalla, as we have seen, caused to be effaced
after his death from all the inscriptions containing it. There
is no doubt, however, that it was originally placed here after
the name of Caracalla, since Severus was careful to pay
equal honour to both of his sons in all respects. The whole
inscription may have been replaced by a new one, or the
fourth line may have been completely effaced and altered.
As it now stands the inscription has been restored as follows :
IMP. CES. L. SEPTIMIUS SEVERUS. PIUS. PERTINAX. AUG. ARABIC.
ADIABENIC. PARTHIC. MAXIMUS. TRIB. POTEST. XI. IMP. XI. COS. III.
P. P. ET IMP. CES. M. AURELIUS. ANTONINUS. PIUS. FELIX. AUG.
TRIB. POTEST. VI. COS. PROCOS. PORTICUM INCENDIO CONSUMPTAM
RESTITUERUNT.

The pediment and tympanum over the inscription are
still preserved, but two of the columns below have been
replaced by a high brickwork arch, probably of the fifth
century, which now supports the inscription and pediment.
Passing round again into the street Via di Pescaria, we find
ourselves in the interior of the gateway. It consisted of
four columns placed on each side between two antæ or projecting piers ornamented with pilasters, and was of larger
dimensions than the colonnades to which it formed the
entrance. The brickwork of the antæ was originally faced
with marble, and they supported arches which led into the
colonnades along the line of the street. The bases of the
columns are now buried in rubbish, but parts of the architecture, frieze, and cornice, which are of a simple description,
may be still traced over the front. The inner side of the
gateway, with the exception of the two columns and the pier
which stand at the entrance of the Via di S. Angelo in
Pescaria, has been removed to make room for the church of
S. Michaele Archangelo.

If we enter the street just mentioned, the capital of a
column may be seen on the right hand over the wall of the
yard belonging to No. 12, and in the yard itself stand
three others, with a portion of the architecture above them.

Their position shows that they formed the corner of a temple.

There is ample proof that we have in the ruins just described, the entrance gateway of the Porticus Octaviæ and the corner of the temple of Juno Regina. For Festus states that there were two Octavian porticoes, one built in honour of Octavia, the sister of Augustus, near the Theatre of Marcellus, and a second close to the Theatre of Pompeius, built by Q. Octavius, the conqueror of Perses. The site upon which the former was built had been previously occupied by the Porticus Metelli, built by Q. Metellus Macedonicus, proprætor in B.C. 146, and the Octavian portico was a complete restoration of this by Augustus.[1]

Pliny also mentions two statues of Apollo near the Porticus Octaviæ, which probably stood in the Temple of Apollo, known to have been situated outside the Porta Carmentalis between the Forum Olitorium and the Circus Flaminius. But the principal evidence is derived from the plan of Rome, now on the staircase of the Capitoline Museum, where the whole design of this portico is laid down, and the temples which it enclosed are named. We learn from this plan that the portico was in form an oblong space enclosed with colonnades, and that the ruins now remaining constituted the principal entrance to this court, and to the Temple of Juno Regina which it enclosed. The line of the Via di Pescaria corresponds to one of the shorter sides of the court, and in the centre of this side the gateway stood. In two points only the Capitoline map fails to correspond with the actually existing ruins. The antæ of the gateway are not represented, and the corner column of the Temple of Juno is omitted. The former of these two omissions may be explained by supposing that the plan was probably made before the restoration of the portico by Severus.

The excavations carried on in 1861 by Pellegrini and Contigliozzi, established the following limits for the Portico of Octavia.

The southern corner of the rectangle was occupied by a quadrifrontal archway, and this was situated near No. 4 in

[1] Festus, p. 178. ed. Müller. Velleius, i. 1, 3; ii. 1, 2.

the Via della Catena di Pescaria. From this the south-western side of the portico ran nearly along the line of the street till it reached the gateway to which the present ruins belong, near the oratory of S. Angelo. The western corner of the portico was also formed by a quadrifrontal archway.

The north-western side passed through the church of S. Ambrogio a little below the high altar, and then skirted the Palazzo Righetti near the Piazza di S. Caterina de' Funari, where it joined the north-eastern and shorter side. In this side there was a pediment with pillars corresponding to the gateway at the opposite end, but not containing the real entrance, which stood near the angle of the Palazzo Caraletti in the Via de' Delphini. The eastern angle was near the Palazzo Capizucchi, and the south-eastern side passed close to the convent of monks of the order of Madre di Dio, attached to the church of S. Maria in Portico in the piazza di Campitelli.

The three Composite columns of marble, which still stand in the house, No. 11 in the Via di S. Angelo in Pescaria, belonged to the Temple of Juno, and stood at the western angle of that temple.

The remains of the Temple of Jupiter are hidden under the church of S. Maria in Portico, and the street which is now called Via della Tribuna dei Campitelli occupies the line of the interval between the two temples. A part of one of the side walls of the Temple of Jupiter rises a little above the ground at the corner of the church of S. Maria in Portico. The school or academy of Augustus was behind the temples, and stood near the centre of the Via della Tribuna di Campitelli. The back of this formed a part of the northern side of the portico.

The interior of the gateway has of late years been cleared of some of the buildings which have blocked it up, and the whole is now visible, with all the columns except one, which has been taken away to enlarge the church door.

A most interesting relic was found near the side door of the church of S. Angelo in Pescaria in April 1878, consisting of a pedestal of marble engraved with the title of Cornelia, the mother of the Gracchi. This was evidently the pedestal of the sitting statue of Cornelia mentioned by Pliny in his 'Natural History' as having been placed in the Portico of Metellus. The statue was the work of Tisicrates.

Excavations which have been made in the repair of houses and for other objects during the six years since 1873, have confirmed the conclusions which have been stated as to the position of the Portico of Octavia, and the temples near it. Some of the columns of the north side of the portico were found along the row of houses in the Via di Pescaria, No. 25–34.

The basement of the Temple of Apollo, between the Theatre of Marcellus and the Portico of Octavia, was found under the Albergo della Catena.

Crypta and Theatrum Balbi.

In the Via di S. Maria in Cacaberis, No. 23, there are two Doric columns of travertine half buried in the ground, with a portion of entablature above them, and between them an ancient brick arch forming the entrance to a stable. In the interior of the stable are two other similar arches and columns, and above these there are indications of an upper story. Other ruins of the same description are built into the next house, No. 22, and into several other houses near. In the sixteenth century, the Bolognese architect Serlio saw more ruins here, and he represents in his sketch an upper story with Corinthian pillars. The name Crypta Balbi, which is found in the catalogue of places in the ninth region, has been given with much probability to these ruins. A crypta, or cryptoporticus, according to Pliny, was a covered corridor with windows, which could be shut or opened at pleasure. Such a building was used for exercise in wet or hot weather. Some were open on one side, others closed on both sides. A cryptoporticus of the latter kind is to be seen in the ruins of Nero's Domus Aurea under the baths of Titus. The ruins in the Via di Cacaberis appear to have had open arches at the sides. This cryptoporticus was probably attached to the Theatre of Balbus, as the porticus Pompeii was to the Theatrum Pompeii, and Venuti thinks that it extended along the back of the scena, and that it was intended as a place of shelter for the spectators in case of the sudden showers of

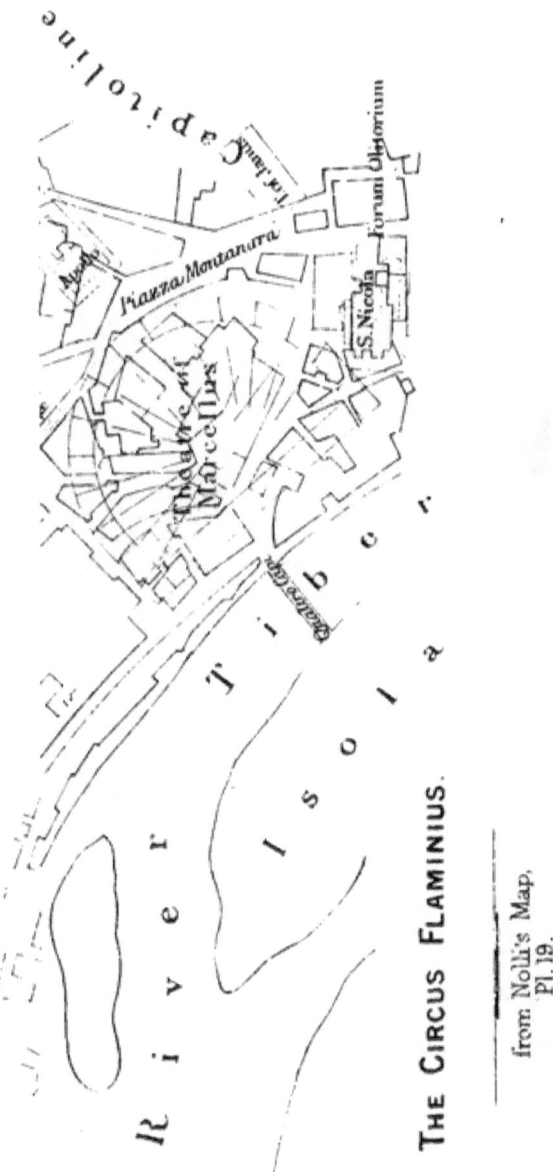

THE CIRCUS FLAMINIUS.

from Nolli's Map, Pl. 19.

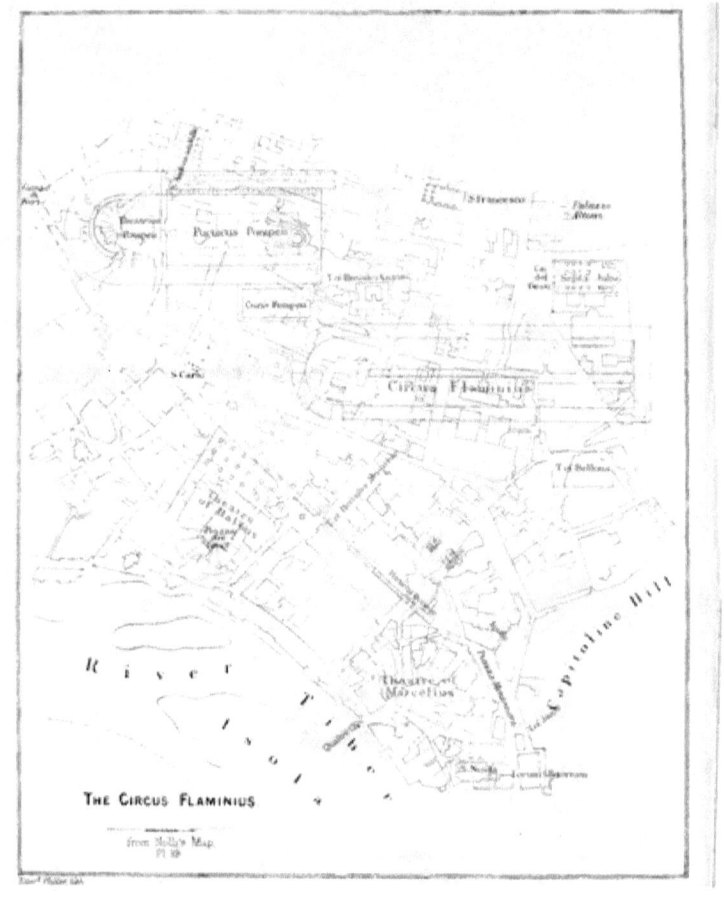

THE CIRCUS FLAMINIUS.

from Nolli's Map.
Pl. 18.

rain peculiar to the Roman climate.[1] The name of the street Cacaberis or Caccavari has been derived from crypticula. The Mirabilia, an ancient list of the sights in Rome, calls these ruins Templum Craticulæ.

The Circus Flaminius, named from the Flaminian family of ancient Rome, lay in the quarter traversed by the Via delle Botteghe Oscure, and in the neighbourhood of the Palazzo Mattei. The Circus was destroyed before the 9th century, and there are now no traces of it left to guide us, but before the erection, in the 15th century, of the larger houses in this quarter, some few ruins appear to have been visible in the neighbourhood of the Palazzo Mattei. These are described by Andrea Fulvio and Ligorio as having belonged to the Circus Flaminius, and according to their account the length of the Circus lay in a direction from west to east, and reached from the Palazzo Mattei, where the semi-circular end was situated, to the Piazzo Margana where the starting-point lay. A tower, now called the Torre Citrangole, was once called the Torre Metangole, and marked the spot where the goal of the Circus stood. Circus Flaminius.

In the district called by the name Circus Flaminius, stand the ruins of a vast range of buildings, the theatre, porticus, curia, and domus Pompeii. That these ruins, which are situated at the back of the church of S. Andrea della Valle, and are plainly those of a theatre, belonged to the Theatre of Pompey, is clear if the proofs given of the situation of the other two theatres in ancient Rome be admitted as sufficient. The place was so familiar to the Romans that we hardly ever find its locality indicated even in any such general terms as in campo Martio or juxta Tiberim, expressions commonly applied to other buildings of less note in the Campus Martius. Theatre of Pompeius.

The remains which are now left of these celebrated buildings are to be seen in the small piazza of S. Maria di Grottapinta behind the church of S. Andrea della Valle. They consist of ranges of travertine walls, converging to a centre, similar to those still visible in the interior of the Theatre of Marcellus and in the Coliseum, and are plainly

[1] Vitruv. v. 9.

the remains of the substructions supporting the cavea of a theatre. Further remains of piers and converging archways of peperino are visible in the cellars of the adjoining Palazzo Pio; and during some excavations made in 1837, a part of the outer walls of the theatre was discovered, with Doric half columns, and a Doric cornice. Most fortunately the ground plan, not only of the theatre, but also of the whole adjoining portico, is given upon some fragments of the Capitoline map.

The first idea of building such a magnificent theatre seems to have been suggested to Pompey by his visit to the theatre at Mitylene, whither he went after the Mithridatic war to be present at a contest of rival poets held in his honour. Only one attempt had before been made to build a permanent theatre in Rome. The Censor C. Cassius Longinus in the year B.C. 154 had entered into a contract for the construction of a stone theatre near the Lupercal, but the senate, by the advice of Scipio Nasica, a rigid Puritan of the old Roman school, and jealous of the introduction of Greek luxury, ordered it when half finished to be demolished, and the materials sold. The same decree inflicted penalties on any one who should, either in the city or within a mile of its walls, venture to place any seats for spectators at the games, or sit down while looking on at them. Tacitus states that even in Pompey's time the conservative Romans retained the same dread lest indolence and luxury should be promoted by the construction of permanent theatres.[1] In carrying out this grand design Pompey was assisted by his freedman Demetrius, who had amassed immense riches during his master's campaigns, and took this opportunity of paying his acknowledgments to the author of his wealth. The capabilities of the theatre must have been very great; nor need we be surprised to hear that it contained 40,000 seats, for the remaining fragments show that it comprehended the whole space between the Via de' Chiavari which corresponds nearly to the line of the scena, the Via di Giubbonari, the Campo di Fiore and the Via del Paradiso. Eastwards from the Via de' Chiavari stretched the long ranges of colonnades of which the Capitoline plan gives the outline, and beyond

[1] Tac. Ann. xiv. 20.

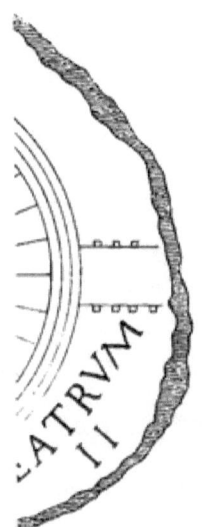

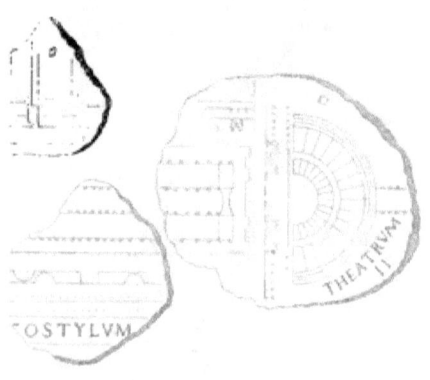

FRAGMENTS OF PIANTA CAPITOLINA
THEATRE OF POMPEY

them the Curia and a temple, with a variety of offices and shops, as far as the Via di Torre Argentina, including the modern Teatro Argentina within their compass. In this theatre Nero gave the grand entertainment to Tiridates, on which occasion not only the scena but the whole interior of the theatre and its furniture was covered with gilding, and a purple velarium stretched over it, upon which Nero himself was represented driving his chariot in the character of the Sun God, with golden stars glittering around him. The scena was burnt in the great fire in A.D. 80, but restored again by Vespasian. Two other conflagrations and restorations are recorded in the first half of the third century, one in the reign of Philippus in A.D. 249, and a second in that of Diocletian.[1] An inscription was found in the Via de' Chiavari in 1551, which commemorates the restoration of one of the colonnades under the name of Jovius, a title which Diocletian often assumed, and in the time of Ammianus Marcellinus the theatre could still be reckoned among the Mirabilia Urbis.[2] Another inscription given by the anonymous writer of the Einsiedlen MS. records a rebuilding by Arcadius and Honorius about A.D. 395. At the time the Notitia was compiled, the number of seats had diminished from 40,000, as given by Pliny, to 27,580 or even less, and the theatre was therefore probably in a ruinous state when the last mentioned restoration took place. The building naturally suffered much in the Gothic wars, and we find that it was again restored by Symmachus in the time of Theodoric, after which it is again mentioned under the right name of Theatrum Pompeii by the anonymous writer of Einsiedlen in the 9th and by the Ordo Romanus in the 12th centuries; but in the 13th the Orsini family had occupied it, and so changed the building that at the beginning of the 14th century it is called in the Mirabilia, Palatium Pompeii. The Florentine Poggio saw the ruins of the outer wall still standing in the Campo di Fiore in the 15th century, but the name of Pompey was then no longer connected with them, until Marliani, Fulvio, and Fauno the topographers of the

---

[1] Hier. Chron. ed. Ronealli, i. 475 ; ii. 247.
[2] Grut. Inscr. cxi. 6. Amm. Marc. xvi. 10.

16th century revived the right designation. Canina, in his work on the buildings of the ancients, has taken the greatest pains to give a full description of the ruins now left, and it is from him that most of our information is derived.

Ponte S. Sisto.

The bridge now called Ponte S. Sisto, near the ruins of the Theatre of Pompeius, stands on the site of an ancient bridge, which was most probably the one named Pons Aurelius in the Notitia. There is no conclusive proof that this was the Pons Aurelius, but the situation of none of the other bridges seems to suit this name, while it is peculiarly applicable to the bridge in question, because it was the principal passage over the Tiber to the Porta Aurelia and the Aurelian road along the coast to Civita Vecchia.

The name frequently given to it by topographers, Pons Janicularis, appears to be a mere invention, as it is not found in any trustworthy authority; and another name Pons Antoninianus, by which we find it called in the Middle Ages, seems to have arisen from the mistaken name Theatrum Antonini, formerly given to the Theatrum Balbi, which is not far distant, and also from the well-known fondness of Severus and Caracalla for the trans-Tiberine pleasure grounds. Marliani gives an inscription which is said to have existed formerly upon this bridge commemorating its restoration under Hadrian by Messius Rusticus, the Conservator of the Tiber. The bridge must therefore have been originally built before Hadrian's time, and cannot be a work of the Antonines.

CHAPTER VI.

PANTHEON, COLUMN OF MARCUS AURELIUS, MAUSOLEUM OF AUGUSTUS, MAUSOLEUM OF HADRIAN, AND NEIGHBOURHOOD.

NEAR the Piazza Venezia and S. Marco, to the east of the site *The Septa* of the ancient Circus Flaminius, stood the Septa, an ancient building erected for the purpose of holding the Roman comitia or elections. Some ruins of a very peculiar kind are situated under the Palazzo Doria and the church of S. Maria in Via Lata. They consist of ancient piers of travertine stone, about thirty-nine inches square, standing in rows at distances of five or six yards, and evidently belonging to the remains of a portico. There are three rows of these, each containing eight piers under the Palazzo Doria, and five rows under the church of S. Maria in Via Lata, containing each five piers. It is plain that these were originally faced with marble, as the exterior surface of the travertine is rough hewn. The situation of these pillars agrees well with the locality in which the Septa are placed by classical writers, and a further proof that they certainly formed a part of that building is given by the Capitoline map, upon which we find a large tract occupied by a building resting upon piers arranged in regular rows exactly corresponding to the piers under the church of S. Maria and the Palazzo Doria. Upon these fragments the letters SÆPT and LIA are legible, which appear to belong to the words SEPTA JULIA.

The shape of the building is very peculiar. It must have reached along the side of the Via Lata from the Piazza di S. Marco to the church of S. Maria in Via Lata, and consisted of a long cloister supported by parallel rows of eight marble piers. This cannot have been the arrangement of the place in the Republican or early Imperial times, for a design less adapted for the orderly meeting of a large body of people can hardly be conceived. It is much more probable that in the present ruins we have the remains of Hadrian's Septa, built when the original purpose of the building, the reception and division of the centuries when they voted, had become an affair of the past.

The design of these spacious covered cloisters seems to have been to afford a sheltered place for various classes of the Roman populace. Even in Domitian's time the Septa had become the common resort of slave vendors, dealers in fancy goods, flâneurs and loungers, and the new arcades were intended possibly for the express accommodation of such persons. The wide court in which the great assemblies of the centuries had previously been held was partly filled up by these new buildings, and partly occupied by private houses, as the Capitoline plan shows. When that plan was prepared, in the time of Septimius Severus, the old Septa had entirely lost their form and original use, and the name only remained attached to the spacious colonnades of Hadrian.

In the early times of the Republic the Septa were simply an enclosed place on the Campus Martius partitioned off into a number of different plots by means of ropes or slight railings, in each of which one division of voters or century assembled, and whence the presidents passed one by one over the pontes to deliver the vote of their respective century. Hence arose the nickname of ovilia, which was given to the septa on account of their similarity to a sheepfold. Julius Cæsar first entertained the idea of setting up marble enclosures for the comitia centuriata, and surrounding them with a magnificent portico. The whole formed a spacious cloistered court, decorated with works of art, and closely connected with the Villa Publica. Cæsar's design was completed after his death by Agrippa in B.C. 27, and he gave the building the name Septa Julia. A rostrum was erected in it, and such was the extent of the space enclosed that gladiatorial shows, and sometimes naumachiæ were held there. This was afterwards altered by Hadrian as above described.

Temples of Isis and Serapis. Westwards from the septa and nearly upon the site now occupied by the church of S. Stefano del Cacco, the little Via di pie di Marmo and a part of the church of S. Maria sopra

Minerva, stood the temples of Isis, Serapis, and Minerva Chalcidica.[1] The names of the three temples are given in the catalogue of the Curiosum in the ninth region, and the sites of the two first, the Iseum and Serapeum, have been sufficiently traced by the numerous Egyptian antiquities which have been found near the church of S. Maria sopra Minerva. Of these the most remarkable are the two obelisks, one of which now stands in the Piazza della Rotunda in front of the Pantheon, and the others on the Piazza della Minerva. The latter of these was found between the church of S. Ignazio and that of S. Maria in the time of Alexander VII. in 1665, and the former had stood, previously to its erection on the present pedestal, in a little piazza near this place, whence it was removed by Clement XI. The antiquarian Fea, in his Miscellanea, gives an account of various other Egyptian relics found on the south-east side of the church of S. Maria sopra Minerva, which undoubtedly belonged to the Iseum and Serapeum.[2]

Among these was a statue of Isis now in the hall of the dying gladiator in the Capitol, the two Egyptian lions now at the foot of the steps of the Capitol; the famous group of the Nile now in the Braccio Nuovo of the Vatican, and two fragments of an altar with Egyptian reliefs, and the inscription ISIDI SACRUM. Further traces of the same Egyptian worship were found by Canina in the year 1852, of which he has given an account in the Annali dell' Instituto of that year. The emperors Commodus and Caracalla were particularly given to the worship of Egyptian deities, and the emperor Alexander Severus is said to have bestowed additional decorations upon those temples. The third temple, that of Minerva Chalcidica, which was restored by Domitian, together with the Iseum and Serapeum after the fire in A.D. 80, stood nearer to the Pantheon, and probably occupied the site of the present church called S. Maria sopra Minerva. The statue of Minerva, formerly in the Giustiniani Palace and now placed in the Braccio Nuovo of the Vatican, was found here. Some few remains of pilasters which are built into the foundations of the houses

---

[1] Juv. Sat. vi. 529.   Joseph. B. J. vii. 5, 4.
[2] Fea, Misc. lxvi. 26; cxxv. 17 : ccliv. 112.

130 *A Handbook to the Ruins of Rome*

between the Via della Minerva and the Via di pie di Marmo may have belonged to this temple.

Pantheon.   At the same time with his Thermæ, which occupied this

district, Agrippa built the famous dome, called by Pliny and Dion, and in the inscription of Severus on the architrave of the building itself, the Pantheon, and still retaining that name, though now consecrated as a Christian Church under the name of S. Maria ad Martyres or della Rotunda. This consecration, together with the colossal thickness of the walls, have secured the building against the waste of time, and the still more destructive attacks of the barons of the Middle Ages, who destroyed most of the other great edifices of imperial Rome by either making them their strongholds or pulling them down for building materials. The pronaos rests upon sixteen granite columns, with marble Corinthian bases and capitals. It was formerly approached by six steps, but two only are now above the level of the surrounding ground. The architrave and frieze are plain, and on the latter stands the inscription, which formerly, as may be seen by the holes for nails, was formed by metallic letters:

M. AGRIPPA . L . F . COS . TERTIUM . FECIT.

Agrippa was consul for the third time in B.C. 27, so that the building is now 1906 years old. Another inscription in smaller characters stands under this upon the two upper ledges of the architrave, commemorating the restoration of the building by Severus and Caracalla. The pediment, as may be seen by the holes of the metal fastenings, formerly contained a bronze relief representing Jupiter hurling thunderbolts upon the giants. The roof of the pronaos was originally arched, but the vaulting has been replaced by strong beams, and on the outside the gilded bronze has been replaced by lead. In the interior of the pronaos, on each side of the entrance are two huge niches which formerly contained the statues of Augustus and Agrippa, but are now empty.

The pronaos is connected with the rotunda by two massive projections of masonry ornamented at the sides with marble pilasters and exquisitely worked reliefs in pentelic marble representing candelabra and sacrificial implements entwined with wreaths. These connecting walls originally rose to an equal height with the walls of the rotunda, but are now hidden by the bell towers, erected by Bernini in the time of Urban VIII. about A.D. 1625.

The doorway is of magnificently carved marble slabs, and

the folding doors, moving on massive hinges fixed in two projecting pilasters, are of exquisitely worked bronze.

The rotunda rests on a rectangular base, similar to those which support the cylindrical part of the mausoleum of Hadrian and the tomb of Cecilia Metella. In the parts where the thickness of the wall is not lessened by niches in the interior, it has the amazing breadth of nineteen feet of solid brickwork. In addition to this it is strengthened with numerous arches built into the wall. Three cornices run round the exterior of the rotunda and divide it into three rings, the lowest of which was faced with marble, and the two upper with stucco. The dome springs from the second cornice, and consists first of a ring of masonry seven feet high, and then of six concentric rings, presenting on the exterior the appearance of six steps. The top is flat, and is pierced in the centre with a large round opening twenty-seven feet in diameter. Round the opening is a ring of ornamental gilded bronze, which is the only part of the old bronze gilt roof now remaining. The masonry of the dome is of wedge-shaped pumice stones, chosen for this purpose on account of their lightness. The same kind of stone is used in several other buildings in Rome where lightness combined with moderate strength is required. The exterior of the dome is flat and heavy, and impressive only from its stern and massive solidity. The proportions of the interior are altogether different, and have been universally admired for their elegance, and the exquisitely simple taste with which they are decorated. The lower part contains eight deep niches, alternately semicircular and square, in one of which the entrance doors are placed, while the others were filled with statues of deities, now replaced by Romish altars. They are decorated with pilasters, and two Corinthian columns stand in front of each, supporting the entablature which runs round the whole interior. Between the eight principal niches are eight smaller ones, now used as altars, faced with aediculae consisting of two small columns with entablature and pediment. The two ring cornices in the interior answer in position to the lower exterior cornices. Above the upper cornice which runs quite round the building there were originally twelve niches surrounded with elegant marbles and stucco work. These were altered in 1747, and their effect injured by the introduction of heavy pediments, and by the removal of the marbles and stucco work. The interior of the roof is relieved by well-designed rectangular coffer work, decreasing in size towards the apex of the dome so as to give the impression of height and space. The floor is laid with slabs of Phrygian and Numidian marble, porphyry, and grey granite, in alternate squares and circles, set in reticulated work. In the centre it has a depression pierced with small holes to carry off the rain water from the aperture above. This drain probably communicated with the great cloaca built by Agrippa to drain the Campus Martius. The proportions of the interior of the dome are admirably adjusted, so that no part of the building has an undue prominence, contrasting favourably in this respect with S. Peter's, where the immense size of the piers on which the dome is supported dwarf the upper part too much. The Pantheon will always be reckoned among the masterpieces of architecture for solid durability combined with beauty of interior effect.

The Romans prided themselves greatly upon it as one of the wonders of their great capital, and no other dome of antiquity could rival its colossal dimensions.[1] The height from the pavement to the crown of the dome is 143 feet, half of which is occupied by the cylindrical wall and half by the dome; this height is insignificant when compared with S. Peter's, the dome of which is 405 feet from the pavement to the base of the lantern, and the exterior appearance of S. Peter's is far finer, but the diameter of the Pantheon is the greater, and the proportions of the interior more harmonious.

The inscription assigns its completion to the year B.C. 27, the third consulship of Agrippa. For a long time the mistaken notion prevailed that the building was dedicated to Juppiter Ultor, a misapprehension arising from a corrupt reading in a passage of Pliny, where the words Jovis Ultoris had been inserted instead of diribitori. The original name, Pantheon, taken in connection with the numerous niches for statues of the gods in the interior, seems to contradict the idea that it

---

[1] Amm. Marc. xvi. 10. Seneca de Ben. iii. 32.

was dedicated to any peculiar deity or class of deities. The seven principal niches may have been intended for the seven superior deities, and the eight aediculae for the next in dignity, while the twelve niches in the upper ring were occupied by the inferior inhabitants of Olympus. Dion hints at this explanation when he suggests that the name was taken from the resemblance of the dome to the vault of heaven.[1]

Originally, to all appearance, the Pantheon was not intended for a temple, but for a part of Agrippa's Thermae. Its shape corresponds very closely with the description given by Vitruvius of the Laconicum or Sudatio attached to all Roman Thermae. He recommends a dome-shaped building, with a round opening like that of the Pantheon at the crown, which can be opened or closed at pleasure, so as to lower or raise the temperature, by the removal or application of a lid (clypeum) moved by chains.

And on an examination of the pronaos it will be found that the stones in its upper part, which abut on the central building, are not bonded into it, but are only placed against it, showing that the pronaos was an after-thought, and was not erected till the rotunda had been finished. Agrippa must have changed the design of the building after the completion of the dome, and, perhaps because he found it too vast for the purposes of a sudatio, or because he thought it too splendid a building to be employed for such a purpose, have determined to dedicate it to the gods of heathendom. The bronze gilt statuary, the work of Diogenes of Athens, with which the temple was decorated, was much admired by the Roman connoisseurs, and in particular the group upon the pediment and the Caryatides. The statue of Venus was adorned with the two divided halves of the famous pearl of Cleopatra, fellow to the one which Cleopatra is said to have dissolved in vinegar in order to win her wager that she could spend ten million sesterces in one dinner.

In the fire of A.D. 80 the Pantheon suffered with the rest of the buildings in this part of the Campus Martius, but from the solidity of its construction the injury done was not great, and was repaired soon afterwards by Domitian. It

---

[1] Dion. Cass. liii. 27.

was damaged by lightning in the reign of Trajan, but restored by Hadrian, who used it frequently as a court of justice.

A hundred years after this, the restoration by Septimius Severus, recorded in the extant inscription, took place A.D. 195. Honorius closed this temple, with the other temples of Rome, in A.D. 399, but it was not consecrated as a Christian church until two hundred years afterwards, when Boniface IV. dedicated it to All Saints in allusion to the pagan name of Pantheon, giving the name of S. Maria ad Martyres. Two acts of plunder perpetrated upon the building deserve mention. In the middle of the seventh century, A.D. 650, Constans II. took off the gilded bronze tiles of the roof, and was carrying them to Constantinople, with the plunder of the Forum of Trajan, when he was intercepted at Syracuse by the Saracens and killed. His act of plunder was imitated by Urban VIII., who in 1632 took away the bronze girders which supported the roof of the pronaos and had them melted down and used partly for the pillars of the baldachino in S. Peter's, and partly for the cannon of the castle of S. Angelo.

Not far from the Pantheon the arches of the Aqua Virgo projected from the side of the Pincian Hill and crossed the Via Lata. Some remains of these arches are still to be seen in the Via del Nazareno (No. 12) at the back of the Fountain of Trevi. They bear an inscription which was copied in the ninth century by the anonymous chronicler of Einsiedlen, recording the restoration of the arches by Claudius after they had been partially destroyed by Caligula, who intended to build an amphitheatre in this neighbourhood. The arches are now entirely covered with rubbish, and the conduit of the aqueduct itself, which formerly was raised upon them, is consequently now upon the level of the ground. The inscription stands on the side of the conduit, and was formerly at the spot where some principal street passed under the aqueduct. Above it is a simple cornice, and below, an architrave, with the upper part of some Doric pilasters, appears above the surface of the water, which is here tapped to afford a washing trough to the laundresses of the neighbourhood. The masonry is of solid travertine blocks, carefully cut and fitted.

Dogana in the Piazza di Pietra.

Some topographers have identified the ruin in the Piazza di Pietra, now the Dogana, with the Posidonium, a portico built by Agrippa in memory of his naval exploits; but unless the ruin in the Piazza di Pietra be a later restoration after the fire of A.D. 80, which is possible enough, the style is not such as to allow us to assign it to the Augustan age. It has eleven fluted Corinthian marble columns supporting a tolerably well-preserved entablature, and plainly belonging to the longer side of a basilica or temple. The architrave, frieze, and cornice, have a heavy and unimpressive appearance, though some of the details of the work are rich and carefully executed. In the courtyard of the building a portion of the wall of the cella, and the spring of the arches of the vaulted roof, can be seen now incorporated into the modern building.

Various conjectures have been made as to the name and history of this building. Some of the older topographers thought that it was the Temple of M. Aurelius, which seems, however, to have been nearer to the column of that emperor than the ruin in question is;[1] nor does the position of this ruin allow us to suppose that it formed any part of a series of buildings placed symmetrically round the column. Palladio gives an elaborate ground-plan, with all the details, and calls it the Temple of Mars; but there does not appear to be any evidence in favour of this appellation; nor is it known how much of Palladio's design is taken from what remained of the ruin in his time, and how much is merely conjectural restoration. The conjecture of Urlichs that the Temple of Marciana, Trajan's sister, stood here, rests on no evidence but that of the Notitia, and is rendered very improbable by the great size of the building, and by the fact that the expression in the Notitia is Basilica Marciani, and not Templum Marcianae. Another hypothesis, which Professor Reber mentions, has more to recommend it. Antoninus Pius is said to have erected a temple in honour of

---

[1] In the Curiosum the temple and column are placed together in the ninth region.

his adopted father, Hadrian. This temple could not have stood in the Forum of Trajan, where there was no room left for such a building, and would most probably be placed near the rest of the Antonine buildings, not far from the Column of M. Aurelius. In the Mirabilia, the Temple of Hadrian is placed near the Church of S. Maria in Aquiro, which corresponded to the modern Chiesa degli Orfanelli; and part of a temple precinct built of travertine has been discovered in the Palazzo Cini, and is, perhaps, a relic of this temple. A medal of the year A.D. 151 contains a representation of the Temple of Hadrian, and corresponds tolerably well with the extant ruins; and in the neighbourhood of the Piazza di Pietra, several statues and fragments of inscriptions bearing the name of Antoninus Pius have been found at different times. When it is added that the style of building and execution of the ornamental work belong to the Antonine era, it will be seen that, although there is nothing more than probable evidence in favour of the above supposition, yet it has more in its favour than any of the other conjectures mentioned.

The present building was erected by Innocent XII. at the end of the seventeenth century in order to prevent the fall of the columns, which had become dangerously disjointed. The entablature has been restored in many parts, and a kind of attica erected over it, which gives the ruin the appearance of being in better preservation than it really is.

North of the Piazza Capranica, in the open space called the Piazza di Monte Citorio, is a large obelisk of red syenite. This is the Gnomon Obelisk, of which Pliny gives an interesting account in his 'Natural History.' It was brought by Augustus from Egypt, with that which is now in the Piazza del Popolo, and was erected on the Campus Martius under the directions of the mathematician Facundus Novus to serve as a sun-dial, by which not only the hour of the day, but also the day of the month, might be shown. For this purpose the pavement of the piazza in which it stood was marked out with a complicated system of lines in bronze; and, to prevent any disturbances caused by the settlement of the foundations, they were laid as deep below the ground as the

Gnomon Obelisk.

height of the obelisk itself. Pliny remarks that when he wrote, the gnomon had ceased for thirty years to mark the time rightly, and he ascribes this inaccuracy to some displacement of the obelisk due to natural causes, such as earthquakes or inundations.[1] It is more probable that the inaccuracy of the Julian calendar gradually produced the change. Ammianus Marcellinus, the Notitia, and the anonymous writer of the Einsiedlen MS., all mention this obelisk as still standing on the place where Augustus placed it. It was then—after the ninth century—lost for a time, but discovered again in 1463 with a part of the figures of the dial. Marliani, in the first half of the sixteenth century, mentions a part of the obelisk as lying neglected in a cellar near S. Lorenzo in Lucina, and it was not erected upon the present site until 1792.

To the east and north of the Monte Citorio lay the great buildings of the Antonine era, of which we still have some remains in the base of the Pillar of Antoninus Pius, now in the Giardino della Pigna of the Vatican, the magnificent Pillar of M. Aurelius in the Piazza Colonna, and the remains of the arch of the latter emperor, now in the Palace of the Conservators on the Capitol.

Pillar of Antoninus Pius.

The first of these, the Pillar of Antoninus Pius, was a monolith of red syenite, resting upon a pedestal of the same stone ornamented with reliefs. These remained upon their original site in the garden of the Casa della Missione near the Monte Citorio, until the time of Benedict XIV., when the pedestal was removed and placed in the Piazza di Monte Citorio near the Gnomon Obelisk, but the monolith was found to be so damaged, as not to be worth the expense of re-erection. Pius VI. when he placed the Gnomon Obelisk in the Piazza di Monte Citorio, removed the pedestal and took it to the Vatican Gardens, and it was finally placed in the Giardino della Pigna by Gregory XVI., who caused it to be carefully restored.

Column of M. Aurelius.

The second of the great Antonine monuments, the Column of M. Aurelius, still stands upon its original site in the Piazza Colonna. Formerly it was the centre point of a group

[1] Plin. N. H. xxxvi. 9, 71, 72.

of massive temples and colossal halls, which have entirely
perished. It is now surrounded by houses of modern construction, and surmounted by a statue of S. Paul, and looks
like a grey veteran clothed in the dress of a later generation,
in which he feels self-conscious and ill at ease. The only
remains of the colonnades, which once enclosed the court in
which it stood, are to be found on the east side of the piazza
in the palace of the Prince of Piombino. They consist of a
triple portico of brickwork, probably faced in ancient times
with marble. The Temple of M. Aurelius, which stood, like
that of Trajan, in front of the column, was probably upon the
western side towards the Piazza di Monte Citorio, and it is
from the ruins of this temple, and not of the Amphitheatre of
Statilius, as commonly supposed, that the mound of ruins called
Monte Citorio may have been formed. But no traces of the
substructions or of the walls or columns have been found.[1]

The column itself, which is a close imitation of that of
Trajan, stands upon a pedestal which was so altered by
Fontana from its original shape as to present a totally different
appearance. The ancient pedestal was much less massive
and better proportioned to the upper part of the monument.
Its base stood at a level thirteen feet lower than the present
pavement of the square, and it consisted of a basement of
solid stonework about sixteen feet in height resting on three
steps, nearly the whole of which is now under the level of
the surrounding ground. On the east side was the door by
which the spiral staircase in the interior was reached. Upon
the basement stood a large square flat stone, ornamented with
genii and triumphal and military ensigns, and above this
the pedestal upon which, before the restorations by Fontana,
only the words CONSECRATIO and D. ANTONINI. AUG. PII.
were legible. The original shape and inscription of this
lower part are only known to us from old prints and
antiquarian notes in Gamucci, Du Perac, and Piranesi's
works. It became necessary for the safety of the pillar, in
1589 to restore the base, and the whole was cased in marble
and repaired by Fontana, under the orders of Sixtus V., who
at the same time placed the statue of S. Paul upon the top.

[1] Annali dell' Inst. 1852, p. 338.

From a want of accurate historical information, however, the old inscription was supposed to refer to the elder of the Antonines, Antoninus Pius, and the new inscription accordingly speaks of the monument as dedicated to him. The error was discovered by a narrower inspection of the reliefs upon the shaft, which clearly relate to the exploits of M. Aurelius.

The plinth is quite simple, and the base of the shaft is formed, like the Column of Trajan, in the shape of a laurel crown. The whole of the shaft is occupied by a spiral series of reliefs, and only a small ring of fluted mouldings separates them from the capital, which is of the Romano-Doric order. The whole pillar measures 122 feet in height, being two feet lower than that of Trajan. The shafts of the two are exactly of the same height (100 Roman feet), and are formed in the same way of solid cylinders of marble, in the centre of which the spiral staircase which leads to the top is hewn.

The great winding wreath of bas-reliefs which twines round the column contains scenes from the history of the German wars in the years from A.D. 167–179, in which a number of the tribes north of the Danube, the Marcomanni, Quadi, Suevi, Hermonduri, Jazyges, Vandali, Sarmati, Alani, and Roxolani, with many others, took part. The representations begin with an army on the march crossing a river (the Danube); then follow, as on the Pillar of Trajan, scenes in which the general harangues his troops, the enemy's encampments are seen, and a great victory is won, accompanied with the usual thank-offerings.

But the most remarkable part of the whole relief is a scene which plainly corresponds to the account given by Dion Cassius of the sudden, and, as it seemed, supernatural relief afforded by a thunderstorm to the Roman army when hard pressed by the Quadi, who had surrounded them and succeeded in preventing all their efforts to escape. "The Roman army," says Dion, "were in the greatest distress from fatigue, many of them were wounded, and they were hemmed in by the enemy, without water, under a burning sun. They could neither fight nor retreat, and would have been compelled to stand in their ranks and die under the scorching heat, had not some thick clouds suddenly gathered, and a heavy rain fallen, which refreshed them, and afforded them drink. This did not happen without the intervention of the gods (οὐκ ἀθεεί), for it was said that one Arnuphis, an Egyptian magician, was with Marcus Aurelius, and that he, by invoking the aid of Hermes, the god of the air, and some other deities by means of incantations, drew down the rain." Xiphilinus, however, from whose abridgement of Dion we have the above account, declares that " Dion has purposely falsified the circumstances, for he must have known that the 'legio fulminata' obtained its name from this incident, the true history of which was as follows. There was a legion in the army of Marcus Aurelius, consisting entirely of Christians. The emperor being told that their prayers in such an emergency never remained unanswered, requested them to pray for help to their God. When they had prayed, God immediately smote the enemy with lightning, but refreshed the Roman army by a copious rain, upon which Marcus published a decree, in which he complimented the Christian legion and bestowed the name fulminate upon it." History however, does not bear out this wonderful tale of Xiphilinus, for the name fulminate is known, from inscriptions, to have been given to the twelfth legion as early as the reign of Augustus.[1]

Upon the pillar the scene is represented by the figure of Jupiter Pluvius dripping with rain, which the soldiers are eagerly catching in their shields.

The drought is followed by an inundation, in which many of the Germans are drowned. A grand battle takes place, followed by the burning of the enemy's huts and the seizure of numerous captives.

The figure of Marcus Aurelius on horseback, accompanying a long train of spoil taken from the German tribes, and a long series of battles, conflagrations of villages and towns, conferences with the enemy's generals follow, and the first campaign ends at a point near the centre of the column, with a procession of trophies and spoils of war, in the midst

[1] Dion. Cass. lv. 23. Orelli, Inscr. 517, 5447.

of which a figure of Victory inscribes the triumph on a shield.

Over this figure of Victory begins the history of the second campaign, in which four battles are represented, and various military scenes, as the crossing of the Danube in boats, the thanksgiving sacrifices after victory, the emperor addressing his army, captures of women and children, and finally a long train of captives and spoils led off in triumph. This great marble history is after the model of that on Trajan's Column. The style of execution is, however, somewhat different: the figures stand out much more from the surface, are more roughly cut, and have a heavier and stiffer look, resembling that of the reliefs upon the Arch of Severus, and the base of the Pillar of Antoninus Pius.

The column is called in all ancient writings Columna Antonini, which may apply to either of the Antonines. But it is perfectly evident from spiral reliefs, representing the frequent crossings of the Danube, and especially from that recording the incident of the sudden storm which extricated the Roman army from their difficulties, that the German wars of Marcus Aurelius are the subject commemorated.

Aurelius Victor and Julius Capitolinus state that temples, columns and priesthoods, were dedicated to this emperor after his death, and some inscriptions discovered in 1777 in the Piazza Colonna establish the conclusion that this pillar was erected in his honour beyond doubt. These inscriptions, now in the Gallery of Inscriptions in the Vatican, contain a petition from Adrastus, a freedman of Septimius Severus, and custodian of the Pillar of Marcus Aurelius, addressed to the Emperor Severus requesting leave to have the miserable hut (cannaba) in which he lived changed into a habitable house (solarium) for himself and his heirs, and also the decree of the emperor, giving the permission and assigning materials and a site. The petition was presented immediately on the accession of Severus, and the decree is dated in the consulship of Falco and Clarus, A.D. 193, two months after the emperor had taken possession of the palace. In this inscription the pillar is called the Columna Centenaria, and exact measurements of the shaft have shown that it is just one hundred Roman feet in height, including the base and capital.[1]

The bronze statue of Marcus Aurelius, which stood on the summit, was probably carried off by the Byzantine emperor, Constans II., to Syracuse, and was there taken by the Saracens from him, and conveyed to Alexandria with the rest of the plunder he had stripped from the buildings of Rome. To distinguish this column from the above-mentioned Pillar of Antoninus Pius, it is called in some of the legal documents of the tenth century " Columpna major Antonina." As recorded in the inscription on the modern base, it was much injured by lightning in the fourteenth century, and restored by Sixtus V.

The Piazza Navona was formerly a stadium, not a circus. The strongest evidence we have in favour of this rests on the shape of the piazza and of the ruins. One of the essential parts of a circus, the spina, is entirely wanting, and the end from which the runners started is at right angles to the longer sides, while in a circus, as in the case of the Circus of Maxentius, the carceres always stood in a slanting direction across the course, in order to equalise the distances round the spina. *Piazza Navona.*

The obelisk, which now stands in the centre of the piazza was brought by Innocent X. from the Circus of Maxentius on the Appian Road. The Circus of Maxentius was not, however, its original site, for the hieroglyphics are of Roman execution and contain the name of Domitian.

The northern part of the Campus Martius, between the Via del Ripetta and the Pincian Hill, contained only one great building of which we have any knowledge. This was the Mausoleum of Augustus, the ruins of which are now buried under the Teatro Correa, and are approached by a narrow entry leading out of the Via dei Pontefici. All that can now be seen of the shapeless mass which this once stately building presents, is a small part of the cylindrical brickwork basement on the left of the entrance to the Teatro Correa, and another fragment of the same at the back of the Church of S. Rocco. The proofs that these are the remains of the *Mausoleum of Augustus.*

[1] Gruter, Inser. 466.

Mausoleum of Augustus are quite indisputable. Suetonius places it between the Tiber and the Flaminian Road, and Strabo speaks of it as standing near the bank of the river, descriptions which, though they are not very definite, agree with the site of the Teatro Correa sufficiently. Complete certainty is, however, afforded by the inscriptions which have been found on the site of the Ustrina Caesarum, where the bodies were burnt before burial. These were found near the Corso, between the Via degli Otto Cantoni and the Via dei Pontefici, a spot answering to Strabo's notice of the site of the Ustrina as standing in the middle of the Campus, which is here narrowed by the approach of the Pincian Hill towards the river.

Augustus had built this magnificent tomb in his sixth consulship (B.C. 28). At that time the course of the Flaminian Road through the Campus was lined with the tombs of many eminent Roman statesmen and public characters, which have all, with the exception of the insignificant Tomb of Bibulus, totally disappeared. The modern city has entirely effaced all traces of these, but we may in all probability suppose that the Flaminian road presented no less striking a spectacle in the days of Augustus than the Appian, which we are accustomed to regard as the great burying-place of Rome.

The name mausoleum was apparently given to this tomb if not immediately, yet soon after its completion, not from any resemblance in the plan of the building of the famous monument of the Halicarnassian queen, which differed entirely in shape and design, but because the expression mausoleum had already become a name used to designate any tomb of colossal proportions. The Mausoleum of Halicarnassus was a rectangular building surrounded with a colonnade, while the Tomb of Augustus was cylindrical and ornamented with deep niches. Strabo gives the following description of the latter monument: "The most remarkable of all the tombs in the Campus is that called the Mausoleum, which consists of a huge mound of earth raised upon a lofty base of white marble near the river bank, and planted to the summit with evergreen trees. Upon the top is a bronze statue of Cæsar Augustus, and under the mound are the burial-places of Augustus and his family and friends, while behind it is a spacious wood containing admirably designed walks. In the middle of the Campus is the enclosure he made for burning the corpses, also of white marble, surrounded by an iron railing, and planted with poplar-trees."[1]

The mound of earth here described by Strabo was probably of a conical shape, and the trees were planted on terraced ledges. The mass of the building was cylindrical, like the central portions of Hadrian's Mausoleum, and of the tombs of Plautius and Cæcilia Metella, and was supported upon a square basement which is now entirely buried beneath the level of the ground. The exterior of the cylindrical part was relieved by large niches which doubtless contained statues, and broke the otherwise heavy uniformity of the surface. At the entrance were the bronze pillars which Augustus had ordered to be erected after his death, on which was engraved a catalogue of the acts of his reign. We now possess a fragment of a copy of this interesting document in the famous Monumentum Ancyranum, found at Ancyra in the vestibule of a Temple of Augustus. Besides these pillars two obelisks stood in front of the entrance door, one of which is now placed in the Piazza of S. Maria Maggiore, while the other stands between the statues of the Dioscuri on the Quirinal. These obelisks were not, however, placed there at the time when the tomb was first built, but at a later period of the empire. The entrance fronted towards the city, i.e., to the south, near the apse of the Church of S. Rocco, and appears to have had a portico with columns, the traces of which are still left.

The interior was formed by massive concentric walls, the spaces between which were vaulted and divided into cells for the deposit of the urns containing the ashes of the illustrious dead. A great alabaster vase found near the Mausoleum in 1777, and placed in the Vatican Museum, was probably one of these. We know from various passages of Roman authors that the first burial which took place here was that of the young Marcellus, the favourite nephew of

[1] Strabo, v. 3, 8.

Augustus, who died at Baiæ [1] in B.C. 23, and the last, that of the Emperor Nerva in A.D. 98. Trajan was buried under his column. The Mausoleum of Hadrian became the Imperial tomb in A.D. 138.[2] During the 160 years which intervened, the ashes of Agrippa, Octavia, the mother of Marcellus, Drusus, Caius and Lucius, Augustus himself and Livia, Germanicus, Drusus, son of Tiberius, the elder Agrippina, Tiberius, Antonia (wife of L. Domitius), Claudius and Britannicus were deposited here. Besides these there must have been a great number of other friends and relations of the Imperial family buried here. Only one of all the inscriptions recording these burials is now extant. It is engraved on a pedestal, which bore the urn where the ashes of the elder Agrippina, the wife of Germanicus and mother of Caligula, lay. In the inscription on this pedestal Caligula is called Augustus, showing that the burial took place after his accession, in accordance with the account of Agrippina's banishment by Tiberius. The pedestal was hollowed out and used in the Middle Ages as a measure for corn, and is still inscribed with the words RUGITELLA DI GRANO. It may now be seen in the courtyard of the Conservator's Palace on the Capitol. At the same time, and at a spot between the Mausoleum and the Corso were found six cippi of travertine, recording the burning of the bodies of four of the children of Germanicus, Tiberius Cæsar, Caius Cæsar, Livilla, and one whose name is erased. The remaining two cippi record the burning of the bodies of a son of Drusus, and of one of the Flavian family. It is evident that these belonged to the Ustrina Cæsarum, a place described by Strabo, as quoted above, where the corpses of the dead were burnt and the formal ceremony of collecting the bones took place. The cippi may still be seen in the Vatican Museum.

The Mausoleum remained closed after Nerva's burial until the capture of Rome by Alaric in A.D. 409, when the Goths broke it open in their search for treasure, and scattered the ashes of the Cæsars to the winds. It was then probably that the alabaster vase mentioned above was removed from the Mausoleum and carried to the Ustrina where it was found.

[1] Dion. Cass. liii. 32, liv. 26.   [2] Dion. Cass. lxix. 23.

In the 12th century the Mausoleum suffered the fate of all the other great buildings of Rome. It became a castle of the Colonna family, and bore the name Augusta. The mound of earth was then probably removed, and a stone or brick tower built in its place. Previously to this, the statue of Augustus, with the bronze decorations of the Pantheon and Forum of Trajan, had probably been carried to Syracuse by Constans, and thence to Alexandria by the Saracens.

The building might, however, still, like the tomb of Hadrian, have long defied the attacks of time, had not the Romans themselves, in the commotions of 1167, demolished the Colonna Castle, and with it the greater part of the walls upon which it was built. Two hundred years later, the body of the last of the Tribunes, Cola di Rienzi, was burned by the Jews before the Mausoleum.[1] At that time the spot was called Campo d' Austa from the ancient site of the Ustrina. The interior chambers seem to have been entirely demolished in the 15th century, and only the exterior wall left. Poggio, the Florentine, describes the building as used in his time (1440) for a vineyard, and before that date its shape was completely changed by the falling in of the vaulting of the interior, so that it presented the appearance of an amphitheatre instead of a lofty conical building. In Donatis' book (1638), it is represented as a funnel-shaped ruin with a garden on the sloping sides of the interior. Much information might doubtless be gained by well-directed excavations, which have apparently never been undertaken on account of the present occupation of the ruin as a circus in winter and a theatre (the Teatro Correa) in summer.

Beyond the Porta del Popolo on the edge of the Pincian hill, there is a very ancient piece of wall, faced in the style called opus reticulatum, which is made of small diamond-shaped blocks of tufa set in the surface of a mass of concrete. These blocks are driven into the concrete before the lime has dried and set. This ruin, which is called the Muro Torto, is often spoken of as having been a part of the house of Sylla, but I do not know upon what authority. It may have formed a part of the substructions of some of the private buildings

Muro Torto.

[1] Reumont, Gesch. Roms, vol. ii. p. 917, A.D. 1354; Gibbon, ch. lxx.

on the Pincian, previous to the time of Aurelian, who incorporated it in his wall. Near the angle of the wall where it turns sharply to the south is a point at which the brickwork leans in great masses considerably out of the perpendicular, whence the name of Muro Torto. Procopius speaks of this as having been in the same state long before his time, and calls it the broken wall.

Pons Ælius. Passing along the bank of the Tiber by the Via Ripetta from the Porta del Popolo we come to the bridge of S. Angelo (Pons Ælius) which crosses the river close to the Castle of S. Angelo, anciently the Mausoleum of Hadrian. This bridge was built by the Emperor Hadrian at the same time with his Mausoleum. The anonymous writer of the Einsiedlen MS. gives an inscription which in his time remained upon the bridge assigning its erection to the nineteenth tribuneship and third consulship of Hadrian, which indicates the year A.D. 135, and in confirmation of this Nardini gives a medal of Hadrian which dates from his third consulship, and has on the obverse a representation of this bridge. The name Pons Ælius, given to it by Dion Cassius in his account of Hadrian's funeral, was probably derived either from Hadrian's praenomen Ælius, or from the name of his son Ælius Cæsar whose burial was the first which took place in the Mausoleum. The piers of the bridge are ancient, but the upper parts have been rebuilt.

Mausoleum of Hadrian. The Mausoleum of Hadrian owes its preservation entirely to the peculiar fitness of the site and shape for the purpose of a fortress which it has served since the time of Belisarius. Had it not been thus made serviceable to the turbulent spirit of the mediæval Romans, the same hands which stripped the great pile of its marble facing, and, after hurling the statues with which it was adorned into the moat, allowed them to lie there in oblivion, would have torn asunder and carried away the whole mass to furnish materials for the palaces and stables of their ferocious and ignorant nobles. The original form of this colossal mausoleum is now greatly changed by the modern buildings which have been piled upon it, by the addition of the corbels round its upper part, and by the loss of the exterior facing of marble, so that the ancient appearance can be only conjecturally restored. The remaining ancient part consists of a square basement of concrete and travertine blocks, the sides of which measured ninety-five yards surmounted by an enormous cylindrical structure of travertine seventy yards in diameter and seventy-five feet high. Procopius tells us that this was cased in Parian marble, and that upon the summit stood a number of splendid marble statues of men and horses.[1] There are several other tombs in Italy constructed upon the same plan with a cylindrical tower placed upon a square base. Two of these are upon the Appian road about three miles from Rome, the celebrated Tomb of Cæcilia Metella, and that of the Servilii, and belong to the Republican Era. Two others are of the Augustan Age, the tomb of the Plautii at Ponte Lucano, near Tivoli, and the beautiful monument of Munatius Plancus, near Gaeta. Hadrian's design was not therefore by any means a new one, as we might have expected in the case of an emperor who was himself an architect, and proud of his artistic designs.

It is plain from the history of Procopius that the statues of men and horses which he describes were upon the top of the building. For the defenders of the mausoleum against the army of Vitiges being hard pressed by the approach of the Goths under shelter of a testudo, in their despair seized these statues and hurled them upon the heads of their assailants, thus breaking down the testudines and repelling the attack. Of the exact order in which they were arranged we have no evidence. Tradition asserts that the twenty-four Corinthian columns destroyed by fire in the Basilica of St. Paul in 1823 formerly belonged to the Mausoleum of Hadrian, and that they were removed by Honorius.[2] A comparison of this tradition with a passage of Herodian, in which he says that the ashes of Septimius Severus were buried in the temple where rest the bones of the Antonini, has led to the conjecture that the columns formed the colonnade of a round temple on the top of the mausoleum in which temple Hadrian's colossal statue stood, and that the bronze fir-cone found here, which is now in the Vatican garden, ornamented the summit. Round

---

[1] Procop. Bell. Goth. 22.
[2] Bunsen's Memoirs, vol. i. p. 208. Hirt. Gesch. der Bauk, ii. p. 373.

this temple, and upon the level top of the cylindrical tower, may have been arranged the various statues of which Procopius speaks.

The colossal head of Hadrian's statue found here is still to be seen in the Museo Pio Clementino, the bronze gilt peacocks in the Giardino della Pigna. The famous Barberini Faun, now at Munich, and the dancing Faun at Florence, were amongst the ornaments of the upper part of the tomb. Another conjecture as to the shape of the upper part of the building is that it was surmounted by a smaller cylindrical tower, with a roof in the shape of a truncated cone, upon the top of which stood the colossal statue of Hadrian. There is not sufficient evidence to give any degree of certainty to either of these conjectural restorations.

The interior of the building, according to the latest discoveries, consists of a large central rectangular chamber (thirty-six by thirty feet wide and fifty-four feet high), approached by an ascending spiral corridor, leading from a lower chamber which communicated immediately with the principal entrance. The entrance was a high arch in the cylindrical tower immediately opposite the bridge; it is now walled up and the lower chamber into which it leads can only be approached from above.

In the central chamber there are four niches in which formerly stood the urns and tombstones of the illustrious persons buried here. A large sarcophagus of porphyry found here was used for the tomb of Pope Innocent II. in the Lateran, and the lid may still be seen in the Baptisterium of St. Peter's, where it is used as a font. The chamber was lighted and ventilated by square passages cut through the stone in a slanting direction, and the rain water was carried off by other channels, which conveyed it into drains at the foot of the building. It does not appear to be certainly known whether other chambers may not exist in the interior which have not been yet discovered. Piranesi gives a number of additional chambers besides the two above mentioned, but his representation is probably conjectural.

After the burial of Nerva no more room was left in the Mausoleum of Augustus for the interment of the imperial ashes. Trajan's remains were deposited under his column in the forum bearing his name, but Hadrian gladly seized the opportunity of adding another to the many colossal structures he had already reared. The mausoleum was begun at the same time with the Ælian bridge in the year A.D. 135. The bricks of which part of the building consists have stamps of various years of Hadrian's reign, and show that the greater part of the building was erected by him, though Antoninus Pius probably completed it. Hadrian's son Ælius, who died before his father, was the first Cæsar whose ashes were placed in this tomb. After him, Hadrian himself was buried here, and then the Emperor Antoninus Pius, and his wife the elder Faustina, three of their sons, Fulvius Antoninus, M. Galerius Aurelius Antoninus, and L. Aurelius Verus, the colleague of M. Aurelius in the empire, and a daughter Aurelia Fadilla.

No record has been preserved of the burial of M. Aurelius, but it seems probable that his ashes were deposited here, as the Mausoleum of Hadrian continued to be the tomb of the Antonines till the time of Severus, who built a third imperial monument, the Septizonium, on the Appian Road.[1] Four children of M. Aurelius were buried here, who died during their father's life, named Aurelius Antoninus, T. Ælius Aurelius, and Domitia Faustina, and also his miserable son and successor the Emperor Commodus. The inscriptions recording all these burials, were copied by the anonymous writer of Einsiedlen in the ninth century, when they were apparently still legible upon the south wall of the square basement. The inscriptions recording the names Hadrian and M. Aurelius may have been placed upon the upper part of the tomb, like those on the Plautian Tomb and the Tomb of Cæcilia Metella, and may therefore either have escaped the notice of the above-mentioned anonymous traveller, or have been stripped off with the marble casing of the exterior.

After the burial of M. Aurelius the tomb was closed until the sack of Rome by Alaric in A.D. 410, when this barbarian's soldiers probably broke it open in search of treasure, and scattered the ashes of the Antonines to the winds. From this

[1] Hist. Aug. Sept. Sev. 19, 24. Herodian iv. 1, 4.

time for a hundred years the tomb was turned into a fortress, the possession of which became the object of many struggles in the wars of the Goths under Vitiges A.D. 537 and Totilas who was killed A.D. 552. From the end of the sixth century, when Gregory the Great saw on its summit a vision of St. Michael sheathing his sword in token that the prayers of the Romans for preservation from the plague were heard, the Mausoleum of Hadrian was considered as a consecrated building under the name of S. Angelus inter nubes, usque ad cælos, or inter cælos, until it was seized in A.D. 923 by Alberic, Count of Tusculum and the infamous Marozia, and again became the scene of the fierce struggles of those miserable ages between popes, emperors, and reckless adventurers.[1] The last injuries appear to have been inflicted upon the building in the contest between the French Pope Clemens VII. and the Italian Pope Urban VIII. The exterior was then finally dismantled and stripped. Partial additions and restorations soon began to take place. Boniface IX., in the beginning of the fifteenth century, erected new battlements and fortifications on and around it, and since his time it has remained in the possession of the Papal Government. The strange medley of Papal reception rooms, dungeons, and military magazines which now encumbers the top was chiefly built by Paul III. The corridor connecting it with the Vatican dates from the time of Alexander Borgia (A.D. 1494), and the bronze statue of St. Michael on the summit, which replaced an older marble statue, from the reign of Benedict XIV.[2]

[1] Gibbon, ch. xlix.
[2] Donati 'Roma vetus ac recens,' 1665, p. 476.

CHAPTER VII.

THE QUIRINAL HILL—BATHS OF DIOCLETIAN—AGGER OF SERVIUS—CASTRA PRÆTORIA.

THE broad flat space to the N.E. of the Quirinal Hill, was occupied by the Thermæ of Diocletian, now converted into the great Church of S. Maria degli Angeli. This enormous group of buildings was the most extensive of all the gigantic edifices of the empire, and the ground plan is not difficult to trace by the aid of the existing ruins. Some idea of their dimensions will be given by remarking that the grand court enclosed a space once occupied by the church, monastery, and spacious garden of the Monks of S. Bernard, the great church and monastery of the Carthusians, two very large piazzas, the large granaries of the Papal Government, part of the grounds of the Villa Montalto Negroni, and some vineyards and houses besides. The north-western side of this grand court is now only marked by the remains of two semicircular tribunes in front of the railway station. The rest of the foundations of this side are hidden under the great cloister of the Carthusian monastery, and in the district beyond. The principal entrance was on this side. The south-eastern side is now occupied by the buildings of the railway station, at the back of which were discovered the ruins of a large reservoir now destroyed (K), in the shape of a right-angled triangle. The peculiar form of this building seems to have been necessitated by the course of a public road of some importance confining it on the south side, and it has been supposed, not without reason, that this was the principal road leading out of the city at the Porta Viminalis. The interior was filled with pillars like those which still stand in the ancient reservoirs at Baiæ and Constantinople.

On the south-western side of the court there are con-

Baths of Diocletian.

siderable remains. In the gardens of the monastery of S. Bernardo, part of the cavea of a theatre (A) with a radius of about seventy yards, may be traced, not unlike that in the

The Quirinal Hill, as seen from the Palatine.

Thermae of Titus. The seats of this are gone, but parts of the back wall with niches remain. On each side of this are traces of rectangular chambers, and at the corners stand two

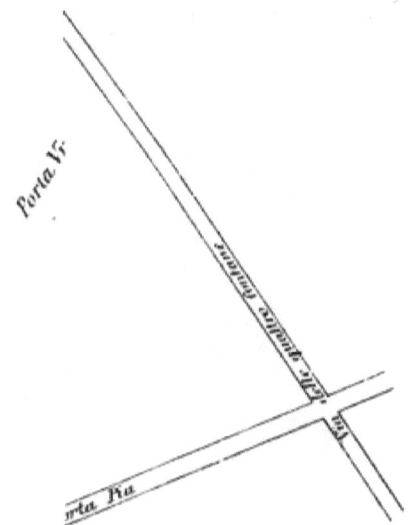

THERMÆ DIOCLETIANÆ. (PALLADIO.)

The red lines mark the conjectural restorations.

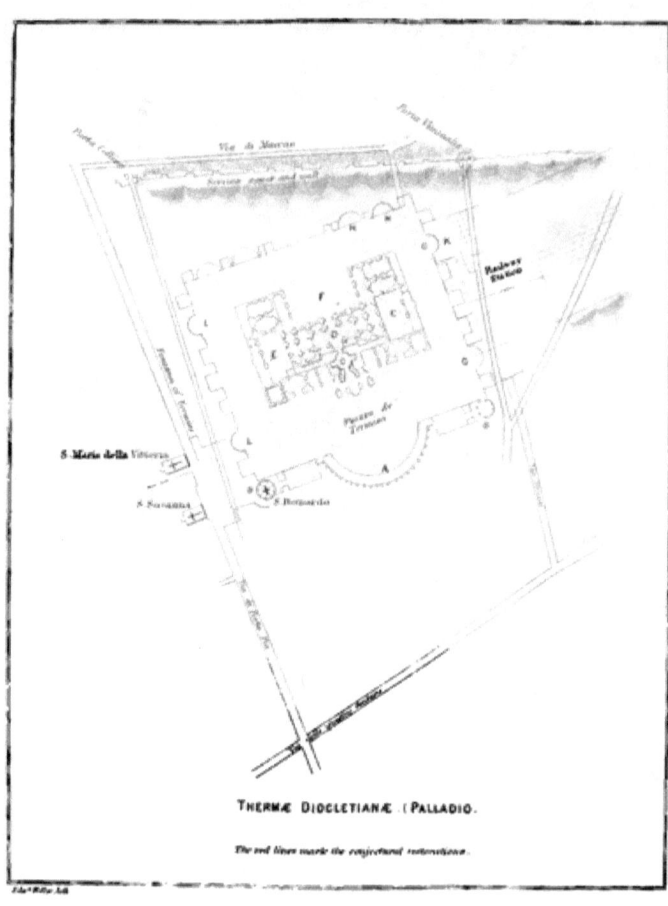

THERMÆ DIOCLETIANÆ (PALLADIO).

The red lines mark the conjectural restorations.

round buildings, one of which is nearly perfect, and has been converted into the Church of S. Bernardo. The ancient domed roof with its octagonal panelled work is still standing. Part of the other rotunda at the southern corner is also left, and has been built into the end of the Via Strozzi.

The north-western side of the court ran parallel to the Via di Venti Settembre from the Church of S. Bernardo. It contained, according to Palladio's plan, two semicircular exedræ (LL) for philosophical conversation or disputation, and some other rooms the purpose of which is not known. The Ulpian libraries are said to have been transferred to these baths from the Forum Trajani. In this spacious court stood a great pile of buildings, the centre of which was occupied by a great hall (D), now the church of S. Maria degli Angeli. The pavement of this was raised above the ancient level of the ground by nearly eight feet, when Michael Angelo undertook to convert the ancient building into a church, and thus the bases of the columns remain buried, and new bases of stucco work have been placed round them. This roof must therefore have been in ancient times considerably more lofty than at present. The ancient roof was 120 feet high, and roofed as now, with an intersecting vault in three compartments, supported by the eight colossal ancient granite pillars. These columns of Egyptian granite with their Corinthian and composite capitals form the sole relic of the magnificence of the hall. In the modern church the transept corresponds to the longer axis of the ancient hall, and the nave to the shorter. Vanvitelli, who altered the arrangement of the church in 1749, threw out an apse for the choir on the north-east side, and made the circular laconicum (C) of the old Thermæ serve as an entrance porch.

Antiquarians are not agreed as to the purpose of this great central hall. Scamozzi, in his edition of Palladio, calls it a xystus for athletic exercises, but, following the analogy of the Thermæ of Caracalla, the baths at Pompeii, and some of the other great thermæ, we should rather suppose it to have been the tepidarium. This view is confirmed when we notice that the laconicum or sudarium (C) is on one side, and the natatio (F) for the cold baths on the other, between which the tepidarium was kept at a mean temperature.

The two wings of the central building were occupied by large peristylia, with cold piscinæ in the centre of each (EE). Round these peristylia were built various rooms for athletic exercises, called sphæristeria and gymnasia.

The style of brick building used in these Thermæ, recalls that of the Basilica of Constantine, where we see the bricks irregularly and hastily laid; and the whole of the architectural details which have been preserved seem to point to the same period. Positive evidence of the date and the builder is not however wanting. An inscription, which was still to be seen two hundred years ago in the thermæ, and which has been partially preserved to us, when compared with three others which were found in the neighbourhood, shows that Maximianus gave orders for building these thermæ when he was absent in Africa, during his Mauretanian campaigns, and intended them to be dedicated to the honour of his brother Diocletian. The dedication took place after the abdication of Diocletian and Maximianus, when their successors Constantius Chlorus and Galerius Maximianus had begun their reign, A.D. 305, but before the death of Constantius in 306. The old chronologers place the date of the commencement of the buildings in 302, which agrees very well with the date of the Mauretanian campaigns of Maximian.

Baronius accounts for the preservation of so large a part of these thermæ by the statement that they were considered to be a monument of the Diocletian persecution. There was a tradition, he says, that Diocletian, after dismissing some thousands of his soldiers because they held the Christian faith, compelled them to work as slaves in the erection of his thermæ, and ordered them to be martyred when they had finished the building. It has also been said that the bricks are in some cases marked with a cross, but this is not well authenticated.

At the end of the fifth century, the baths are mentioned by Sidonius Apollinaris as still used, but at the time of the visit of the anonymous writer of the Einsiedlen MS., probably

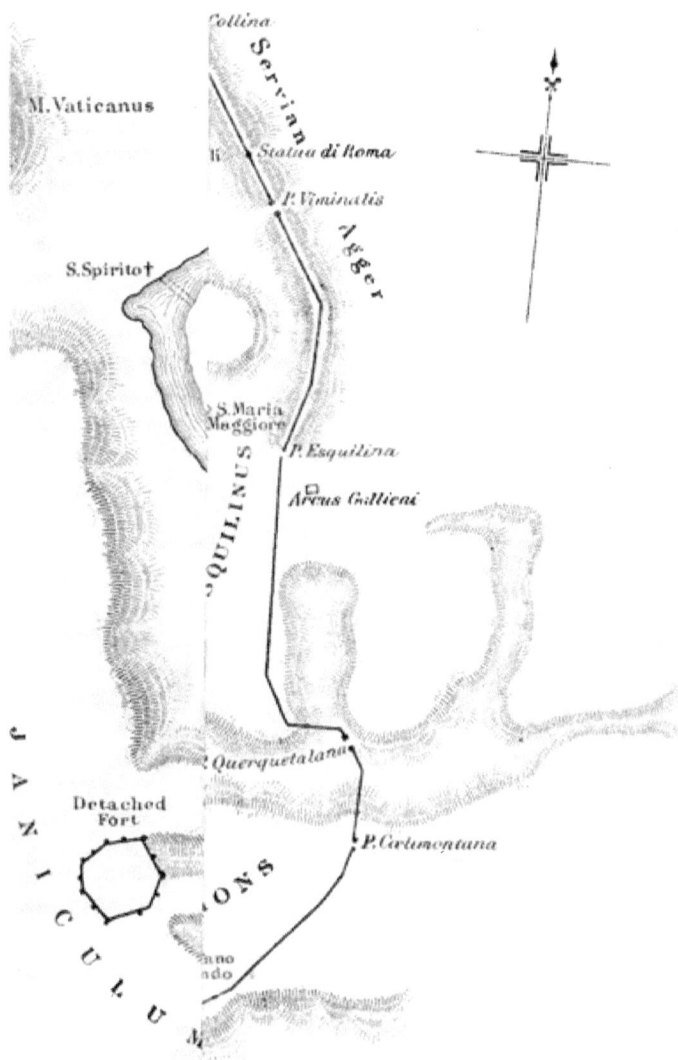

THE SERVIAN WALLS.
Chapter IV.
SCALE OF HALF AN ENGLISH MILE

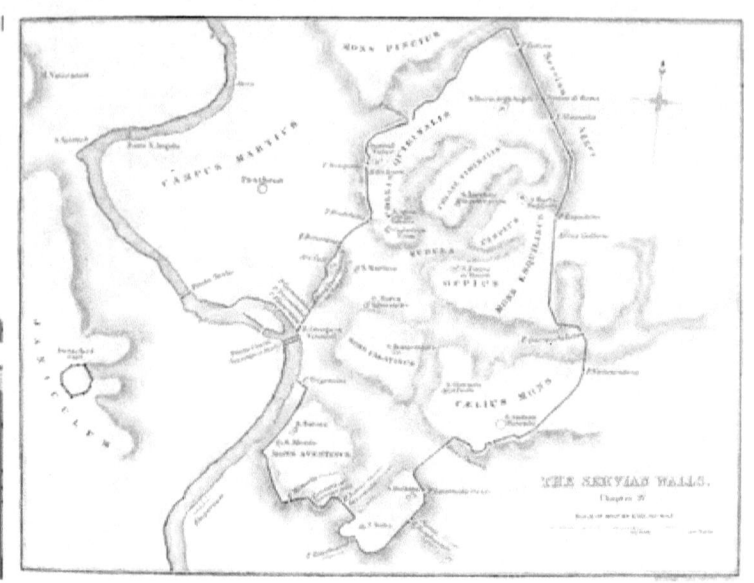

about A.D. 850, they were evidently in ruins. Among the ruins have been found, from time to time, a number of busts of the Emperors Diocletian, Maximian, Galerius, and Constantine, and also the well-known busts of philosophers now in the Farnese collection at Naples.

The great fountain now in front of the railway station is supplied by the water brought along the course of the ancient Aqua Marcia.

The Agger of Servius, which has now been so much levelled and destroyed, ran between the Church of S. Maria degli Angeli and the present walls. This enormous rampart has been described by Dionysius. He says that the ditch outside was more than one hundred feet broad at the narrowest part and thirty feet deep, and that a wall stood upon the edge of the ditch supported by the agger, which was of such massive strength that it could not be shaken down by battering rams or breached by undermining the foundation. Dionysius gives the length of the agger as seven stadia, and Strabo as six, which, taking the stadium at 202 yards, nearly corresponds to 1400 yards. The breadth he states at fifty feet. That this ditch and wall were the work of some of the later kings there can be no doubt, but it cannot be determined what part each took in their erection. The final completion of the whole undertaking is ascribed to Tarquinius Superbus, who deepened the ditch, raised the wall, and added new towers. The additions made by him can be distinguished in the portion brought to light by the modern excavations in the railway cutting.[1]

The Servian Agger.

Excavations which have been made in this part of the agger from time to time, and the extensions of the city in this direction have brought to light an enormous wall buried in the earth, constructed of huge blocks of peperino. This is probably the wall mentioned by Dionysius, which in his time stood outside the rampart on the edge of the ditch. The remains of buildings of the imperial times have been found placed upon and outside of this wall, and it is probable that the whole ditch is now filled with such remains, and most part of the wall buried in them.

[1] Dionys. ix. 68. Brocchi, Suolo di Roma, p. 144.

The central railway station stands close to this agger, and cuttings have lately been made through it to make room for the station, by which new portions of the wall have been disinterred. All these excavations have proved the truth of Dionysius's description, the wall having been found on the outer side of the original agger, which is easily distinguishable from the rubbish in which it is buried by being composed of clean soil unmixed with potsherds and brickbats. The wall probably ran from the southern end of the agger along the back of the Esquiline and Cælian in the direction of the modern Via Merulana and Via Ferratella. In this portion must be placed the Porta Querquetulana and the Porta Cælimontana, but their exact situation is unknown.[1]

The Prætorian Camp.

Near the Porta Pia, to the north-east of the church of S. Maria degli Angeli, the square of the Castra Prætoria projects from the walls. This permanent camp was established under Tiberius by Sejanus; subsequently Aurelian made use of the four outer walls of this camp as a part of his fortification, and therefore Constantine, when he abolished the Prætorian Guard, pulled down the side towards the city only. The porta decumana of the camp is still to be seen though it is now walled up, and also the porta principalis dextra, but the porta principalis sinistra has disappeared or perhaps never existed. The camp was enclosed by a wall at least as early as the time of Pertinax and Julian, for here occurred that memorable and most melancholy scene in Roman history, when the Prætorian guards shut themselves within their camp after the murder of the reforming Emperor Pertinax and put up the throne to auction. Julian and Sulpicianus were the bidders. The soldiers let down a ladder and allowed Julian to get up upon the wall, says Herodian, for they would not open the gates before they heard how much would be offered. Sulpicianus was not allowed to mount the wall. They then bid one against the other, and at last they ran up the price little by little to five thousand drachmas to each soldier. Julian then impatiently outbid his rival by offering at once six thousand

[1] Ann. dell' Inst. xxxiv. 133. Festus, p. 261. Varro, L. L. v. § 49.

two hundred and fifty, and the Empire was knocked down to him. This was not by any means the first or only time that the fate of the Empire had been decided here.[1]

The chief power in the Roman state had lain within these walls of the Prætorian camp since the time when Tiberius consented to allow their designing colonel, Sejanus, to establish the Prætorian guards in permanent quarters, and the readers of the historians of the Empire will recall the many vivid pictures of their rapacity and violence. To go to the Prætorian camp and promise a largess to the guards was the first duty of a Roman emperor.

The eastern side of the camp, which is probably the only one now retaining its original form, measures 500 yards, and the southern 400 yards. The latter seems to have been partly pulled down, and the northern side has also been altered. Aurelian's Wall did not exactly meet the two angles of the camp towards the city, but its course was here determined by the houses and buildings in the vicinity which it was desirable to protect. The walls of the camp were, according to Bunsen, at first only fourteen feet high, but were raised by Aurelian and fortified with towers. Some parts of the walls doubtless consist of the original brickwork of Aurelian's time, as the masonry bears the marks of great age, and is of a most regular and solid style. A few of the soldiers' quarters are still left, consisting of rows of small low arched rooms similar to those on the Palatine and at Hadrian's Villa near Tivoli.[2]

In the angle formed by the projecting wall of the Prætorian camp and the Aurelian Wall, there is a gate now walled up and called simply by the name of the Porta Chiusa. This gate is one of the mysteries of Roman topography. It is not mentioned by Procopius or by the anonymous writer of Einsiedlen, yet it seems too large and important to have been altogether omitted. That a gate would be required here in Aurelian's Wall, at least before Constantine's reign, while the camp was still occupied, seems probable. No passage would be allowed to the public through the camp, and besides the Porta Nomentana, another gate would be wanted for the

Porta Chiusa.

[1] Herodian, ii. 6. [2] Bunsen, Beschreibung Roms, iii. 2, 359.

convenience of persons resorting to the camp from the country with supplies of provisions, or on business of various kinds, or for the shopkeepers who would naturally live within the walls near the camp. It may have been closed when the camp was abolished by Constantine, and that part of the city became comparatively empty, and it would thus in the time of Procopius, or the anonymous writer of Einsiedlen, have been long blocked up and forgotten or perhaps concealed by other buildings. This may account for their silence.

CHAPTER VIII.

THE AVENTINE AND CAELIAN HILLS.

BEFORE the end of the regal period there was an enlargement of the limits of the city in which the Aventine and Caelian were comprehended. Dionysius, Livy, and Aurelius Victor all relate that Tarquinius Priscus undertook the building of a new stone wall for the defence of the whole of the new quarters of the city, but that he did not live to finish it. The design was carried out by Servius Tullius, who also constructed the enormous agger called by his name, and still partly remaining at the back of the Esquiline, Viminal and Quirinal Hills. Before this great work was accomplished we must suppose that each suburb, as it grew out of the original settlement, was defended by a new piece of fortification, but these fortifications were, as Dionysius describes them, only temporary and hastily erected for the nonce. The expressions of Livy and Aurelius would lead us also to the conclusion that they were not of stone, but probably were entrenchments of earth. Rome then became the capital of Latium; she had lately united all her citizens, the Montani, the Collini, and the other freeholders living within the districts of Servius by a complete military organisation, and her powers were directed by a form of government which has always proved best calculated for the production of great public works. A new stone wall was accordingly planned on a vast scale, and the drainage of the low-lying parts of the city was effected about the same time by colossal sewers. The king having the whole control of the finances of the state could appropriate large sums of money for works of public utility, and could also doubtless command the labour of immense gangs of workmen. The Servian walls and the Cloacae of Rome are to be looked upon as the parallels in the

The Servian walls.

History of Rome to the pyramids of Egypt, the walls of Babylon, and of Mycenae and Tiryns. They point to a time of concentrated power and unresisting obedience, when the will of one man could direct the whole resources of the community to the accomplishment of a comprehensive design.

With the exception of a small portion which has been discovered in the depression between the north-western and south-eastern parts of the Aventine, another portion upon the Servian Agger, and a few remnants on the Quirinal in the Barberini and Colonna Gardens,[1] no remnants of the Servian walls are now to be seen, and we have to infer their probable extent from the nature of the ground, the rough estimate given by Dionysius of the space which they enclose, and the positions of the gates as described by various ancient authors. It may be safely concluded that, wherever it was possible, advantage would be taken of the sides of the hills, and the wall would be made to run along their edges. Thus the course of the wall on the outer side of the Capitoline, Quirinal, Esquiline and north-eastern part of the Aventine can be ascertained with tolerable certainty, and the agger serves as a guide along the back of the Viminal and Quirinal. The principal difficulty lies in the portions between the Capitoline and Aventine along the river bank, in the space to the south of the Caelian, and at the Hill of S. Saba and S. Balbina, where there is but little indication in the nature of the ground to guide us.

In the time of Dionysius, who died about B.C. 10, the Servian Wall was already so much covered with buildings of various kinds, that he speaks of it as difficult to trace, and therefore, naturally enough, we find at the present day that nearly the whole has disappeared under heaps of rubbish. The portion brought to light in 1855 under the south-eastern slope of the Aventine was accidentally discovered by digging in the vineyards not far from the Porta S. Paolo, for the purpose of clearing the ground from masses of brickwork. This portion, some of which has since been covered with earth again, was 104 feet in length, 50 feet high, and 12 broad. The breadth shows the great solidity and strength of the construction.

[1] Bull. dell' Inst. 1855, p. 87.

The original height was probably greater, as Mr. Braun remarks, and a parapet was placed upon the top. Some parts of this ruin are covered with reticulated work, and on others great masses of masonry have been placed which belonged to dwelling-houses. Mr. J. H. Parker has since been able to clear this fragment of wall, thus doing a very great service to Roman Archæology. No monumental antiquities have been found in these excavations earlier than the imperial times. A stamp bearing an inscription was discovered near one of the more modern arches, and dates from the reign of Trajan.

At the time when these walls were built, the stone generally used for such purposes was the hard tufa. The greater part of the Cloaca Maxima, and the remnants of these Servian walls, are composed of this material. It is hewn into long rectangular blocks, which are placed (in builders' phrase alternately headers and stretchers) sometimes across and sometimes along the line of the wall, in order to gain greater strength. No cement is used, but the stones are carefully fitted together and regularly shaped.

It must here be observed that the rectangular shape and horizontal position of the blocks in this stonework by no means disprove its high antiquity. It is true that the so-called Pelasgian walls are built in a totally different style, for the stones in them are polygonal. But this difference of shape in the stones arises from a difference in the material. All the so-called Pelasgian walls in Italy are built of a stone which naturally breaks into polygonal masses; but tufa stone is found in the quarry in horizontal layers, and is most easily cut into a rectangular shape. The inference sometimes drawn from horizontally laid masonry that it indicates a more advanced state of art than polygonal cannot be relied upon as certain. The arch in this ruin is of a later date and may have been an embrasure for a catapult.[1]

The situation of no gate in the Servian walls can be determined so completely as that of the Porta Capena. We know that part of the Aqua Marcia passed over it, whence

Porta Capena

[1] Abeken, 'Mittelitalien,' p. 143.

it was called the dripping gate (Madida Capena) by Martial and Juvenal. It was therefore in the valley below the Caelian Hill, and we should, judging from the form of the ground, naturally place it where the hill, on which S. Balbina stands, approaches the Caelian most nearly. A striking confirmation of this conjecture has been discovered. The first milestone on the Appian Road was found in 1584 in the first vineyard beyond the present Porta S. Sebastiano — the Vigna Naro — and, measuring back one mile from it, we come exactly to this spot. This milestone is now placed on the steps leading up to the Capitoline Museum. Milestones and horse-blocks were erected on all the great roads by Caius Gracchus before the milliarium aureum was put up in the Forum by Augustus, and it is probable that the distances were always measured from the gates. Mr. Parker carried on excavations for some time to find the exact position of the Porta Capena, and he discovered some of the piers of the aqueduct which passed over the gate in the garden of the Convent of S. Gregorio. These excavations have unfortunately been more or less filled up again.

Monte Testaccio. Near the Porta S. Paolo, between the Aventine and the river, stands the hill called Monte Testaccio from its being composed almost entirely of potsherds mixed with rubbish. The hill is 150 feet high, and one-third of a mile in circumference. Many conjectures have been hazarded about its origin, which still, however, remains a mystery.

The hypothesis which has gained most credit rests upon a passage in Tacitus, in which that historian, after giving an account of the Neronian fire, proceeds to say that Nero intended to have the rubbish carried to the Ostian marshes, and, therefore, gave orders that the corn-ships, after discharging their freight at the Emporium, should take a load of rubbish on their return to Ostia. This explanation appears satisfactory until the peculiar composition of the hill is examined. Nearly the whole mass consists of pieces of broken earthenware, and is not such as we should expect the rubbish left after a fire to be. The absence of bricks may perhaps be explained by the supposition that they were saved in order to be used a second time; but the immense quantity of potsherds still remains to be accounted for. Further, it is said that a coin of Gallienus has been found in such a position on the smaller portion of the hill as to leave no doubt that the accumulation of that part could not have been anterior to Gallienus. A medal of Constantine has also been found in the interior of the larger portion. Bunsen's explanation that the hill is composed of the rubbish cleared away by Honorius when he restored the walls of Aurelian, and other ingenious hypotheses of the same kind, do not sufficiently account for the peculiar composition of the hill.

M. Reifferscheid, in a paper communicated to the Roman Archæological Institute, has propounded the most natural and proper solution of the problem.[1] He observes that it is not necessary to go farther than the magazines of the neighbouring Emporium for an explanation of this immense mass of potsherds. Every kind of provisions brought to Rome in ancient times was stored in earthenware jars, not only wine, but corn, oil, and other articles of commerce. A fire, therefore, which consumed any part of the Emporium would leave rubbish composed in great part of fragments of earthen jars (dolia); and, since many such fires must have taken place in the course of ages, and immense quantities of earthen jars must have been broken in the process of unloading, it does not seem at all impossible that so large an accumulation of matter should have taken place. At Alexandria and at Cairo similar heaps of potsherds are to be seen outside the walls, and their extent, though less, as might be expected, than that at Rome, is such as to create astonishment in the traveller's mind when he sees them for the first time. An attempt has been made by M. Reifferscheid to determine the earliest date at which we can suppose this gradual deposition of potsherds to have taken place, but the data upon which he builds his conclusion, that the accumulation forming the Monte Testaccio first began to be deposited in the time of the decay of the Empire, about the third century, are not by any means such as to produce conviction.

Near the Monte Testaccio, and close to the Porta S. Paolo, stands a pyramidal monument, measuring about 97 feet on

Tomb of Cestius.

[1] Bull. dell' Inst. xxv. 85, 116; xxxvii. 235.

each side, and 120 feet in height. It is placed upon a square basement of travertine, and the rest of the building is of rubble, with a casing of white marble. It is built into the Aurelian Wall, no pains having been taken to avoid the injury which this might cause to the building. It has, however, suffered but little from this except in appearance. The ancient entrance, which was probably on the north-east side, has been walled up. No trace is now to be seen of it, and the present entrance on the north-west was made in 1663. The interior consists of a small plastered chamber 16 feet long by 13, and 12 feet high, the corners of which are ornamented with paintings of winged genii. No coffin or sarcophagus was found when the tomb was opened, but the inscription on the outside gives the name of C. Cestius, the son of L. Cestius, of the Publilian tribe, as the person who was buried in it. It further appears that this C. Cestius had been Prætor and Tribune of the commons, and one of the seven epulones who superintended the sacrificial banquets to the gods. The date of his burial has been discovered by means of two marble pedestals containing inscriptions which were found near the pyramid. On one of these the foot of a colossal bronze statue is still fixed. They show that C. Cestius's death took place in the time of M. Agrippa, and, therefore, of the Emperor Augustus, and that the statues were erected from the proceeds of the sale of some costly robes of cloth of gold (attalica), which Cestius had by his will ordered to be buried with him. Such burial being forbidden by law, the robes were sold and the statues erected from the proceeds by order of his heirs. They probably stood at the corners of the pyramid. Two fluted Doric pillars, the fragments of which were found near the spot, have now been placed at these corners. Cestius may possibly have been the same person who is mentioned by Cicero as a Roman knight.

Baths of Caracalla.

To the south-east of the hills of S. Saba and S. Balbina, between the Aurelian walls and the Via Appia, lie the most colossal ruins in Rome, covering a space each side of which measures more than a thousand feet. It is certain, from the arrangement of these buildings, that they were destined for

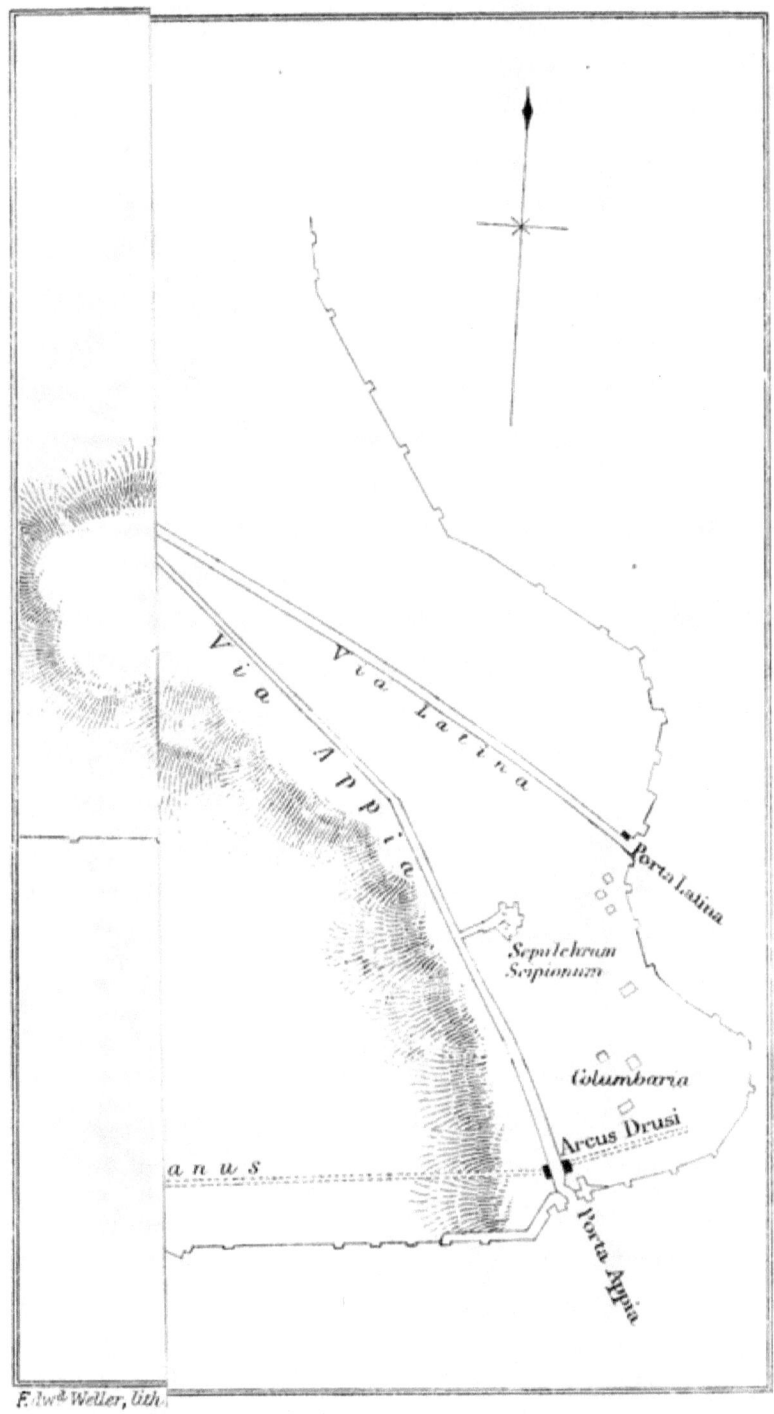

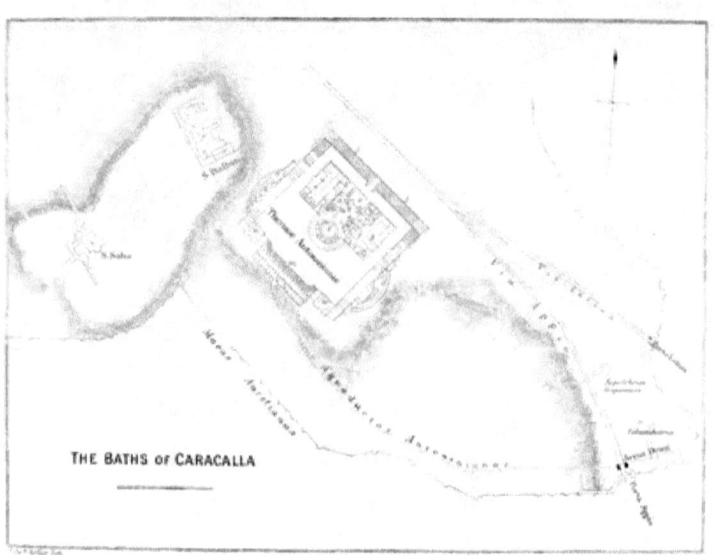

THE BATHS OF CARACALLA

public baths; and as tradition and the catalogue of the twelfth region both assign the name of the Thermæ Antoninianæ to them, and the style of the masonry is that of the Antonine era, we may feel satisfied that they belonged to the baths mentioned by Cassiodorus and Hieronymus as already partially built by Caracalla in the year A.D. 216, and finished by Heliogabalus and Alexander Severus.[1]

This enormous mass of building consisted of a central oblong block, containing all the halls and chambers appropriated more immediately to the baths, and a surrounding court, the sides of which were formed by gymnasia and other places of amusement, and the area of which was laid out in gardens, with shrubberies, ornamental colonnades, and fountains. A similar arrangement is found in the Thermæ of Titus and Diocletian.

The central block of buildings contained four immense halls and a rotunda, around which numerous smaller rooms were grouped. The first of these large halls (a) was entered from the north-eastern side by two wide doorways. Rows of niches for sculpture broke the broad inner surfaces of its walls, and it communicated with the chambers on each side by open passages filled with columns of splendid marble and granite. The floor formed an immense basin shaped hollow, showing that the purpose for which it was used was that of a cold swimming-bath. The steps by which the bathers descended into it have been found at the two shorter sides, and on both sides are chambers for dressing and undressing.

In the centre of the group of buildings is another hall (b) of nearly the same dimensions as the cold bath, with large recesses at both ends. The floor of this was paved with the richest marbles. The four lateral circular recesses formed hot baths, and were fitted with steps and seats of various kinds for bathers. In the recesses at the ends stood two enormous porphyry basins, one of which is now preserved in the Museum at Naples. This hall was probably the tepidarium and had a very lofty roof supported by eight granite pillars of colossal size, and by a network of brazen or copper rods. One of the pillars was given to Duke

[1] Hist. Aug. Car. 9. Hel. 17. Al. Sev. 25.

Cosmo I. by Pius IV., and stands in the Piazza di Trinità in Florence. The smaller chambers (c) (d) (e), at the western and southern angles of the tepidarium, contained the apparatus for heating water.

These chambers, the purpose of which is unknown, separate the tepidarium from the rotunda (f). The position of this latter and its shape would seem to indicate that it was a laconicum or hot-air room, but the state of the ruins is at present such as to preclude any positive assertion as to its purpose.

On each side of the above-mentioned three chambers is a similar range of halls. The south-eastern wing (g), being the most perfect, serves as the better guide to the arrangement of this part of the building. We pass through two chambers (h) (i) containing fine mosaic pavement, and then reach a large long hall (g), which apparently consisted of three aisles and two semicircular tribunes, divided from each other by rows of columns, somewhat in the manner of a basilica. A considerable portion of the mosaics on the floor of this hall have been laid bare and may be seen amongst the ruins of the roof and upper part. In the larger tribune was discovered the great mosaic pavement of the Athletes, now preserved in the Lateran Museum, whence it has been inferred that this side hall as well as the corresponding one on the north-west side were used as gymnasia or ball courts (sphaeristeria), with galleries for spectators. The purpose of the rooms situated on each side of the rotunda is not known, but it has been conjectured that they were additional tepidaria, since even the magnificent central tepidarium is hardly large enough to furnish the accommodation spoken of by Olympiodorus, who stated that there were 1600 marble seats for bathers in the Antonine Baths.[1]

There were numerous chambers in the upper stories in and about these large halls, to which the staircases led, one of which has been restored. These were perhaps used as libraries, picture galleries, and museums of curiosities.

The whole north-eastern side of the court which surrounded these central halls consists of ranges of rooms built of brick

[1] Olymp. ap. Phot. Bibl. 80, p. 63. Bekker.

and opening outwards. Many of these are still standing, and the traces of an upper story are to be seen over some of them (j, j). Different opinions have been held as to their use. Some writers think that they were offices and rooms for the slaves belonging to the establishment, others that they were separate baths for women. The principal entrance to the enclosure was in the centre of this side of the court.

On the north-western side of the court the remains can be traced of a large shallow tribune in the shape of a segment of a circle and surrounded by a vaulted corridor or cloister (k). Within this were three large apartments, probably used as lecture and conversation rooms. The rest of this side has entirely disappeared, as has also the opposite south-eastern side with the exception of one of the large apartments. These two sides of the court probably correspond in the same way as the wings of the central building.

The fourth side of the court was occupied by an immense reservoir of water divided into numerous compartments (l), in front of which was the cavea of a stadium (m), and on each side two large halls, possibly used as dressing-rooms and gymnasia (n, n).

The reservoir was supplied with water by a branch aqueduct from the Aqua Marcia.

The numerous magnificent works of art, sculptures, bronzes, lamps, cameos, and coins, which have from time to time been discovered in these ruins, are now dispersed through the museums of Italy. Some of the larger sculptures, including the Hercules of Glykon and the group called the Toro Farnese are in the Naples Museum, and two large porphyry fountain-basins are in the Piazza Farnese at Rome.

Some excavations have been lately made in the Vigna Guidi, a vineyard on the south-east side of the Court of these Thermae. The ruins of a large house have been found which had been demolished and covered with earth, to make room for the Thermæ. Nothing is known of the history of this house, but various conjectures have been hazarded, taken from the catalogues of the Regionaries.

The vast Necropolis of Rome stretched along both sides of

the Appian Road from the Porta Capena nearly as far as the Alban Hills.

Tomb of the Cornelian Scipios.

Conspicuous among these burial-places is the tomb which remained in possession of the great family of the Cornelian Scipios for nearly four centuries.[1] The entrance to this is near the gate of one of the vineyards, on the north-east side of the Appian Road, about two hundred and fifty yards from the Porta S. Sebastiano. The tomb itself consists of a number of passages roughly hewn in the tufa stone, as the catacombs are, without any apparent plan of arrangement. Unfortunately, the original state of the catacomb has been so altered by the substructions which have been found necessary to support the roof that it can hardly be recognised at the present day, and the sarcophagi and inscriptions have been removed, and placed for greater security in the Vatican Museum. Those now seen in situ are modern copies. Anciently there were two entrances, one from the Via Appia, and the other from the road which here unites the Via Appia and Via Latina. The present entrance has been cut for the convenience of access from the Appian Road.

Columbaria.

The catacomb of the Scipios differs from most of the other burial places which surround it, on account of the retention by the gens Cornelia of the old Latin custom of burying in coffins, instead of burning the corpse of the deceased. Most of the burying places on the Monte d'Oro are arranged in the manner called a columbarium by the Romans, from the resemblance of the niches in it to the holes in a pigeon-house.[2] Four of these columbaria have been excavated in the Vigna Codini, near the Porta S. Sebastiano, and are now to be seen in almost perfect preservation. They consist of a square pit roofed over, and entered by a staircase. The roof is supported by a massive square central column, and the whole of the sides of the pit and of the central column are pierced with semicircular niches, containing earthenware jars filled with ashes. In one of the columbaria in the Vigna Codini there is room for 909 jars. Most of the names which are inscribed above each niche upon a marble tablet are those of imperial freedmen, or servants of great families or public officers, and

---

[1] Cor. Insc. Lat. vol. i, p. 12.   [2] Marini, Frat. Arv. p. 674.

other persons of the middle class of life, and are therefore of little historical interest. The ashes of some few of a somewhat higher grade, are placed in small marble sarcophagi or urns, but no persons of distinguished rank appear to have been buried in this way. There are, however, few places in Rome where the ordinary manners and customs of the ancient Romans are more vividly placed before the eye than here, and the very insignificance of some of the details exhibited is somewhat striking. In one corner we find the ashes of a lady's maid attached to one of the imperial princesses; in another, those of the royal barber; and in another, a favourite lapdog has been admitted to take his place among his mistress's other faithful servants.

Not far from these columbaria, and close to the Porta S. Sebastiano, the Via Appia is spanned by a half ruinous archway, of which little but the core remains, the marble casing having long been torn off. It was probably originally ornamented with eight columns, two only of which now remain standing on the side next the modern gateway. These have shafts of Numidian marble (giallo antico), and composite capitals with Corinthian bases. Arch of Drusus.

Upon the top of this arch is a brick ruin apparently belonging to the Middle Ages, as the style of building is similar to that called opera saracenica by the Italians. It was probably a part of a fortified tower, placed upon the arch, resembling that which formerly surmounted the Arch of Titus.

On each side of the arch are some remains of the branch aqueduct, which brought water from the Aqua Marcia to the Baths of Caracalla, and it is natural to conclude that this arch carried the aqueduct over the Via Appia, and was built by Caracalla for that purpose. The costly nature of the materials used has, however, induced most topographers to reject this explanation, and to assume that the arch is one of the three mentioned by the Notitia in the first region, as built in honour respectively of Drusus, Trajan, and Verus. The composite capitals seem to point to the earliest date of these three, and as the building bears a resemblance to a representation of the Arch of Drusus, which has been discovered upon a coin,[1] the arch has been thought identical with that erected to Drusus, the father of Claudius, mentioned by Suetonius.

Sessorium and Amphitheatrum Castrense.

Two ruins standing near the Basilica of S. Croce in Gerusalemme may be reckoned as belonging to the district of the Cælian Hill. They are called by the topographers the Sessorium and the Amphitheatrum Castrense. The first of these consists of a ruin built of brick, containing a large semi-circular apse with round-headed windows, from which two walls project. No excavations having been made in order to ascertain the further extent of the buildings, any opinion formed as to their purpose must necessarily be highly uncertain. The most probable conjecture which has been made is that they are the ruins of a tribunal called the Sessorium. Such a court of justice is mentioned by the Scholiast on Horace as situated on the Esquiline near the place where criminals and paupers were buried. Further notices of the same name as applied to an edifice in the neighbourhood of the Basilica of S. Croce are to be found in Anastasius's Life of S. Silvester, and in a fragmentary history of certain passages in the Life of Theodoric, printed at the end of the work of Ammianus Marcellinus. Theodoric is there said to have ordered a criminal to be beheaded in palatio quod appellatur Sessorium, using the same phrase which Anastasius also employs.

The authors of the Beschreibung Roms supposed that this ruin was the Nymphæum Alexandri of the Notitia, but this has been disproved by Becker, who shows that the Nymphæum was near the Villa Altieri.

The opinion that it was the Temple of Spes Vetus, which Frontinus places near the commencement of the branch aqueduct of Nero, is more likely to be correct, but the shape of the building, so far as it is at present known, does not agree with such a supposition. The ruins are commonly known by the name of the Temple of Venus and Cupid, a name which was given to them from the discovery of a statue near them representing a female figure. But it is a fatal objection to this that the name of the Roman matron (Sallustia) whose statue was supposed to be that of Venus, has been discovered

[1] Eckhel, Num. Vet. ii. 6. 176.

to be engraved upon the pedestal. The statue may be seen in the Museo Pio Clementino.

On the other side of the Basilica, and forming a part of the Aurelian wall, is a portion of an amphitheatre. The interior, now used as a garden, may be seen by entering the door on the right hand of the basilica. The larger axis of the amphitheatre was apparently about one hundred and ten yards, and the shorter eighty-five or thereabouts. It is entirely constructed of brick, even to the Corinthian capitals which ornament the exterior, and the workmanship shows it to belong to the best age of Roman architectural art. The second tier of arches has almost entirely disappeared, and of the lowest tier only those are left which are built into the city wall. But to suppose, as Becker does, that it was not an amphitheatre, but the vivarium, where the wild beasts used in the games were kept, seems out of the question. The only difficulty is to determine what the special history and purpose of the building, manifestly an amphitheatre, placed so far from the populous parts of the city, was. The Notitia here comes to our aid, for it records the existence of an amphitheatrum castrense in the fifth region; and there can be little doubt that we have here the remains of the amphitheatre built for the entertainment of the prætorian troops quartered in a fortified camp beyond the Porta S. Lorenzo. Aurelian made use of the outer side of the building as a part of his walls, and it is most probable that when Constantine pulled down the inner portion of the prætorian camp, he also destroyed the greater part of this amphitheatre. *[marginal note: Amphitheatrum Castrense.]*

In consequence of the sinking of part of the wall which supports the apse of the Basilica of St. John Lateran, excavations became necessary in the year 1876 which disclosed the foundations of some ancient buildings between the baptistery and the Via della Ferratella, and of some others under the apse itself. These were carefully examined, and it became evident that they belonged to the extended ruins of a large villa, probably that called the House of the Laterani, which was occupied and enlarged by the emperors of the second and third centuries, and finally given by Constantine to the Bishop of Rome. The House of Verus, *[marginal note: House of the Laterani.]*

also mentioned by Julius Capitolinus, was probably on this site.

<small>Claudian Aqueduct.</small> Not far from the Sessorium, and springing out of the angle of the wall close to the Porta Maggiore, a series of lofty arches begins which extends throughout the whole length of the Caelian Hill. This is a branch aqueduct of the Aqua Claudia, built by Nero to supply the Caelian and Aventine Hills at a higher level than the Aqua Marcia and Aqua Julia, on which they had previously depended for their supply. It passed over the road leading from the Porta Maggiore to the Basilica of S. Croce, and thence ran along the higher ground, through the vineyards of the Scala Santa, whence it skirted the Via di S. Stefano, and, at the Arch of Dolabella, was divided into three branches, one of which crossed the valley to the Palatine, the second ran towards the edge of the hill over the Coliseum, and a third towards the Porta Capena.

<small>Arch of Dolabella.</small> The arch of Dolabella stands a little to the north-west of the Piazza della Navicella, and spans the road leading down from thence into the valley between the Caelian and Palatine, formerly called the Clivus Scauri. The archway consists of a single arch of travertine, without any ornamentation, but carrying an inscription to the effect that Publius Cornelius Dolabella, when consul, and Caius Julius Silanus, when Flamen Martialis, erected the arch by order of the Senate. The consulship of this Dolabella falls in the reign of Augustus A.D. 10, and therefore the arch can originally have had no connection with the Neronian aqueduct. It is possible, however, as Becker and Reber suggest, that the arch may have been originally built to carry the Aqua Marcia and Julia, which, as we know from Frontinus, supplied the Caelian before the building of the Neronian branch of the Aqua Claudia.[1] On one side the Arch of Dolabella is still completely hidden by the brickwork of the Neronian arches, and the other side was probably covered in a similar manner until after 1670, as we find no mention of this arch in Donatus, who could not have omitted to notice it in his description of the Neronian aqueduct had it been visible in his time.

<small>Navicella.</small> The marble representation of a ship, which stands now in

[1] Frontin. 76.

Arch of Dolabella.

the Piazza della Navicella and gives its name to the place, was probably a votive offering to Jupiter Redux, and there may be some connection between these and the Castra Peregrinorum, as having perhaps been the place where the troops employed on foreign service were quartered. An inscription seems to allude to this connection between the Temple of Jupiter Redux and the camp.

Houses on the Cælian. In the time of the empire many palaces of the richer classes stood upon the Cælian. Among them we have distinct mention of the houses of Claudius Centumalus, which was visible from the Arx, of Mamurra, and of Annius Verus, in which Marcus Aurelius was born. Tetricus also, the unsuccessful rival of Aurelian, built a magnificent residence on the Cælian, in which, on his readmission to the emperor's favour, he entertained Aurelian.

Palace of Commodus. It seems probable, as Bunsen has conjectured, that the Vectilian Palace in which Commodus lived, occupied the part of the Cælian next to the Coliseum. The ruins there consist of arches of travertine, forming a rectangular space upon the northern end of the hill. They are massively constructed, so as to bear a great superincumbent weight, and would be in every way suitable for the terraces of a large imperial villa such as Commodus may have built, when, as Lampridius tells us, he removed from the Palatine, where he found himself unable to sleep, to the house of Vectilius on the Cælian. He was afterwards murdered there. The position may have pleased him from its immediate vicinity to the Coliseum, where he was so fond of superintending the exhibitions, and displaying his own skill in killing wild animals. The story that he had an underground passage made from his villa to the Coliseum is also a strong confirmation of the conjecture of Bunsen, and some additional probability is given to it by the course of the branch aqueduct which leads from the Arch of Dolabella in the direction of this garden, and would certainly be required to supply the luxuries of a large Roman palace.

APPENDIX TO CHAPTER VIII.

MONUMENTAL ANTIQUITIES IN THE MUSEUMS, PIAZZAS AND OTHER PLACES.

BESIDES the ruins which are still standing in Rome and the Campagna, many historical monuments may be seen in the Roman museums, and in some of the gardens and piazzas. The principal among these are as follows:

1. Numerous Egyptian antiquities were found near the Churches of S. Maria sopra Minerva and that of S. Stefano in Cacco, on the site of the ancient Temples of Isis and Serapis. Of these the most remarkable are the two obelisks, one of which now stands in front of the Pantheon, and the other in the Piazza della Minerva. The statue of Isis, now in the Hall of the Dying Gladiator at the Capitoline Museum, the Egyptian lions on the steps of the Capitol, and the famous statue of the Nile now in the Braccio Nuovo of the Vatican, were also found here. *Egyptian antiquities.*

2. At the corner where the Strada della Vite crosses the Corso is a tablet recording the improvements made by Alexander VII. in the Corso at that point, whence he removed the ruins of an ancient triumphal arch which impeded the thoroughfare. A view of this is given by Donati, who calls it the Arcus Domitiani. But Nardini and all topographers since his time are agreed that the arch which stood here till 1662, must have been erected at a later time in honour of M. Aurelius. When it was pulled down, for public convenience as the inscription tells us, there were still four columns of verde antico standing, two of which are now used to adorn the principal altar in the Church of S. Agnese in Piazza Navona, and two are in the Corsini Chapel of the Lateran Basilica. The keystone of the arch is preserved in the Collegio della Sapienza; on each side of the arch there were two reliefs, now placed in the Capitoline Palace of the Conservators on the landing places at the top of the stairs. One of these represents M. Aurelius standing on a suggestus to deliver an harangue, and the other the apotheosis of the younger Faustina, his wife, who is being carried up to heaven by a genius, while the emperor is seated below, and at his feet the genius of Halala, a town at the foot of Mount Taurus where Faustina died. *Bas-reliefs from Arch of M. Aurelius.*

These two reliefs were removed into the Palace of the Conservators in order that they might be placed near four other reliefs, which had been found in the sixteenth century in the Church of S. Martina on the Capitol. A fifth, also found in the same church, is now in the Palazzo Torlonia in the Piazza di Venezia. The earlier history of the removal of these last five reliefs is not known, but it seems certain, from their style and subjects, that they belonged to the Arch of M. Aurelius. The four which are now in the Conservators' Palace represent Marcus Aurelius on horseback with his army, a group of barbarians kneeling before him, the goddess Roma, receiving the emperor who comes on foot to the gates, and presenting him with the globe, the symbol of empire, the triumphal procession of M. Aurelius in a quadriga crowned by Victory, and his thanksgiving sacrifice on the Capitol. The fifth relief, which is now in the Palazzo Torlonia, represents either M. Aurelius, or his brother Lucius Verus in conference with some barbarians who kneel as suppliants before him. Even supposing that the last mentioned five reliefs do not belong to this arch, yet the two first which are known to have stood upon it are quite sufficient to prove that it was the arch of M. Aurelius. The similarity between the representation of the apotheosis of the younger Faustina and that of Antoninus Pius and the elder Faustina is too evident to be overlooked, and the whole style of sculpture and architecture points to the Antonine Age.

3. With the bas-reliefs from the Arch of M. Aurelius must be compared that on the pedestal of the column of Antoninus Pius now placed in the Giardino della Pigna at the Vatican. On one side of this is an inscription recording its dedication to Antoninus Pius, and on the other sides are reliefs, the principal of which represents the apotheosis of Antoninus and Faustina, while the others represent groups of cavalry and infantry.[1] One fragment of the column now placed upon the pedestal has a Greek inscription upon it showing that the stone of which the column was formed was originally cut in the ninth year of Trajan, and after lying for a long time in the imperial stoneyard was subsequently used for this column. In the same place, the Giardino della Pigna, is to be seen the gigantic bronze fir-cone which may have formed the summit of Hadrian's Mausoleum, now the Castle of S. Angelo, and also the bronze peacocks which ornamented the same building.[2] The colossal head of Hadrian from his mausoleum is now in the Museo Pio Clementino.

4. The inscription cut upon the pedestal of the urn of Agrippina, the mother of Caligula, may still be seen in the courtyard of the Palazzo dei Conservatori on the Capitol, and also the cippi recording the burials of some of the imperial family. The pedestal was hollowed out and used as a measure for corn in the Middle Ages, and hence it was called Rugitella di grano.

[1] See Woodcut on p. 179.
[2] Ibid. p. 180.

Other colossal fragments are also kept in this courtyard, and on the staircase are the fragments of the inscription on the Duilian column found near the arch of Septimius Severus, and a bas-relief of Curtius leaping into the gulf, found in the Forum Romanum near the Church of

Pedestal of Antonine Column.

S. Maria Liberatrice. The bas-reliefs mentioned above, No. 2, are also there.

5. The fragments of the ancient register of Consuls from A.U.C. 272 to the end of Augustus' reign, which were found in the Forum Romanum,

near the Temple of Castor, are arranged on the wall of the fourth room in the Halls of the Conservators on the Capitol. These are printed and discussed in the Berlin 'Corpus Inscriptionum,' Vol. I.

Cone from the top of Hadrian's Mausoleum.

6. The famous bronze figure of the wolf and twins is placed in the gallery of bronzes on the Capitol. It was found, according to Flaminius Vacca, who wrote in 1594, near the Arch of Janus Quadrifrons. Urlichs, who has discussed the probable history of this figure in the

Rheinisches Museum, thinks that it is the figure dedicated by the Ogulnii, Ædiles in B.C. 297, and mentioned in the tenth book of Livy.

7. A stupendous sarcophagus brought from Vico Varo, with a bas-relief representing the Calydonian boar hunt, stands in the Museum of the Capitol, and in the next room is the sepulchral monument found at the Porta Salaria in 1871, recording the young Greek scholar who won the prize at the Agon Capitolinus in A.D. 86. Another most interesting sarcophagus, which was found at the Monte del Grano on the road to Frascati, and contained the vase called the Portland Vase now in the British Museum, stands in the Hall of the Urns in the Capitoline Museum.

8. On the wall of the staircase in the Capitoline Museum are the fragments of the celebrated marble plan of Rome cut in the time of Septimius Severus, which shows the sites and ground plans of the Portico of Octavia, the Theatre of Pompeius, the Basilica of Trajan, the Basilica Julia, and the Theatre of Marcellus.

9. The Dying Gladiator, or more properly the Dying Gaulish Herald, was found in the gardens of Sallust, near the Porta Salaria. It now stands in the room called the Hall of the Dying Gladiator at the Capitoline Museum.

10. In the Hall of the Faun at the Capitoline Museum may be seen one of the most beautiful ancient bas-reliefs in Rome, representing the battle of Theseus, and the Amazons. This is on a sarcophagus which was found near Torre Salona on the Via Collatina.

11. In the Capitoline Museum, the Halls of Busts of the Emperors and of Illustrious Men, the Venus of the Capitol, and the Doves of Pliny, are monuments connected with several celebrated spots in Rome and the Campagna.

12. The places, however, at which most of the important antiquities have been found are the Villa of Hadrian, near Tibur, and the ruins of Veii and Ostia. The following is a list of the chief monuments which were found there and are now placed in the Vatican Museum.

A. From Hadrian's Villa.
1. Faun. No. 84.
2. A Vestal. No. 120.
3. A Niobid. No. 176.
4. Clotho. No. 498.
5. Bacchic bas-reliefs. No. 642.
6. Hercules. No. 732.

} Museo Chiaromonti.

7. Baths of granite and masses of alabaster in the 4th portico of the Cortile di Belvedere.

8. Mosaics on the wall in the Hall of the Animals and in the Cabinet of the Masks.

9. The Candelabra on each side of the Ariadne in the Gallery of Statues.

10. Colossal bust of M. Aurelius in the Hall of the Busts. No. 288.
11. Corinthian columns in the Hall of the Muses.
12. Colossal Hermæ at the entrance of the Rotonda and bust of Faustina, No. 541 in the Rotonda.
13. Granite statues at the doorway of the Hall of the Greek Cross.
14. Discobolus, No. 618 in the Hall of the Biga.
15. Ephesian Diana, No. 81, and Female Statue No. 222, in the Gallery of Candelabra.
16. Egyptian figures in the Egyptian Museum.

B. From Veii and the North-Western Campagna.

1. Statue of Tiberius. No. 400. } Museo Chiaromonti.
2. Head of Augustus. No. 401.
3. Statue of Augustus from Prima Porta, in the Braccio Nuovo.

C. From Ostia.

1. Antoninus. No. 6.
2. Winter. No. 13.
3. Bust of young Augustus. No. 416.
4. Bust of Julia. No. 418.
5. Juno. No. 534.
6. Head of Neptune. No. 606A. } Museo Chiaromonti.
7. Boy and Swan. No. 651.
8. Sarcophagus of Nonius Asprenas. No. 685.
9. Æsculapius. No. 684.
10. Bust of Antoninus Pius. No. 700.
11. Ganymede. No. 38.
12. Ceres. No. 83. } Braccio Nuovo.
13. Bust of Commodus. No. 121.

The other principal ancient monuments now in the Vatican Museum besides those from the Villa of Hadrian, from Ostia, and Veii, above-mentioned, are:—

1. The statue of Demosthenes from the neighbourhood of Cicero's Tusculan villa. No. 62. Braccio Nuovo.
2. The Torso Belvedere found near the ruins of the Theatre of Pompeius. No. 3, Museo Pio Clementino.
3. The Laocoon found near the Baths of Titus. Cortile di Belvedere. No. 74.
4. The great porphyry basin found at the Baths of Diocletian. Rotonda.
5. Sarcophagi of S. Constantia and S. Helena, and cippus of Syphax found on the road to Tibur. Hall of the Greek Cross.
6. Sarcophagus of L. Scipio Barbatus, from the Tomb of the Scipios, near the Porta S. Sebastiano. Museo Pio Clementino.

In the Capitoline Museum are placed:—

A. From Hadrian's Villa.

1. Colossal head of Cybele. No. 9 in the courtyard.
2. { Psyche. No. 53.
    Cupid of Praxiteles. No. 13.   } In the Gallery.
    Euterpe. No. 32.
3. Roman Matron. No. 3.
4. An Amazon. No. 5.
5. Flora. No. 11.   } In the Hall of the Dying Gladiator.
6. Antinous. No. 13.
7. The Faun. No. 1 in the Hall of the Faun.
8. Centaurs in bigio antico. No. 2.
9. A Gymnasiarch. No. 27.   } In the Saloon.
10. Harpocrates. No. 34.

Some other great ancient monuments are placed as follows:—

1. The first milestone on the Appian Road, found in 1584, is now placed in the Piazza del Campidoglio at the top of the steps leading up from the Piazza d'Ara Coeli on the right hand. The seventh milestone is placed opposite to it.

On the stairs of the Capitol are also placed the marble sculptures called the trophies of Marius which were brought from the ruin on the Campus Esquilinus, not very far from the Arch of Gallienus. At the top of the steps stand two equestrian figures of the Dioscuri, said to have come from the neighbourhood of the Theatre of Balbus, and the statues of Constantine and his son Constans from the Baths of Constantine on the Quirinal. At the foot of the staircase are the two Egyptian lions found as above mentioned near the Church of S. Stefano in Cacco. The history of the bronze equestrian statue of M. Aurelius, now in the Piazza of the Capitol, cannot be traced as Palladio states to the Temple of Antoninus and Faustina, but it was more probably found as Fea has recorded, near the Arch of Septimius Severus.

2. A bronze cista mistica found at Praeneste is in the Kircherian Museum.

3. The wooden beams from the Villa of Caesar in the lake of Nemi, are kept partly in the Kircherian Museum, and partly in the Gallery on the right hand of the Vatican Library.

4. The caricature of Alexamenos from the Palatine is in the Kircherian Museum.

5. The mosaics from the Baths of Caracalla are in the Hall of Mosaics at the Lateran.

6. One of the white marble columns from the Basilica of Constantine is placed in front of the Basilica of S. Maria Maggiore.

7. The history of the great pair of figures on the Piazza del Quirinale called the Dioscuri and their horses, cannot be traced further back than the time of Constantine, in whose baths they stood, as we are told by Bufalini. The style of sculpture is of the Imperial

Age of Rome, and the inscriptions ascribing them to Phidias and Praxiteles are erroneous.

8. Many good specimens of columns, ancient ornamental sculpture, and other monuments may be seen in the following places. The Churches of S. Lorenzo and S. Agnese fuori le Mura; S. Maria in Cosmedin, di Aracœli, degli Angeli, and in Trastevere. The Villas Ludovisi, Borghese, Albani, and Spada.

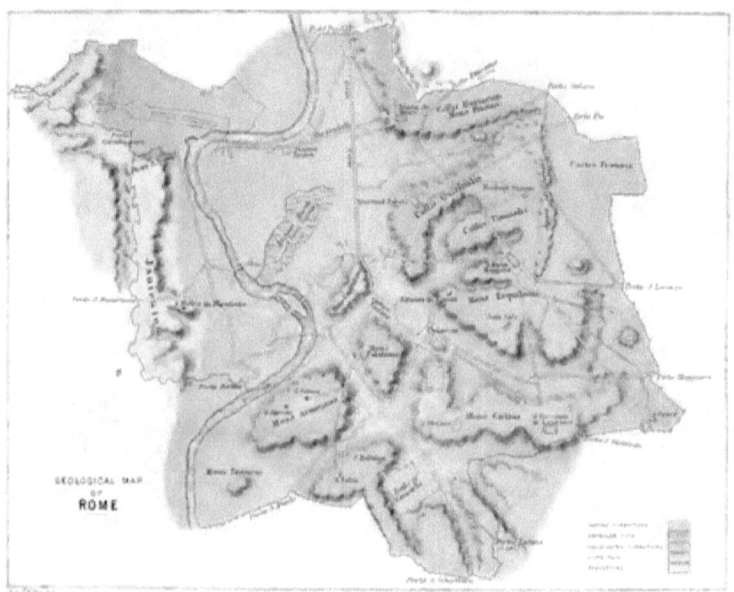

INTRODUCTION TO CHAPTER IX.

THE geological strata found on the site of Rome and in its immediate neighbourhood divide themselves into three principal groups. The oldest of these is a marine formation, and exhibits itself upon the Vatican, Janiculum, and Monte Mario. The second, of which all the hills on the eastern bank and the district of the Campagna are composed, is of volcanic origin, and consists chiefly of beds of tufaceous matter erupted from submarine volcanoes and more or less solidified. The third, which appears in the hollows of the Tiber valley, is a fresh-water formation, and is found on the slope of the hills on both banks of the river.

The oldest of these three groups belongs to the division of the tertiary period, called by Lyell the older pleiocene, as having had a fauna and flora in which the greater number of species were identical with those now living on the earth. These strata are of marine formation, and are similar to those which extend over a great breadth of Italy on both flanks of the Apennine mountains, reaching as far south as the point of Reggio in Calabria. Their lower bed consists of a bluish-grey clayey marl, which will be found in the valley between the Janiculum and the Vatican. Its marine origin is sufficiently proved by the fossils found in it, and the remains of sea-weed. This bed of clay is of a plastic nature, and is still used for making pottery, as it was in the time of Juvenal. Above it lies a stratum of yellow calcareous sand, which sometimes takes the form of loose sand with boulders, sometimes of a stratified arenaceous rock, and sometimes of a rough conglomerate. This may be seen outside the Porta Angelica, on the left, under the walls of the city, and in the Belvedere Gardens on the Vatican Hill. The Church of S. Pietro in

<small>Marine formation.</small>

Montorio is said to derive its name Montorio, monte aureo, from the yellow colour of this sand.

On Monte Mario an abundance of fossil shells, of the Ostrea hippopus and other varieties of sea shells, may be seen, plainly indicating the marine origin of this formation.

The only places within the actual walls of Rome where these tertiary marine strata are to be found, are the Vatican and the Janiculum. At the base of the Capitoline, in the subterranean vaults of the Ospitale della Consolazione, under the volcanic rock which forms the upper part of the hill, Brocchi found a stratum of calcareous rock and clay, which he affirms to be of marine origin, and to resemble the limestone of the Apennines.

Volcanic formation. The second group of strata found on the site of Rome is one which is not confined to the neighbourhood of Rome, but is most extensively spread over the whole of the Campagna, the district of Campania, and a considerable part of southern Italy. The great mass of the Capitoline, Palatine, Aventine, Esquiline, Cælian, Viminal, Quirinal, and Pincian Hills, is composed of this formation. Geologists give it the general name of tufa, and divide it into two kinds, the stony and the granular. It is distinguished from lava by not having flowed in a liquid state from the volcano, and is a mechanical conglomerate of scoriæ, ashes, and other volcanic products which have been carried to some distance from the crater of eruption, and then consolidated by some chemical re-arrangement of their constituent elements. The harder kind of tufa, the tufa litoide, is a reddish brown, or tawny stone, with orange-coloured spots. These spots are embedded fragments of scoriaceous lava. It is hard enough to be used as a building stone, and has been quarried largely under the Aventine Hill near S. Saba, at Monte Verde, on the southern end of the Janiculum, and at other places near Rome, as at Torre Pignatara on the Via Labicana, at the bridge over the Anio, on the Via Nomentana, and at the Tarpeian rock.

This tufaceous stone presents itself in very thick banks, traversed by long vertical and oblique fissures, probably produced by the contraction of the mass on passing from a humid and soft to a dry and hard state. The Arch of the

Cloaca Maxima, near S. Giorgio in Velabro, is built of this stone, and the inner part of the substruction of the so-called tabularium on the Capitol. Portions of the Servian wall were also built of it, and many stones which were taken from this wall are to be seen at the present day in the walls of Aurelian, near the gate of S. Lorenzo; and others have been laid bare by the railway excavations in the Servian Agger. Brick-shaped masses of it are found in the ambulacra of the Theatre of Marcellus, so that the use of it must not be restricted to the earliest times of Roman architecture. In fact, several buildings of the Middle Ages in or near Rome consist of this stone, as may be seen at the Fortress Gaetani, near the Tomb of Cæcilia Metella, and in the large tower at the side of the palace of the Senator.

Fresh-water formations cover the bottoms of all the valleys in the district of Rome and in the whole of the Campus Martius, and ascend to a considerable height on the flanks of the hills and into the Campagna. They consist chiefly of sand, clay, gravel, and the stone called travertine, and of tufa beds which have been disturbed and then re-deposited. This re-deposited tufa has been the subject of some controversy. It was at one time thought to indicate that the lower tufa was also a fresh-water deposit, since it is sometimes found overlying the fresh-water formations. But no doubt now remains that it must have been formed by a re-arrangement in fresh water of previously deposited marine tufa beds. The water of the Tiber, at the time when these fluviatile formations took place, stood at such a height as to leave deposits upon the intermontium of the Capitol, and as high as the Church of S. Isidoro on the Pincian, and it must have partially removed and shifted the previously existing light and porous volcanic soil of the sea-bottom. Even the top of the Pincian was covered by this fresh water; for modules of calcareous matter, such as are deposited in fresh water alone, were found in digging the excavations for the fountain on the public promenade.

Freshwater formation.

The surface of the broad river which then existed, seems, in fact, to have been at from 130 to 140 feet above the present surface level of the Tiber, and its water must have been more surcharged with alluvium, derived from sources with which the present river is no longer connected.

Among the fluviatile deposits, argillaceous marl beds now play an important part. They intercept the water as it descends from the hills, and impede its descent to the river, thus furnishing supplies to the wells in Rome, but rendering the soil less dry and healthy. The greater portion of these strata consist of a mixture of sand and clay. The ridge between the Campo Vaccino and the Coliseum, on which the Arch of Titus stands, is formed almost entirely of these mixed strata of clay and sand. To prove the fresh-water origin of these deposits, we need only refer to the nodules of travertine and the shells of lacustrine animals which they contain. Such species of fresh-water shell-fish could not live in turbid and rapid water like that of the Tiber as it now is, and we must therefore conclude from their presence that the waters of the Tiber valley where such fossils are found were once in a semi-stagnant state. That there was also a period of violent movement during the prevalence of this lacustrine era is testified by the quantities of matter brought from a distance and accumulated at considerable altitudes, and by the size of the pebbles and boulders which have been rolled along by the stream. But before a more accurate investigation of facts shall have been made, it will be impossible to distinguish these two periods of stagnation and rapid movement from each other.

Tiber water. The river water has no longer the power which it once possessed of depositing the travertine which we find lying in thick beds upon the slopes of some of the hills of Rome, and from which the larger ruins are all built. This travertine is formed from carbonate of lime which the waters take up as they pass through the soil containing it. In order to give the water the power of holding this carbonate of lime in solution, a certain quanity of carbonic acid gas must be present in it. When by means of the rapid movement of the water or from other causes this gas becomes disengaged, it leaves the carbonate of lime behind in the shape of a hard stony deposit. This natural process of petrifaction is familiar to all who have seen the Falls of the Anio at Tivoli.

and the way in which the artificial canals of running water in that neighbourhood are choked by limestone concretions, and it may be seen in all vessels made use of to boil water which is impregnated with lime. The more violent the agitation of the water the more rapid is the disengagement of the carbonic acid gas, and the consequent settlement of the lime. This process is accompanied, in most places where it can be seen, by the presence of sulphuretted hydrogen, which produces a white colour in the water by depositing the sediment called gesso by the Italians. Hence an explanation of the ancient name of Albula given to the Tiber is easy. In the period when the Tiber had the power of depositing travertine, its waters were much more strongly impregnated not only with carbonate of lime, but also with gesso, which gave a white tinge to the water as it now does to the sulphureous waters near Tivoli. The same colour was characteristic of " the white Nar, with its sulphureous stream," Virgil's description of the chief stream of the central Apennines.

The subject of the climate of Rome is naturally connected with that of the nature of the soil and configuration of the hills and valleys. *Climate.*

It is not difficult to see why the peculiar geological formation of the Campagna proves, without careful drainage, extremely deleterious to health. We have there a district containing numerous closed valleys and depressions in the soil without outlet for the waters which naturally accumulate. The tufa which composes the surface seems commonly to take the shape of isolated hills with irregular hollows between them, so as to impede the formation of natural watercourses. Under this tufa is a quantity of marl and stiff clay, which retains the water after it has filtered through the tufa, and sends it oozing out into the lower parts of the country, where it accumulates, and, mixed with putrescent vegetable matter, taints the surrounding atmosphere. A want of movement in the air caused by the mountainous barriers by which the Campagna is enclosed is another source of malaria.

The sites of Veii, Fidenæ and Gabii, once the rivals and equals of Rome are now entirely deserted except by a few shepherds and cattle stalls. Along the coast stood Ardea, Laurentum, Lavinium and Ostia, all of them towns apparently with a considerable number of inhabitants. Of these Ostia is now a miserable village, Ardea contains about sixty inhabitants, while Laurentum and Lavinium are represented by single towers. During a part of the year the ancient Roman nobility lived in great numbers on these very shores now found so deadly. Pliny the younger describes the appearance of their villas near Laurentum as that of a number of towns placed at intervals along the beach, and he writes an enthusiastic letter in praise of the salubrity and convenience of his own house there.[1] Lælius and Scipio used to make the seaside at Laurentum their resort, and to amuse themselves there with collecting shells.[2] Nor was it only on the seacoast that the country villas were placed. Six miles from Rome on the Flaminian Road, at the spot now called Prima Porta, there stood a well-known country house belonging to the Empress Livia, part of which has lately been excavated.[3] This was a highly decorated and commodious house, as the rooms which have been discovered, in which was found a splendid statue of Augustus, and the busts of several members of the imperial family, amply testify. The views from this spot over the Campagna and the Sabine Hills are most lovely, but the contrast between the beauty of nature and the haggard and fever-stricken appearance of the modern inhabitants is melancholy enough. A few squalid houses occupied by agricultural labourers stand by the roadside. Among their tenants not a single healthy face is to be seen, and even the children are gaunt, hollow-cheeked, and sallow in complexion. No wealthy Roman would now consent to live on the site of Hadrian's stately villa in the Campagna near Tivoli. Tivoli itself, which Horace wished might be the retreat of his old age, and which was celebrated as a healthy place in Martial's

[1] Plin. Ep. ii. 17. The depopulation of the Campagna began even in the time of the later Republic. See Appian, B.C., i. 7. In the Antonine era and the following reigns, pestilence and famine swept off millions of inhabitants. Zumpt, 'Stand der Bevölkerung,' p. 84, quoted by Merivale, vol. vii. p. 610.

[2] Cic. de Or. ii. 6. Val. Max. viii. 8. See Mommsen, R. H. i. 13, p. 200.

[3] Suet. Galb. i. Plin. N. H. xv. 40, 136, 137.

time, has now lost its reputation for salubrity, and is known as—

> Tivoli di mal conforto,
> O piove, o tira vento, o suona amorto.

Strabo speaks of the now desolate district between Tusculum and Rome as having been convenient to live in. But there is no need to multiply proofs which might be gathered from all sides of what is an acknowledged fact, that the malarian fevers of the present day were not nearly so deadly in the classic times of Rome, or even in the Middle Ages. The troops of labourers who, fearing to pass the night in the country, are met returning to Rome every evening, the forsaken towers and buildings which stand rotting everywhere about the Campagna, all tell the same tale of a pestilence-stricken district.

The peculiar physical features of the district have had no little influence in determining the mode in which the population was grouped in ancient times. Everywhere we find the hills of Rome reproduced on a reduced scale. Small isolated flat-topped hills, irregularly divided by deeply cut watercourses, and edged with steep low cliffs, afford numerous sites for the settlement of limited independent communities. Such are the hills on which Laurentum, Lavinium, Fidenæ, Antemnæ, Ficulea, Crustumerium and Gabii stood, and similar places abound in many parts of the district. Such hills afforded suitable sites for the small fortified towns with which ancient Latini was thickly studded. Their sides can be easily scarped so as to afford a natural line of defence, and they are in general fairly supplied with water from numerous land springs.

Thus, although the general aspect of the Campagna is that of a plain country, yet the main level of its surface is broken by numerous deep gullies and groups of hillocks.

The tertiary marine strata, already described as forming the Janiculum and other hills upon the right bank of the Tiber, do not rise to the surface in the Campagna, except on the flanks of the Æquian and Sabine hills. These hills themselves consist of great masses of Apennine limestone jutting out here and there into the spurs upon which some of the more considerable cities of the Latin confederacy stood, as Tibur, Præneste, Bola and Cameria.

The Alban Hills form a totally distinct group, consisting of two principal extinct volcanic craters somewhat resembling, in their relations to each other, the great Neapolitan craters of Vesuvius and Somma. One of them lies within the embrace of the other, just as Vesuvius lies half enclosed by Monte Somma. The walls of the outer Alban crater are of peperino, while those of the inner are basaltic. Both are broken away on the northern side towards Grotta Ferrata and Marino, but on the southern side they are tolerably perfect.

From the legendary times, when Latinus, Evander, Æneas, and the rest of Virgil's heroes are supposed to have occupied the great plain of Latium, down to the final settlement of the district by its subjection to Rome in B.C. 338, the Roman Campagna was peopled by communities chiefly living in towns. Etruria on one side and Latium on the other, contained confederacies of independent cities, with one or other of which the Romans were constantly at war. Etruria gave way first, and after the fall of Veii in B.C. 395, the Roman dominions extended northwards as far as the Lago Bracciano and Civita Castellana.

At that time the great confederacy of Latium, though Alba was destroyed, still existed under the Hegemony of Rome as the successor of Alba, and numbered Tibur, Præneste, Tusculum, Aricia, Antium, Lanuvium, Velitræ, Pedum, and Nomentum among its members. But after the victories gained by the consuls of the year B.C. 338, the absorption of the Latin cities made rapid progress, and the character of the population of the Campagna began to be completely changed.[1] In this, the second period of the history of the Campagna, the towns were gradually reduced to mere villages, the small farmers disappeared, and the land was occupied by the immense estates (latifundia) of rich proprietors cultivated by hordes of slaves. Such is the condition in which we find the Campagna in the time of Cicero.[2] The great villas which

[1] Plin. N. H. xxxiv. § 20. Rutilius de Red. 224. Strabo, v. 3.
[2] Cic. pro Planc. 9. De Leg. Agr. ii. 35.

strew the ground everywhere in the neighbourhood of Rome with their ruins were then constructed, and the colossal aqueducts which served not only to supply Rome with water but also to irrigate the farms and country seats of the Campagna.

There seems to have been a constant tendency during the later republic and early empire to reduce the amount of arable land, and to increase the extent of pasturage in the Campagna. Thus the country was rendered less and less healthy, and Rome became gradually more dependent than ever on foreign countries for her supply of corn.

The last phase of the history of the Roman Campagna is the most melancholy. The aqueducts were nearly all destroyed by the Gothic army at the siege of Rome under Vitiges in A.D. 536, and the great country seats of the Roman nobles and princes must have been ruined by the successive devastations of Roman territory during the fifth and sixth centuries in which the Lombards were the principal actors. Agriculture ceased, and the few villages and country houses which remained soon became uninhabitable during a great part of the year, in consequence of the increase of malarious exhalations arising from the uncultivated state of the soil, or were rendered unsafe by the lawless bands of ruffian marauders who infested the open country. Such is in the main the condition of the Roman Campagna at the present day, for the most part a waste of ragged pastures without human habitations, and wild jungles tenanted only by foxes, bears, and other wild animals.

The above remarks will serve to show that after B.C. 338 the Campagna became deprived of all historical interest except as the summer residence of the great Roman proprietors. Its history belongs almost entirely to the early times of the Roman Republic.

CHAPTER IX.

(A) THE VIA APPIA AND THE ALBAN HILLS.

The Appian Road. OF the great roads along which the principal traffic from ancient Rome passed, the Appian Road may perhaps be said to have been the most important, as it led to the southern and oriental provinces of the great empire; and it is on the line of this ancient road that the greatest number of ruined tombs and other buildings are still left. Two hundred ruins are said to stand on the sides of the Appian Road between the site of the Porta Capena, by which this road left the Servian walls, and Albano, a distance of fourteen miles. The tombs were of the most varied and fantastic shapes and designs, the most common forms being those with square or circular bases, cylindrical superstructure, and conical roof. Some were square with several floors, and surmounted by a pyramid, others consisted of chapels in brick, placed upon a cubical base, or of sarcophagi in various shapes, mounted upon brick substructions.

Many fragmentary inscriptions have been found which once belonged to these tombs, but not one of any historical importance. The greater part of them record the names of freedmen, and other obscure people, as the larger and more highly decorated tombs were plundered first, and their marble casing and inscriptions completely destroyed at an early period. The older fragments which have been saved may be studied in the Berlin Collection of Inscriptions where they are learnedly and ably edited by Th. Mommsen.

There were also many fountains and semicircular ranges of seats by the side of the road designed as resting-places for travellers.

The commencement of the ancient Appian Road now lies between the Porta S. Sebastiano and the site of the old Porta

Capena. From this part of the road the Via Latina diverged on the left, and the Via Ardeatina on the right. Beyond the Porta S. Sebastiano, the first monument now visible is a mass of stonework on the left hand, about one hundred yards from the gate. From its form and the style of masonry there can be little doubt that it was a pyramidal tomb similar to that of Caius Cestius at the Porta S. Paolo, and that it was built in the Augustan era. The road then crosses the Almo, and the remains of another pyramidal tomb are to be seen on the left. This is sometimes called the Tomb of Priscilla, mentioned by Statius, but that name more probably belongs to the larger tomb further on, beyond the Church of Domine quo Vadis. This latter ruin agrees better with the description of Statius, as it had a cupola and loculi for the reception of unburnt corpses. The immense number of ruined tombs and other buildings which crowd the sides of the road beyond this point, make it necessary to restrict our remarks as much as possible, and we shall therefore only notice a few of the most prominent ruins upon the road or in the immediate neighbourhood.

The brick building called the Temple of the Divus Rediculus stands half a mile to the left of the road at the second milestone in the Caffarella valley. The legend which connects it with Hannibal's march on Rome is altogether unworthy of credit,[1] and it is plain that the building, which had no rows of surrounding columns, but is constructed with Corinthian pilasters, had two stories, and cannot therefore have been a temple. Professor Reber considers that it was a chapel tomb similar to that to be seen further on the road at S. Urbano, near the Tomb of Cæcilia Metella. Divus Rediculus.

The Grotto of Egeria, as it is called, lies in the valley of the Almo about half a mile above the building just mentioned. It is an arched nymphæum of brick, at the back of which a plentiful stream of clear water issues. The mutilated statue of the nymph still remains, but no other parts of the decorations. There is little doubt that it was the nymphæum of some suburban villa. Grotto of Egeria.

On the hill above it stands the Church of S. Urbano, pro- Temple of Bacchus or Honos.

[1] Festus, p. 232.

bably an ancient tomb in the shape of a chapel. It is commonly called the Temple of Bacchus from the discovery under it of an altar of Dionysus with a Greek inscription. But this altar seems to have been moved here from some other spot. The building is in the form which has a projecting porch with four Corinthian columns and capitals. These are now built up into the modern wall. The whole, except the entablature and columns, is of brickwork of the Antonine era, as appears from the stamps of the bricks. The triple frieze, forming a kind of attica between the architrave and cornice, seems to contradict the notion that this was a temple, though the great antiquary E. Q. Visconti considered that it was the Temple of Honour built by Marius outside the Porta Capena.[1] The interior is tolerably well preserved, and has a vaulted roof with coffers and reliefs in the form of trophies.

The Circus of Maxentius and Temple of Romulus. On the left of the Appian Road, where it dips suddenly into a valley near the Church of S. Sebastian, lies a group of ruins, the principal of which consist of a circus, a building enclosed in a large square court, and some remains of rooms apparently belonging to an ancient villa. The walls of the circus are still in such preservation that they can be easily traced round the whole enclosure, and are in some parts nearly of the original height. They are built of rubble mixed with brickwork, and with jars of terra-cotta to lighten their weight, as in the case of the masonry in other walls of the same date. The towers at each side of the Carceres, or starting post, the curved line of Carceres themselves, and the spina, or central division line, can be easily traced. An inscription in honour of Romulus, son of Maxentius, found here in 1825, and now placed at the entrance to the ruins, seems to show the circus was built in honour of Romulus, son of Maxentius, who died before his father, A.D. 309. This is confirmed by a statement in one of the ancient chronicles published by Roncalli, in which it is said that Maxentius built a circus near the catacombs, evidently referring to the neighbouring catacombs of S. Sebastian and others, and also by the style of masonry used in the circus. The adjoining ruined temple,

[1] Visconti, op. Milan 1829, vol. ii. p. 387.

with its enclosing court, seems to belong to a somewhat earlier style of construction, but some reasons derived from the coins of Maxentius and Romulus have been given for supposing that it was the temple dedicated to Romulus after his apotheosis by his father.[1] The ruins are not sufficiently preserved to make it certain that the building was a temple, and there is nothing to contradict the hypothesis that it was a tomb. Nor is anything whatever known about the adjoining villa.

On the end of the mound formed by the great lava stream which ages ago flowed down from the Alban Hills, and along the top of which the Via Appia runs from this point, stands the conspicuous Tomb of Cæcilia Metella, the daughter of Metellus Creticus, and wife of Crassus, but whether of the Triumvir Crassus, or of the orator, or of some other less well known Crassus is uncertain. The inscription on the tomb is Cæciliæ, Q. Cretici Filiæ, Metellæ Crassi. The shape of the tomb is the same as that of the Mausoleum of Hadrian, and the Tomb of the Plautii at Tivoli; a cylindrical towerlike edifice, resting on a square base of concrete with massive blocks of travertine. The upper part has been destroyed, and the marble casing stripped off, with the exception of a band of ox skulls and garlands which surrounds it, and some trophies carved in relief above the inscription. The roof was probably conical. Mediæval battlements, erected by the Caetani family, who held it as a fortress in the 13th century, now crown the upper edge. The remains of their castle are still visible on each side of the road beyond the tomb. *Tomb of Cæcilia Metella.*

After passing the third milestone, the Appian Road is fringed with ruins of innumerable tombs, and here and there the relics of a suburban villa. Scarcely any of these can have names attached to them with any certainty. The spot is now called Roma Vecchia, and the Campus sacer Horatiorum, the Fossa Cluilia, and the Villa Quintiliana Commodi lay here. The suburban villa in which Seneca committed suicide by opening his veins was at the fourth milestone, as we learn from Tacitus, and near this was found *Roma Vecchia, Villa of Seneca.*

[1] Hobler, Roman coins, p. 821. No. 2035. Eckhel, Num. Vet. viii. p. 59.

in 1824, by Nibby, a marble slab with the name of Granius, a military tribune. A tribune of this name was employed by Nero to compel Seneca to kill himself, but whether the stone refers to him or not is of course doubtful.

<small>Tomb of Atticus.</small>

At the fifth milestone on the right hand of the road is a round mass of ruins with a rectangular chamber inside, which has been supposed to be the tomb mentioned by Cornelius Nepos, as the burial place of Atticus, Cicero's friend. Near this is the great platform of peperino blocks which are thought to have been used as a burning place (ustrina) for the bodies interred at the sides of the road.

<small>Villa Quintiliana.</small>

On the left hand, a little way beyond the fifth milestone, the remains of the Villa Quintiliana of Commodus begin, and reach along the side of the road for at least half a mile, extending also towards the left into the adjoining fields as far as the edge of the great lava current, on the top of which the Via Appia is here carried. The whole of this space, nearly two miles in circumference, is covered with fragments of costly marbles, of sculpture, and bits of mosaic, showing that it was covered with handsomely decorated buildings. The style of construction, says Nibby, belongs to three different epochs. The buildings nearest to the Appian Road, comprising the great reservoir, on the foundation of which the farmhouse of S. Maria Nuova is built, are of brickwork and reticulated work of the time of Hadrian, the great mass of the ruins which lies on the left towards the new road to Albano, exhibits workmanship of the Antonine era, and amongst them have been found numerous fragments of sculpture, also belonging to the reigns of the Antonines. The third style of building is that called opera mista by the Italian antiquarians, which prevailed in the Constantinian times, at the beginning of the fourth century. The buildings of the Antonines have been repaired and overlaid in many places by this later work. The stamps of most of the bricks found here belong to the reigns of Antoninus Pius, Marcus Aurelius, and Commodus, and were made chiefly in the imperial brickyards. Thus the date of the principal parts of the building is decided, and it is seen that the villa was most probably an imperial villa. But all doubt on this point was completely cleared away by the discovery in 1828, of a number of large leaden pipes bearing the inscription, II. QUINTILIORUM CONDINI ET MAXIMI, from which it became evident that the villa was the same place which Vopiscus and Dion Cassius mention as the property of the Quintilii, consuls in the year A.D. 151, under Antoninus Pius, and victims of the spite of Commodus in A.D. 182.[1] Commodus seized their property, and the villa became one of his favourite residences. The great extent of the ruins explains the circumstance related by Herodian, that the emperor, being in the back part of the villa, could not hear the shouts of the infuriated mob on the Appian Road, who were demanding the life of Cleander.[2]

The ruins which extend along the side of the road, are plainly fragments of a kind of vestibule or grand entrance to the imperial villa. They consist of a nymphæum or grand fountain, and a row of chambers intended for slaves' lodgings. The fountain is supplied with water by an aqueduct, the arches of which can be seen at the seventh milestone, where it leaves the lava rocks, and crosses the country towards Marino, at a higher level than even the Aqua Claudia. This nymphæum and aqueduct are built of opera mista, which shows that they are probably the work of the Constantinian Age.

The principal mass of the villa itself stood nearly half a mile from the old Appian Road, on the edge of the rocks of basaltic lava. Between them and the road the space was occupied by gardens and ornamental summer-houses and ponds. Nibby describes the chief ruins as having belonged to a richly ornamented fountain, and a suite of bathing-rooms of great grandeur.

One spacious saloon, the walls of which form a picturesque ruin, as seen from the new post road to Albano, stands on the edge of the rising ground, and commands a magnificent view of the whole of the Alban and Sabine Hills and the city of Rome. Near this was a small theatre, from which the cipollino columns of the entrance to the Tordinone Theatre in Rome were taken.

An immense quantity of valuable sculpture, now in the

[1] Hist. Aug. Flor. 16. Dion Cass. lxxii. 5, 13.   [2] Herodian, i. 12.

Roman museums and palaces, was discovered by excavations here in 1787 and 1792. Among these sculptures was a splendid statue of Euterpe, now in the Galleria dei Candelabri, a tiger now in the Hall of Animals; and the busts of Lucius Verus, Diocletian, and Epicurus, Socrates, the Isis and Antinous in the Vatican, with numerous Sileni, Fauns, and Nereids.

Casale Rotondo. Between the sixth and seventh milestones from the Porta Capena there is a large round ruin 300 feet in diameter, called Casale Rotondo, now supporting a house and olive orchard upon the top. The fragments of sculpture found here have been arranged on the face of a wall, close to the pile of ruins. The name Cotta was found on an inscription belonging to this, and hence it has been supposed to be the tomb of the gens Aurelia, who bore the surname of Cotta. On the left are the arches of the aqueduct which supplied the Villa of Commodus.

At the eighth milestone there was a Temple of Hercules erected by Domitian. Martial mentions this temple in several passages. There are considerable remains of a tetrastyle temple on the right hand of the road, consisting of columns of Alban peperino; but this, which was once supposed to be the Temple of Hercules, is now said to have contained an altar to Silvanus.

The Villa and Farm of Persius the poet is said by his biographer to have been near the eighth milestone. At the ninth stood the Tomb of Gallienus, and perhaps the ruins there belong to his suburbanum. At the tenth milestone, the Rivus Albanus, formerly the Aqua Terentina, is crossed; and at the eleventh, the road begins to ascend the slope towards Albano. At the twelfth, the circuit of the walls of *Bovillæ.* the ancient town of Bovillæ is approached. Dionysius says that Bovillæ was situated where the hill before reaching Albano first begins to be steep, and this answers to the position of the modern Osteria delle Frattocchie. The ruins which are now generally held to be those of Bovillæ lie on the cross road, called Strada di Nettuno, a little way above Frattocchie.[1] They consist of a small theatre built of brick-

---

[1] Ann. dell' Inst. 1853, 1854.

work and opus reticulatum, and a somewhat larger circus, the enclosure of which and the carceres are still pretty well preserved. The town did not lie close to the road. It was founded by a colony from Alba Longa, and was a flourishing place until Coriolanus destroyed it. For centuries afterwards we find but little notice taken of it. In Cicero's time it was a very insignificant village, and had it not been immortalised by the assassination of Clodius there, which led to such important results, it could hardly excite any interest in later times.[1]

The honour of being the native place of the gens Julia gave it some artificial importance in the imperial times. Tiberius is mentioned by Tacitus as erecting a sacrarium of the Julian family and a statue of Augustus there, and founding Circensian games in honour of the gens Julia. Some inscriptions found on the spot show the town still existed in the 2nd century A.D. It is now occupied by plots of land laid out as gardens. The Villa of Clodius, Cicero's enemy, appears to have been at or near the thirteenth milestone from Rome, close to the left side of the Appian Road, between Bovillæ and the modern Albano. It was raised on immense substructions, the arches of which were capable of concealing a thousand men, and Cicero declares that Clodius had not respected even the confines of the Temple of Jupiter Latiaris or the sacred groves of Alba.[2] The ruins which lie under Castel Gandolfo, on the left side of the road towards the Porta Romana of Albano, may have formed part of the substruction of which Cicero speaks. The estate of Clodius passed after his death, when the family of the Claudii Pulcri became extinct, into the hands of the Claudii Nerones, from whom Tiberius inherited it, and thus it became imperial property.

The Villa of Pompey was between that of Clodius and Aricia, and therefore occupied the site of the present town of Albano. Nibby thinks that the walls of reticulated work in the Villa Doria belonged to Pompey's house, and that the great tomb, near the Roman gate of Albano was Pompey's burial place. Plutarch states that Pompey was buried at his

Villa of Pompey.

---

[1] Cic. pro Planc. 9; Propert. v. 1, 33.
[2] Cic. pro Mil. 10, 19, 20, 31.

Alban villa. The tomb, with five truncated cones, usually called the Tomb of the Horatii and Curiatii, has also been called the Tomb of Pompey. It is more probably an imitation of the old Etruscan tombs executed at a later time. After the death of that great general, the estate became the property of Dolabella, and subsequently of Antony, who held it till the battle of Actium, when Augustus took possession of it. After the adoption of Tiberius, it was united with the Clodian grounds, and thus formed the nucleus of the Albanum Cæsarum.

Albanum Cæsarum. Augustus and some of the early emperors found the Albanum a convenient halting-place on their journeys to the south, but it was in the time of Domitian that the place was extended so much as to contain a military camp, enormous reservoirs of water, thermæ, a theatre, an amphitheatre, and a circular temple. It is called Arx Albana by Juvenal, Tacitus and Martial.

The plan of the camp can still be traced. It resembled that of the Prætorian camp at Rome, in being a quadrangular space rounded off at the corners. The two longer sides extend from the Church of S. Paolo at Albano to the round Temple, now the Church of S. Maria. One of the shorter sides was parallel to the Appian Road, and the other ran near the Church of S. Paolo. There were four terraces or levels in the camp rising towards the hill behind. The Porta Decumana was in the north-eastern side, and the Porta Prætoria on the south-western. The great reservoirs for water stand on the northern side near S. Paolo, and the thermæ towards the south-east on the opposite side of the Appian Road. At the western corner is the round building usually called the Temple of Minerva, and supposed to be that alluded to by Suetonius as annually visited by Domitian. This round building is in good preservation, but its purpose cannot be determined with certainty. Nibby says that the ancient mosaic pavement still remains at a depth of six feet below the present surface. The amphitheatre is situated between the Church of S. Paolo and that of the Capuchin Convent. It is principally constructed of opus quadratum, but the interior parts are of a mixed masonry, consisting of

Plan of the
ALBAN HILLS & GABII

bricks and fragments of the local stone. This amphitheatre is supposed to have been the scene of the feats performed by Domitian, in killing with his own hand hundreds of wild beasts with arrows and javelins, and also of the degradation of Acilius Glabrio, who was forced, according to Juvenal, by Domitian to join him in these sports of the arena.

Between Castel Gandolfo and Albano four magnificent terraces, rising one above the other, were traced by Cav. Rosa as forming part of the Albanum Cæsarum, and in the Villa Barberini there is a considerable part of a cryptoporticus, ornamented with stucco reliefs, which probably stands over the old substructions of the Villa Clodi.[1] On the side towards the lake there were open balconies for viewing the mock naval engagements; and near the entrance of the Barberini Villa the ruins of a theatre have been discovered. It appears probable from the numerous ruins found upon the edge of the lake that the whole of it was surrounded with quays and tiers of stone seats, and chapels of Nymphs, making it resemble a gigantic natural naumachia, or sheet of water for sham naval fights. These ruins may possibly, however, have belonged to separate private villas placed at different points round the water.

To the south of Albano, in the grounds of the Villa Doria, there are the ruins of an extensive Roman villa. Whether this was a part of the Albanum Cæsarum or not, is uncertain. Some of the bricks bear the stamps of Domitian, others those of the third consulship of Servianus (A.D. 134), Hadrian's brother-in-law, others of Commodus.[2]

The Alban lake belongs to the water system of the Tiber, and has most of its outlets on the western side. It has been supposed that a subterranean communication exists between this lake and that of Nemi, but Nibby asserts that this is impossible, as the level of the lake of Nemi is higher than that of the Alban lake. The circumference of this sheet of water is more than six miles, and it is nearly elliptical in shape. The story of the sudden rise of its waters in the

Lago Albano or Di Castello.

---

[1] The mock council held over the gigantic turbot described in the Fourth Satire of Juvenal was at the Albanum.
[2] Ann. and Mon. dell' Inst. 1854, p. 101.

sixth year of the siege of Veii is well known, and the response of the Delphic oracle as given in Livy.

Cicero gives a distinct account of the drainage of the lake. "We are told, he says, by the Annalists, that during the siege of Veii, when the Alban lake had risen to an unusual height, a Veientine noble fled to Rome as a deserter, and declared that it was written in the books of fate which were kept at Veii, that Veii could not be taken, so long as the lake was overflowing its banks, and that if the lake were tapped, and flowed into the sea by its own channel and stream, it would be fatal to the Roman nation, but that if the water were so discharged as to make it impossible for it to reach the sea, then the Romans would be victorious. In consequence of this our ancestors contrived that admirable plan for drawing off and dispersing the water of the lake."

From this passage it would seem likely that the whole object of the drainage of the lake was to obtain a constant supply of water for the irrigation of the Campagna. In another passage Cicero states his opinion still more clearly, that the work was really undertaken for the benefit of suburban agriculture. "The Veientine prophecy that if the water of the Alban lake rose above its margin and flowed into the sea, Rome would perish; but that if it were checked, Veii would be taken, in consequence of which the Alban water was diverted, was intended to benefit the suburban farms, and not to secure the safety of Rome." What appears strange, is that it should have been necessary to appeal to a superstitious motive in the case of a people evidently so far advanced in civilization as to be capable of carrying out an engineering work of such difficulty in a single year.[1]

Emissarium of the Alban lake.

The tunnel which still carries off the superfluous water of the lake is cut through solid peperino and occasional masses of still harder basaltic lava. It is more than a mile and a half in length, from seven to ten feet in height, and never less than four feet in breadth. The height of the edge of the lake basin above the level of its water at the part which is pierced by the tunnel is 430 feet. Three vertical shafts are still discoverable, by which a draft of air was created and the

[1] Cic. de Div. I. 44; ii. 32.

rubbish was removed, and one slanting shaft for the entrance and exit of the miners. The rock was cut with a chisel an inch wide, as may be seen from the marks left upon the sides of the tunnel.

At the points where the water enters and leaves the tunnel, considerable pains have been taken to regulate the flow. The channel of stonework at the mouth is placed in a slanting direction so as to break the force of the rush of water. At the end of this first channel is a cross wall with openings, protected by gratings to catch the leaves and floating rubbish. Behind this is a reservoir, similar to the cisterns in use in the Roman aqueducts, allowing the mud to settle before the water entered the tunnel. Next to the tunnel itself there is a closed building to protect the canal from the fall of rocks and stones, and the actual entrance into the rock is faced with a massive portal of wedge-shaped blocks of stone. The water in this enclosure is now used by the fishermen of the lake as a receptacle for keeping fish, and is for this purpose provided with sluices. Hirt thinks that these arrangements at the mouth are very ancient.[1] Others ascribe them to the imperial era.

The point where the tunnel emerges from the mountain on the west of Castel Savelli, nearly a mile from Albano, is called Le Mole. The water was there received in a long troughlike reservoir arched over with a stone vaulted roof. From this it ran through five smaller openings into five separate channels, and was so dispersed into the fields for irrigation. At the present time the whole stream is united, and after passing the road to Anzio, thirteen miles from Rome, takes the name of Rio d'Albano, receives the brook from the valley of Apiolæ, and joining the Acqua Acetosa and Cornacciola crosses the Ostian way near Tor di Valle, three miles and a half from Rome, and then discharges itself into the Tiber.

It is the opinion of some archæologists that the Romans brought engineers from Greece to superintend the Alban tunnel. This supposition, however, is not necessary. If the Italian engineers could construct the Cloaca Maxima they would be fully equal to the task of tapping the Alban lake.

[1] Hirt, Gesch. der Bau, ii. p. 106.

The physical conformation of Central Italy compelled its inhabitants to turn their attention at an early period to the construction of drains and other hydraulic works. Considerable artificial channels were rendered necessary in order to regulate the flow of the Arno and Tiber in the neighbourhood of Chiusi. In southern Etruria, the district now known as the pestilent Maremma, could only have been rendered healthy by systematic artificial drainage. The sites of Populonia, Saturnia, Cosa, Veii, and Cære were thus rendered habitable and fertile, and a great part of Latium Maritimum, the Pomptine marshes, and the tract about Suessa Pometia must have been artificially and skilfully drained at the time of the greatest prosperity of those places. Many of the ancient cities of Central Italy had tunnels bored underneath their streets which served as thoroughfares connecting the different parts of the city, or as secret passages leading out into the country. Such tunnels are found at Præneste and Alba Fucensis. An account of the attempted escape of Marius from Præneste, by means of the tunnels, is given by Velleius. The catacombs show that the same genius for tunnelling operations existed at a later time among the Italians of the empire.

Alban Mount.

The triumphal route by which the festal processions from Rome ascended the Alban Mount diverged from the Appian road at the ninth milestone. It probably passed by Marino to Palazzuolo and thence ascended to the summit by a series of zigzags. The stones which mark its course have the letters N V. (numinis via) cut upon them. On the summit stood the Temple of Jupiter Latiaris, the ancient sanctuary of the Latin league. The sole remains of this famous building are now built into the wall of the reservoir of the convent of Palazzuolo. They consist of fragments only.

Most of the stones employed by Cardinal York in 1783 in the erection of the convent of Palazzuolo and the church of the Trinity, on the site of the temple, were taken from the ruins, but nothing can be learnt from them regarding the ancient buildings. The summit of the hill is not broad enough to have supported any large building, and we may therefore conclude that the temple was of small size, and

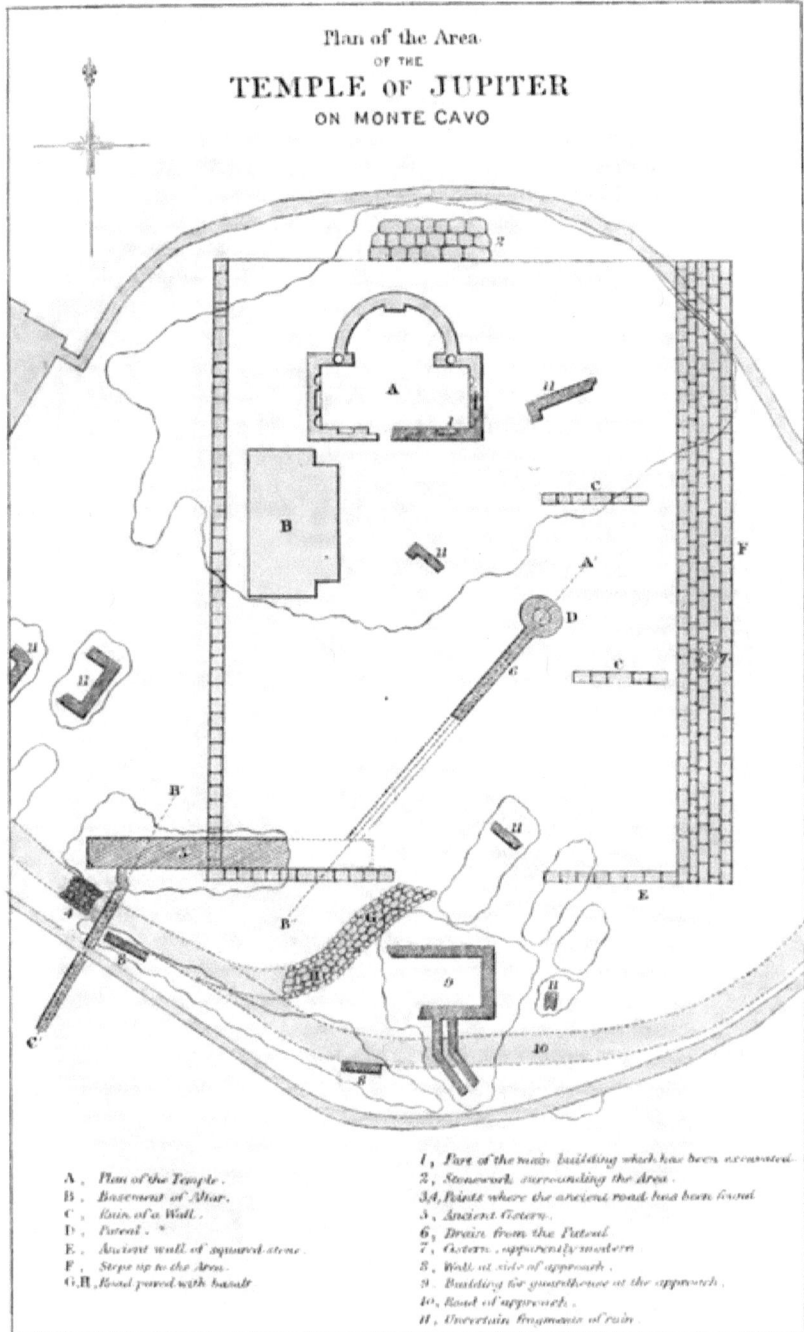

that the great festival games at the Feriæ Latinæ were held in the Prati d'Annibale below. The inscriptions on some of the stones are merely the freaks of some modern stonemasons. The fragments which remain were probably used for the area round the temple.

The explorations carried out in 1876 seem to have proved that the buildings consecrated to Jupiter Latiaris on Monte Cavo were a walled area of about sixty-five yards long, and fifty wide, a fragment of the wall of which was found; a chapel dedicated to Jupiter, one corner of which was excavated; a large altar, and some other chapels dedicated as votive offerings. A tracing of the shape and position of the area, chapels and altar was found by M. S. De Rossi in a seventeenth century MS. in the Barberini Library, and was published in the Annali dell' Instituto for 1876. This traced sketch agrees with the excavations. (See Plan.)

The early destruction of Alba Longa, so famous in Roman legendary lore, has completely deprived us of the means of tracing its site by the discovery of any remains of the walls or buildings which it contained. It was razed to the ground by Tullus Hostilius in B.C. 667 and never rebuilt. Dionysius thus describes the site: "The city was built close to the mountain and lake, upon a site between the two. They serve as defences to it, and make it almost impregnable, for the mountain is very steep and lofty and the lake deep and wide." Livy says that the city was named Longa because it extended along a ridge of the Alban hills. The words of Dionysius seem to imply that Alba stood immediately between Monte Cavo and the lake on the site of the convent of Palazzuolo, and Cav. Rosa, the highest modern authority on the topography of the Campagna, who has made the neighbourhood of Albano and Nemi the subject of special study, holds this opinion. Nibby thought that the whole edge of the crater from Palazzuolo nearly to Marino, a distance of more than two miles, was occupied by the city of Alba. Sir William Gell discovered an ancient road running along the edge of the crater above Monte Cuccu, and a few blocks of stone on the top of the precipice bordering the lake further eastwards, which he thought must have belonged to the gate of Alba.

Alba Longa

At the sixteenth milestone on the Appian road beyond Albano, in the valley below the modern town of Ariccia, is the massive causeway 700 feet in length and 40 in width, upon which the old Appian road was raised. It is built of blocks of peperino and is a solid mass of masonry, except where three archways give passage to the water which descends from the Alban hills and the neighbourhood of Nemi.

Lake of Nemi.

Beyond the ancient viaduct we come to the tunnel through which the lake of Nemi discharges its waters.

The name of this lake and of the village on its margin, is derived from the great grove of Diana (Nemus Dianæ) whose temple probably stood on the site of the present village of Nemi. The wooded cliffs which surround the crater here are steep and descend immediately into the water, except on the side near Genzano, where they slope magnificently and are planted with vines. Their average height is 300 feet. In the Latin poets frequent mention is made of this lake as one of the principal ornaments of the neighbourhood of Rome, and in connection with the widely celebrated temple of Diana. Hence it was called Speculum Dianæ, lacus Triviæ and Stagnum Dianæ.

Whether the name Lacus Aricinus also belonged to this lake is doubtful, for Pliny speaks of a lake which formerly occupied the valley of Ariccia, and the water in this valley was certainly called Lacus Aricinus in the middle ages.

The water of the lake is supplied partially at least from a small spring near the road from Genzano to Nemi, and also from the copious stream which turns the mills of the village of Nemi. The latter is probably alluded to by Strabo when he says that the sources whence the lake is filled are visible, and are near the temple of Diana.

Nibby gives the following account of the Lake of Nemi, and of the investigations carried on in his time for the purpose of discovering the real nature of the curious wooden fabrics said to have been found at the bottom of the lake:

"The situation of Nemi is picturesque, and the view from it of the crater, and of the lake, which resembles an enormous mirror spread below, is magnificent. But beyond the historical reminiscences of the Temple of Diana, it presents nothing worth particular mention. The baronial castle near it has all the appearance of a feudal fortress. It was built by the famous Colonna family, once the lords of the estate, who also built the round tower or keep which surmounts it. By ascending the side of the mountain which rises above it, a splendid panoramic view of the coast of Latium and of the adjacent Rutulian and Volscian territory may be enjoyed The eye ranges along the whole coast line of the Tyrrhenian Sea, from the Circæan promontory to the mouths of the Tiber, and the situations of Astura, Antium, Ardea, Lavinium, Laurentum, Ostia and Porto are clearly distinguishable, together with many other points."

"The crater is surrounded in parts by rocks of the hardest basaltic lava, in others by conglomerated cinders and scoriæ, and in some places by banks of tufa. Its circumference is about five miles; and the level of the water is higher than that of the Alban Lake. The story of the ship discovered at the bottom of this lake and said by some authors to have belonged to the time of Tiberius, by others to that of Trajan, is well known. Biondo, Leon Battista Alberti, and particularly Francesco Marchi a celebrated architect and military engineer of the sixteenth century, who went down into the lake himself, have spoken of it.[1] Fresh investigations have been carried on of late, at which I was present, and saw and examined everything which was brought to the surface, and inquired of those who went down what they saw there. I consider myself in a position to assert that the pretended ship was nothing more than the wooden piles and timbers used in the foundations of a building. The beams are of fir and larch, and are joined by metal nails of various sizes. The pavement, or at least the lowest stratum, of the remains is formed of large tiles placed upon a kind of grating of iron, on which the name CAISAR, in ancient letters, is marked. Some of these tiles and nails and gratings are now kept in the Vatican Library.

"'The name Caisar seems to explain the history of the building, for Suetonius in his 'Life of Julius Cæsar,' as an illus-

[1] Fea, Miscellanea, pp. cccxvii. cclxxiv.

tration of Julius Cæsar's extravagance, asserts that after having built a villa on the lake of Nemi at an enormous expense, he had the whole destroyed because it did not quite suit his taste. It is my belief that the pretended ship was nothing else than the piles and wooden framework upon which this villa was supported, and that after the upper part was destroyed the foundations under the water still remained, partly covered by the fragments of the demolished building above."[1]

The mention of paving tiles, marbles, and leaden pipes as among the objects raised from the bottom of the lake, renders the notion that they belonged to a ship improbable, and Nibby's conjecture that a Roman villa, partly built out into the water, stood here, seems much more likely, though his application of the passage of Suetonius is very doubtful.

Cav. Rosa, who examined the neighbourhood of Nemi and Genzano with a special view to the solution of the question of the site of the Temple of Artemis, has given a careful account both of the ruins under Genzano and those to the west of Nemi. The former he pronounces undoubtedly to belong to a villa, the latter he thinks belonged to a temple with a large court in front, and an ancient road leading to it from the western side of the lake. These ruins are just above the lower road leading from the Capuccini convent at Genzano to Nemi, at the point where a cross road leads to the left and joins the higher road to Nemi, not far from the place called le Mole.[2] Genzano is a town of mediæval origin.

(B) THE VIA LATINA AND TUSCULUM.

Latin road.   The modern Porta Giovanni is now the point at which the new road to Albano, and also that to Frascati, leave Rome. The Latin road anciently diverged, after passing the Porta Capena, from the Alban road and had a gate of its own in the Aurelian wall, called the Porta Latina, now walled up.

The old Via Latina is unfortunately now almost lost, and can only be traced by the lines of ruined tombs which mark

---

[1] Nibby, Analisi, ii. 305.
[2] Annali and Monumenti dell' Inst. 1856.

its former course. After leaving the old Porta Latina it runs along the edge of the hills which fringe the right bank of the Caffarelli valley, and crosses the new road to Albano at the second milestone, at a point on the other side of the valley almost opposite to the so-called fountain of Egeria. Not far from this spot some very interesting tombs were excavated in 1860. A full account of them has been given in the 'Annali dell' Instituto di Corrispondenza Archeologica' for 1860. The sarcophagi and stucco ornaments are the most perfect remains of the kind in the neighbourhood of Rome. These sepulchral monuments are near the remains of the Basilica of S. Stefano, a ruin of the fifth century, and on the farm which bears the name of Arco Travertino from the travertine arches of the Claudian Aqueduct which cross it. The ancient pavement of the Latin road has been uncovered in some places near the tombs, and also some traces of a villa, which probably belonged to the Servilian and Anician families, have been excavated. The portico of the tomb which faces the southern side of the road leads down to two large vaults, in the outer of which stand the mutilated remains of a marble sarcophagus in a niche, while the inner vault is decorated with well-preserved stucco ornaments in relief, representing sea-monsters and nymphs. Some of the marble casing which covered the walls remains, but no name has been found on the bricks or stones. In the tomb on the opposite side of the road there is a well-preserved mosaic with figures of sea-monsters at the entrance, and below are paintings of birds upon the arches which support the sarcophagi in the outer chamber, and an inscription which gives the name of the Pancratii as the owners of the tomb. The family figures and profiles are only sketched roughly in outline, as is common in the catacombs. The roof of the inner chamber in this second tomb is exquisitely ornamented with paintings and stucco reliefs, representing mythological subjects and landscapes. In the centre a large marble sarcophagus containing places for two bodies is left standing. This sarcophagus is plain and without any decoration. The date of this tomb cannot precede the Antonine era, as there are no cinerary urns in it.

Tombs on Latin road.

Torre Fiscale.

At the fourth milestone from the Porta Capena, the Latin road passed under the arches of the Claudian and Marcian aqueducts, at the tower now called Torre Fiscale. At this point the two aqueducts cross each other, and present a most magnificent series of arcades running along the side of the old Latin road for more than a mile. The arches of the Claudian aqueduct are here more than fifty feet in height. The railway to Naples runs very close to the line of the old Latin road here.

A great number of ruins are still to be seen at a place called Sette Bassi, four miles and a half from the Porta S. Giovanni and near the Osteria del Curato. This spot, as well as the district near it on the Appian road, bears the name of Roma Vecchia. The scattered ruins occupy a space of nearly three-quarters of a mile in circumference, and appear to have been built at two different epochs. The bricks of which one portion of them is constructed have the dates A.D. 123 and 134 upon them, the years when Pœtinus and Africanus and Servianus and Juventius were consuls. The other part of the building is evidently contemporaneous with the ruins on the Appian road and belongs to the Antonine era. All the bricks were made at one of the imperial kilns, and it has therefore been generally supposed that the villa was an imperial residence, forming a part of the already-mentioned Suburbanum Commodi. The marbles found on the spot show that it was decorated with great magnificence, and a particular kind of breccia, numerous fragments of which have been picked up there, obtains its name, Breccia di Sette Bassi from the place.

The plan, according to Nibby, was that of a large oblong area, the longer sides of which ran north and south. In the centre there was room for a large pleasure garden. The front of the buildings was at the northern end towards Rome, and the remains of a portico can be traced, which supported a terrace on a level with the first floor rooms of the mansion. One of these rooms with three doors and the same number of windows can still be traced. In some of the walls the remains may be seen of terra-cotta pipes for heating the rooms. The ground floor apartments were without decorations, and are therefore supposed to have served as storehouses for grain and farm produce.[1]

Circus of Maxentius, with Torre Fiscale beyond it and the hills above Praeneste and Tusculum.

Behind this front building, on the eastern and western

[1] Nibby, Anal. iii. p. 736.

sides, are long ranges of building, the eastern consisting of two suites of rooms, probably intended for baths or for gymnasia, and the western forming a long ambulacrum terminated by an exedra. On the south side there is a cryptoporticus and a reservoir for water which was supplied by a branch of the Claudian aqueduct.

About a quarter of a mile farther south, near the Latin road, there is an outlying building which seems to have been intended to command a view of that road. The railway to Frascati now runs between the Claudian aqueduct and these ruins.

The castella of the Aqua Marcia, the Tepula, the Julia, the Claudia, the Anio Vetus, and the Anio Nova lie on the right of the old Latin road here, at the sixth milestone, where the arcades make a right angle. The old road then runs to the right of the present road to Frascati, nearly on the line of the modern Strada di Grotta Ferrata, and ascending the slopes of the Alban Hills, passes behind Tusculum and Corbio, along the valley called Vallis Albana.

Tusculum. Since the excavations carried out by Lucien Bonaparte at the beginning of this century, there has been no doubt left as to the site of the ancient city of Tusculum. The ruins lie from about a mile and a half to two miles above Frascati, upon the ridge forming the edge of the most ancient crater of the Alban Hills. Between this ridge, which bore the name of Tusculani Colles, and the hills upon which Marino and Rocca di Papa stand, the great Latin road ran. Tusculum stands just over this road and was approached from it by a steep path ascending the northern side of the valley. The main road entered the city on the other side, from the direction of Frascati and Rufinella, leaving the Via Latina at the tenth milestone, between Morena and Ciampino. The ancient pavement of this road can be clearly traced on the slope of the hill above Frascati, and it leads us along the top of the hill through what has plainly been the main street of the town to the citadel, which stood at the eastern extremity.

The site of the citadel is a platform nearly square and 2700 feet in circuit, standing about 200 feet above the level of the surrounding parts of the hill. Its walls were

completely demolished by the Romans in 1191 and not a
vestige of them is left. Sir William Gell thought, however,
that he could discover the traces of four ancient gates, one
on the west, another on the side of the Alban valley, a
third on the eastern side, and not far from this last, a
postern communicating with a steep and rocky path which
descended to the Alban valley. Most of the ruins now
visible belong to the mediæval fortress of the Dukes of
Tusculum, and a few only of the quadrilateral blocks of the
ancient enclosure are visible. In the Æquian and Volscian
wars this citadel playëd an important part. It must therefore
have been a fortress of considerable strength from
very early times. Dionysius describes it as a very strong
position, requiring but a small garrison to hold it, and adds
that the whole country as far as the gates of Rome, is
plainly visible from it, so that the defenders could see the
Roman forces issuing from the Porta Latina. The city
itself lay on the ridge of the hill westwards from the citadel.
The area which it occupied is an oblong strip of ground
about 3000 feet long, and from 500 to 1000 feet in width.
On the north and south sides the limits of the city are
clearly marked by the edges of the hill, but on the west
they are not so easily defined. At the foot of the descent
from the citadel are the ruins of a large water tank of an
oblong shape divided into four compartments by three rows
of piers, and immediately under this tank is a small theatre
built of peperino, which was excavated by the dowager
Queen of Sardinia Maria Christina in 1839 and 1840. This,
with the exception of the theatres at Pompeii, is the most
perfectly preserved in Italy. The walls of the scena are
unfortunately destroyed, but the ground plan of it can still
be traced. The stage, which abuts closely on the western
side of the semicircular cavea, is 110 feet in length, and 20
feet in depth. It has the three usual entrances from the
back, and one at each end. These open into a corridor and
communicate with two chambers, probably used as dressing
rooms by the actors. Nearly the whole of the fifteen rows
of seats in the lower division are still preserved unbroken,
but the upper part which contained, to judge by the height

Theatre.

of the outer walls still remaining, about nine rows of seats, is entirely destroyed.

Other ruins. The curved walls on the northern side of the theatre were supposed by Nibby to have belonged to another theatre, but are now generally believed to have been a part of a fountain connected with the above-mentioned reservoir. Along the northern side of the reservoir are two parallel walls, which apparently enclosed the street leading to the citadel. The roadway must have been here carried by an arched corridor under the side of the theatre. Near the ancient road from the theatre westwards is a mass of ruins the plan of which cannot be determined, and beyond these, not far from the point where the road divides, and on its right-hand branch, is one of the gates of the city, marked by *Gate and walls.* two fragments of ancient fluted columns which perhaps formed a part of its architecture. Near this are the remains of the ancient north wall of the city, consisting of blocks of peperino of great size more or less regularly laid, and of restorations here and there in reticulated work, partly of the later republic, and partly of more modern times. The pavement of the street is here perfectly preserved, and near the gateway there is a wide space left, probably as a turning place for carts or carriages.

Tank and fountain. In the walls near this point is a stone doorway leading into a stone water-tank, with a pointed roof formed by overlapping stones, on the same principle as the roof of the so-called Mamertine prison at Rome, the gate of Arpinum and the treasuries of Mycenæ and Orchomenos. The doorway is about ten feet high and five wide, and the tank of the same dimensions. In the interior are three divisions or basins for water, and at the back an aqueduct enters by means of which the water was supplied. At the side of this tank there is a small ancient fountain under the wall which was supplied from the tank by a leaden pipe. An inscription on the fountain records that it was made by the Ædiles Quintus Cœlius Latinus, son of Quintus, and Marcus Decumo, by command of the Senate of Tusculum. Not far from the fountain was found the fifteenth milestone from Rome.

On the road to Frascati, near the point where the western

gate of the city has been supposed to have stood, the remains of an amphitheatre can be discovered. The seats are entirely destroyed, and it is only by the oval shape and by the position of the substruction that the ruins can be recognized as those of an amphitheatre. A round tomb stands a little above the amphitheatre, and beyond this the ruins of a large villa called Scuola di Cicerone cover the side of the hill towards the Alban valley.

The legend which ascribes the foundation of Tusculum to Telegonus, the son of Circe and Ulysses, is familiar to all readers of the Latin poets. It is remarkable, however, that Virgil, who mentions most of the towns of Latium, has entirely omitted to notice Tusculum. This may be mere accident, or it may be attributable to a grudge similar to that which led him, according to Aulus Gellius, to omit Nola from the lines in the Georgics celebrating the fertility of Campania, but it certainly cannot be due to the fear of making an anachronism, as Nibby supposes. In the times of the Latin league, from the fall of Alba to the battle of the Lake Regillus, Tusculum was the most prominent town in Latium. It suffered, like the other towns of Latium, a complete eclipse during the later republic and the imperial times, but in the ninth, tenth, eleventh and twelfth centuries under the counts of Tusculum it became again a place of great importance and power, no less than seven Popes of their house having sat in the chair of St. Peter. The final destruction of the city is placed by Nibby, following the account given in the records of the Podesta of Reggio, on the 1st of April, A.D. 1191, in which year the city was given up to the Romans by the Emperor Henry VI., and after the withdrawal of the German garrison, was sacked and razed to the ground. Those of the inhabitants who escaped collected round the church of S. Sebastian on the foot of the hill, in the district called Frascati, whence the town of Frascati took its origin and name. They founded their new town upon the remains of an ancient villa, which stood near the round tomb which still remains on the road to the Villa della Ruffinella. The name of Lucullus has been attached to this villa and tomb from the statement of Plutarch that Lucullus was buried by his brother at his Tusculan villa. It is however, much more probable that the larger round tomb in the vigna Angelotti on the road towards Rome was the burial-place of Lucullus.

Scuola di Cicerone.

The building now called Scuola di Cicerone is not far from the ruins of the western gate of Tusculum. The ground floor is apparently about 270 feet in length and 100 in depth, but the upper parts of the buildings have now completely disappeared. The materials were of brick and reticulated work, similar to that now found in the gardens of Sallust at Rome, and generally considered as belonging to the last age of the Republic or the early Empire. The ground floor had a cryptoporticus along its whole length, and above this on the first floor was probably an open portico with a colonnade. Eight large rooms opened out behind the cryptoporticus, in the second of which are the remains of some stairs, and at the back of the eighth a recess. At the ends of the cryptoporticus are the remains of some more rooms. There are no signs of decoration on any of the walls, and therefore this lowest story of the building is supposed to have been used as a storehouse for corn and farm produce.

There is, however, no evidence whatever to connect these ruins with Cicero's Villa. The only indication we have of its site is given by the Scholiast on Horace, who speaks of it as situated near Tusculum on the upper slopes of the hill.[1]

This will agree either with the ruins just described or with those found in 1741 under the modern Villa Rufinella, which is a little way lower down the western slope. That Cicero's Villa was upon the upper part of the hill is confirmed by his own statement that it was so near that of the consul Gabinius, that at the time of Cicero's exile, not only the furniture but the trees in his garden were transferred to the Villa of Gabinius, and we also find that this latter villa was upon the upper part of the hill. Nibby accordingly places the Villa of Gabinius on the site of the modern Villa Falconieri close to the Rufinella.

Villa of Gabinius.

Several particulars about his villa are mentioned by Cicero

[1] Schol. ad Hor. Ep. i. 29.

himself. It contained two rooms called gymnasia, to the upper of which he gave the name of Lyceum, and which contained his library. The lower gymnasium was called the Academy in honour of Plato.

The Lyceum seems to have been used in the morning, and the Academia in the afternoon, as being more sheltered from the heat of the sun.

The Hermathena, a double-headed bust of Hermes and Athena, mentioned in the letters to Atticus, was probably placed in the Lyceum, for the phrase he uses there seems to refer to Apollo as the patron of the gymnasium, in which it was placed. There were also some Hermæ of Pentelic marble, bronze busts, and Megarian statues placed in the gymnasia, and Atticus had a general commission to buy up anything which he might think suitable for these rooms.

Another part of the villa was called the atriolum. Nibby has shown from one of the letters to Quintus that the atriolum of a villa was a small courtyard surrounded with bedchambers and offices. The Tusculan atriolum was decorated with stucco reliefs on the walls, like those in the tombs on the Latin Road.

(c) Gabii and Præneste.

The road to Gabii and Præneste leaves Rome at the Porta Maggiore. The most conspicuous ruin, which it passes at about one mile from the walls of Rome, is a very large circular sepulchral monument more than a hundred feet in diameter, to which the name of Quintus Atta has been attached. Beyond this, at a distance of two miles and a half from Rome, we come to the remains of a vast villa, which has been identified with that spoken of by Julius Capitolinus in his history of the Gordian family. That historian says that their "country house was situated on the road to Præneste, and was remarkable for the magnificence of a portico with four ranges of columns, fifty of which were of Carystian, fifty of Claudian, fifty of Synnadan and fifty of Numidian marble. There were also three basilicas in it, each of a hundred feet in length, and other buildings of corresponding size, in particular some

Tomb of Atta.

Villa Gordiana.

Thermæ more magnificent than any others in the world except those at Rome." The ruins of this great imperial villa extend for nearly a mile along the road, consisting chiefly of some huge reservoirs for water, two spacious halls belonging to the Thermæ, a round temple or Heroon, and a stadium surrounded with arcades. The style of construction in most of these is the irregular brickwork with thick layers of mortar which is known to be characteristic of the third century. Gordian III. was killed in A.D. 244. The great reservoirs are close to the road, two on the left and two on the right-hand side, beyond the depression in which the stream called Acqua Bollicante runs, where the ground rises towards the hill of Torre de' Schiavi. Some of them appear to be of an earlier date than the reigns of the Gordians, and are referred by Nibby to the Antonine epoch. The brickwork of these last is more regular, and they contain a good deal of reticulated work and layers of squared tufa stones. The two large halls which belonged to the Thermæ are to the east of the reservoirs. One of them was a spacious octagonal building with round windows. It was occupied as a fortress or watch-tower in the middle ages, and has been repaired in the style called Saracenesca. In the walls of this may be seen the earliest instances of a mode of construction afterwards, as in the Circus of Maxentius, very common, the introduction of jars of terra-cotta in the walls to make the work lighter. The interior is ornamented with niches alternately square and circular headed, and retaining some of their ancient stucco decorations.

The other hall of the Thermæ stands not far off, and is circular with a domed roof.

The Heroon, or circular temple, of which mention has been made, is similar to that near the Circus of Maxentius. The diameter of this is fifty-six feet, and it was lighted by four large round windows. The front was turned towards the road according to the rule laid down by the architect Vitruvius. Underneath, there is a crypt supported by a massive round pillar, and containing six niches. In this, Nibby thinks that the ashes of the dead were placed, as their statues were in the temple above, and that the building was the Heroon of the reigning family. In the middle ages this Heroon was used as a church, and some of the paintings then introduced are still visible on the interior walls. Not far from the Heroon are the ruins of the arcades which surrounded the stadium and bounded the domain of the villa on the east side.

In this district, but along the ancient Via Labicana which runs in the direction of Frascati, stands the conspicuous tower now called Torre Pignatara from its construction with pigne or earthen pots. It surmounts a large circular hall and a catacomb to which the titles of S. Helena's Mausoleum and the Chapels of SS. Peter and Marcellinus have been given, but the real history of the building is unknown. *Torre Pignatara.*

At the ninth milestone on the road to Palestrina, where the road crosses a small brook, is a magnificent monument of ancient Roman architecture, consisting of an arched viaduct built of peperino and tufa blocks. The length of this viaduct is 105 yards, and the highest of the seven arches about fifty feet. The blocks of stone used are in some cases ten feet in length, and they are firmly fitted together without any kind of cement. This viaduct is now called Ponte di Nono.[1] The ancient roadway of polygonal fragments of basalt still remains, but the parapet on each side has been destroyed. *Ponte di Nono.*

At a distance of about three miles beyond the Ponte di Nono are the ruins of Gabii on the edge of the lake called Lago di Pantano in the district of Castiglione. Numerous traces of the ancient city are still visible. It occupied a long strip of ground extending from the sepulchral mound on the right of the road near the outlet of the lake to the tower of Castiglione. Nibby thinks that this tower stands on the spot formerly occupied by the citadel of Gabii, the original stronghold founded according to the legend by a colony from Alba. In the year 1792 extensive excavations were made on the site by Prince Marcantonio Borghese at the suggestion of Mr. Hamilton a Scotch painter, and a quantity of sculptures and inscriptions now in the Louvre at Paris were discovered. The principal ruins now remaining are those of the cella of a temple built of the famous lapis Gabinus, and some steps in *Gabii.*

[1] Canina, Mon. dell' Arch. ant. tav. 183.

a semicircular form, probably the remains of a theatre. The temple is generally supposed to have been that of Juno alluded to by Virgil.

The form of this temple was almost identical with that at Aricia. The interior of the cella was twenty-seven feet wide and forty-five feet long. It had columns of the Doric order in front and at the sides, but none at the back. The walls of the chamber at the back were here, as at Aricia, prolonged on each side, so as to close the side porticoes at the back. The surrounding area was about fifty-four feet in breadth at the sides, but in front a space of only eight feet was left open, in consequence of the position of the theatre, which abutted closely upon the temple. On the eastern side of the cella are traces of the rooms where the priests in charge of the temple lived.

The shape of the forum can only be partially made out. From the plan published in the 'Monumenti Gabino-borghesiani,' it appears that it was a rectangular quadrilateral space, traversed by the Via Praenestina at the southern end, and that it was surrounded with a portico of Doric columns except at the end along which the Via Praenestina was carried. It was believed at the time when the excavations were made that the Curia and Augusteum could be distinguished among the surrounding buildings, but this seems now to be very doubtful. In the centre stood the statue of Titus Flavius Ælianus, the patron of the borough town. The pedestal of this statue with its inscription was found in situ in 1792.

"The stone of Gabii quarried near the lake and the product of its extinct volcano, is used in many of the Roman buildings and especially in the building called the tabularium at the head of the Forum Romanum. It is a hard species of peperino, of a brownish-grey colour, which when exposed to the air becomes paler than the common peperino of Albano. It resists the action of fire, and is a compound of volcanic ashes mixed with small fragments of black, brown, and reddish lava, scales of mica, and bits of Apennine limestone."[1]

The city of Gabii lost its independence soon after the beginning of the Republican era of Rome. It was restored

[1] Nibby, Anal. vol. ii. p. 87.

as a colony of veterans by Sylla, but sank into obscurity, and became almost proverbial for its desolate condition in the Augustan era. It afterwards recovered its prosperity in some degree by means of the celebrity of its cold baths, and in the time of Hadrian was patronised by the Emperor, who built an aqueduct and a Curia Ælia there. The inscriptions found on the spot belong chiefly to the Antonine era, and the busts of Severus and Geta also found there show that in the first part of the third century Gabii was still a flourishing borough town.

The most conspicuous outlying hill of the volcanic district Labicum. not far from Gabii is that of La Colonna, about three miles below Rocca Priora. It stands apart from the rest of the range, and is easily seen from Rome. From Strabo's description of the site of Labicum there can be but little doubt that this hill must be considered to be the place to which he refers in his account of the Via Labicana. "That road," he says, "begins at the Esquiline Gate, at which the Prænestine Road also leaves the city, and leaving both this latter and the Esquiline plain on the left, proceeds for more than a hundred and twenty stadia (fifteen and a half Roman miles) till it reaches Labicum, an old, dismantled city, lying on a mount. The road leaves it and Tusculum on the right, and ends at the station called ad Pictas, where it joins the Latin Road." There are no ancient ruins now on the spot. In Strabo's time it was apparently ruined and deserted, and at an earlier date Cicero says that it was difficult to find any inhabitant to represent Labicum at the Feriæ Latinæ. It seems probable, therefore, that it suffered severely in the civil wars of Sylla and Marius, and did not recover itself until the establishment of an imperial villa there gave it some importance.

Beyond La Colonna, the ancient Labicum, by far the most Præneste. important place on the Æquian frontier was the strong fortress-town of Præneste, now Palestrina, which commands the passage from Latium into the valley of the Sacco. Præneste is placed on one of the projecting spurs of the mountainous district which intervenes between the Anio and the Sacco. Standing, as the city does, more than 2400 feet above the sea level, it forms a very conspicuous object in the view from the hills of Rome.

After its eventful history as the great border fortress of Latium, we can only wonder that it has been found possible to restore the ancient plan of Præneste with tolerable accuracy, as has been done by Nibby and other archæologists. The modern town, an agglomeration of filthy narrow alleys, occupies little more than the space on which stood the great Temple of Fortune and its approaches. Nearly a mile distant from this, on the summit of the hill, stood the citadel united with the town by two long walls of polygonal masonry, traces of which are still to be seen, though they do not rise to any height above the ground. The site of the citadel is now occupied by a wretched little suburb called Borgo di S. Pietro, and by a ruined mediæval castle of the Colonnas built in the style called opera Saracenesca. On the side towards the town the walls of the citadel are still easily traced, and present admirable examples of polygonal structure, rising in some places to a considerable height. On the other side, where the steepness of the hill made artificial defences less necessary, the walls have almost disappeared.

The original fortifications of the city may be followed from the Porta del Sole, where the ancient polygonal masonry is visible. "In this part of the walls," says Nibby, "are some towers of opus incertum, standing between the Porta delle Monache and the Porta Portella. Near the latter gate the polygonal wall is nearly fifteen feet in height, and on one great block may be read in very ancient letters the words FED. XXX. After having surrounded the summit of the hill of S. Pietro, the wall descends to the Porta S. Martino, where it was strengthened at the time of the Punic wars with additions of quadrilateral structure, and where an ancient gate now closed may be seen. From this point the wall proceeds in a nearly straight line in the direction of the upper garden of the Barberini Palace and the Via di S. Girolamo towards the Porta del Sole. This circuit of about three miles in length was intersected at different points by at least three other lines of fortifications above the Contrada della Cortina, and hence perhaps the city bore the name of 'many crowns,'

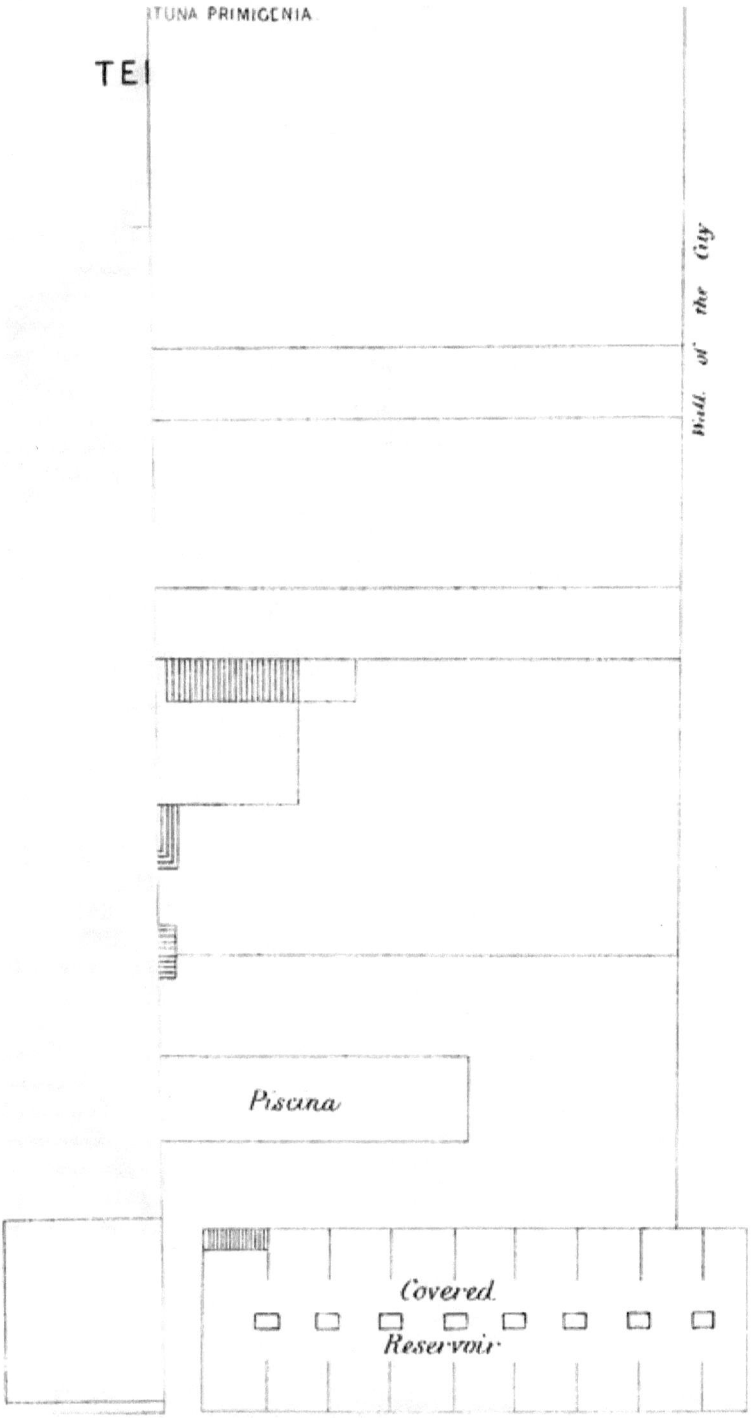

TUNA PRIMIGENIA.

TE

Wall of the City

Piscina

Covered
Reservoir

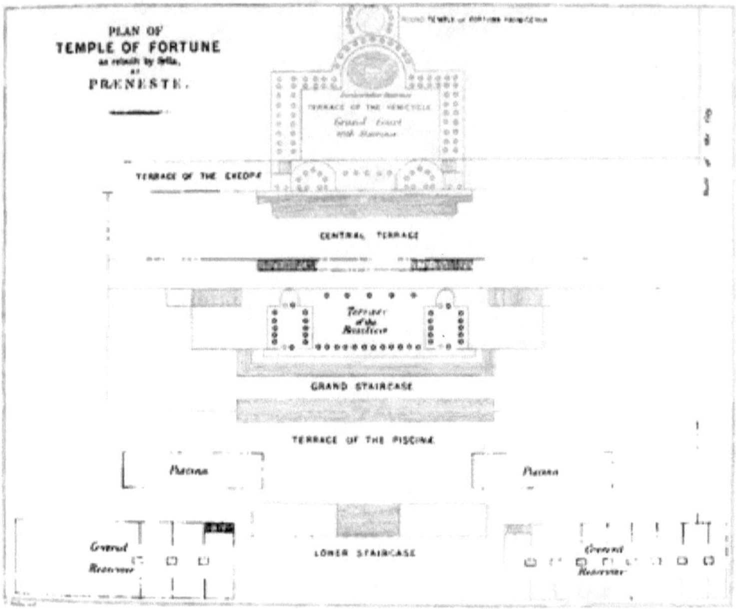

PLAN OF
TEMPLE OF FORTUNE
as rebuilt by Sylla,
at
PRÆNESTE.

TERRACE OF THE HEMICYCLE

Grand Court
with Staircase

TERRACE OF THE CHEOPS

CENTRAL TERRACE

Terrace
of the
Basilica

GRAND STAIRCASE

TERRACE OF THE PISCINA

Piscina   Piscina

Grand   Grand
Reservoir   LOWER STAIRCASE   Reservoir

given it by Strabo, forming, as it were, four separate inclosures, besides the various terraces of the great temple, which could almost be regarded as so many divisions of the town."[1]

The original foundation of the Temple of Fortuna Primigenia at Præneste is lost in obscurity; but the ancient polygonal substructions which support it show that it was a very large temple even in early times.

Cicero in his description of the Prænestine lots, calls it a splendid and ancient temple, and Valerius Maximus speaks of it as the most celebrated oracle of Latium at the end of the first Punic war.

The original extent of the temple appears to have included only that part of the lower town, which lies between the modern streets of the Corso and the Borgo, and the ancient city principally lay on the side towards the citadel. But after Sylla had rebuilt the temple, its precincts reached as far downwards as the modern Contrada degli Arconi, and upwards to the Contrada Scacciato behind the baronial palace. The whole of this space was filled with a gradually ascending series of flights of marble stairs and terraces, arranged in a pyramidal form, at the summit of which stood the tholus or round temple of the goddess, 450 feet above the lowest terrace. The base of this pyramidal approach was 1275 feet broad, and the upper terraces gradually diminished in width. The temple faced the south, like those of Diana at Aricia, of Juno at Gabii and Lanuvium, and of Jupiter Capitolinus at Rome. The modes of construction found in the ruins are referred by Nibby to four different epochs—the polyhedral stonework of the primitive temple, which was incorporated in the buildings of the new; the squared stonework of the time of the Punic wars; the structures composed of smaller polygonal stones erected by Sylla; and the brickwork of the imperial times. There were five principal terraces or platforms rising one above the other. Nibby calls these the terrace of the cisterns, the terrace of the halls, the central terrace, the terrace of the recesses, and the terrace of the hemicycle. In front of the lowest terrace was a large

[1] Nibby, Anal. ii. 496.

open space on which the boundary of the sacred precincts was marked out by stone landmarks, some of which have been found on the spot. This open area was on the right of the Contrada degli Arconi, which takes its name from the arches still remaining. The sides of the area were bordered by two immense reservoirs. One of these is still entirely preserved, but the other is filled with rubbish. On the side of the open area towards the hill were twenty-nine arches, five of which in the centre projected, forming a kind of portico with fountains in niches, while the other twenty-four completed the sides towards the reservoirs. The style of these arches seems to indicate that they were built by Sylla as an addition to the older temple precincts. One arch on the left hand, and all the twelve on the right, still remain intact. They were probably used as rooms for the slaves belonging to the temple.

Reservoirs. The two reservoirs, as may be seen by the brickwork of which they consist, were added after Sylla's time. They served to collect and keep the water which flowed from the fountains of the upper terraces, and to distribute it to those parts of the city which lay below the temple. The western reservoir, which can still be seen, is one of the most remarkable of such edifices now extant. It is 320 feet in length and 100 in width, and is divided internally into ten compartments, in the same manner as the Sette Sale at Rome, each communicating with the next to it by three apertures, and each lighted by two openings in the roof covered with circular well-mouths of stone. The interior walls of this reservoir are covered with the finest cement. On the exterior to the south, the walls are decorated with niches, one of which, with a square head, was intended to contain the inscription stating the names and titles of the builder of the reservoir.[1] The brickwork, which is similar to that of the Prætorian camp at Rome, and the fact that an inscription dated A.D. 18, when Tiberius was consul-designate for the third time, has been found near, seem to point to Tiberius as the builder. On the western side there are no niches, but a doorway, with a stair leading

[1] Cecconi, 'Storia di Palestrina,' p. 162.

down to the bottom of the reservoir, and ornamented with two brick half-columns of the Doric order.

From the area between the reservoirs just described, two staircases built by Sylla ascended to the level of the first principal terrace 1275 feet in breadth, containing two large basins for water, of rectangular shape, each 250 feet by 90 in size. They were intended for the purpose of the ceremonial ablutions commanded by the religious rites of the temple. That on the western side can still be seen in the Barberini garden, though it is now filled with rubbish. The rim or edging of these basins was of white mosaic. Terrace of cisterns.

Above this terrace two flights of stairs conducted to the next principal esplanade, which was of the same length as the first, but narrower. At the back of this esplanade, against the side of the hill, stood two magnificent halls, with an open area between them. The eastern hall is now entirely destroyed, but that on the western side, now serving as the kitchen of the modern seminario, is partly preserved. The front, which may be seen near the cathedral in the Piazza Tonda, was decorated with four Corinthian half-columns, the capitals of which still remain in their original position. The interior had seven recesses on each side, separated by half-columns and pilasters, and probably intended for statues. In front of the side recesses ran a low wall or podium, ornamented with triglyphs like a Doric frieze. These decorations are executed in a style which Nibby considers equal to that of any of the ancient Doric buildings now extant. At the end of the hall there was a large rectangular recess, with niches for statues. In the easternmost of these recesses was found the celebrated Prænestine mosaic, now in the Barberini Palace at Palestrina. The rest of the floor was composed of white mosaic work. Between the fronts of the two halls ran a row of columns, three of which still stand in their original positions in the wall of one of the chapels near the cathedral, and at the back of the area between them was a corridor with nine windows, some of which may still be seen in the court of the seminario. Terrace of halls.

Above the terrace of the halls rose the central grand terrace, supported by a great wall of polygonal masonry, which Central terrace.

Q 2

at the point called the Rifolta still stands at its full height. This terrace is now occupied by the Contrada del Borgo. On the eastern side it reached to the wall of the city, where the ancient gate, now closed, near the Porta Portella, stands. Two lofty arches stood, one at each end of the back of this terrace, containing fountains and statues.

It was upon this level, according to Nibby, that the original temple stood, before the alterations made by Sylla.

Terrace of Recesses. The whole of the two uppermost terraces were the work of the great dictator. They were supported by walls of opus incertum, and the lower of them contained two large semi-circular recesses, for the accommodation of the persons who came to consult the oracle. Hence it may be called the terrace of the recesses. The eastern recess is still remaining under the name of the Grotta Petrelli. It is supported in the interior by four Corinthian columns, and the roof preserves the traces of decorative designs in bronze. It is probable that the chamber in the centre, between the two recesses, was the spot where, as Cicero narrates, the mysterious Præstine lots were originally discovered by Numerius Suffucius, and where the statue of Fortuna, mentioned by him, stood. On each side of the recesses were arched chambers, probably appropriated to the priests of the temple and the interpreters of the lots.

Terrace of Hemicycle. Above the terrace of the recesses, rose that of the Hemicycle. This was divided into two parts, the lower consisting of a great rectangular sacrificial court, with porticoes surrounding it, and the upper, of a semicircular recess, somewhat similar to those which existed in the fora of the emperors at Rome, having at the back of it a smaller raised terrace on which stood the actual ædes, or shrine of the goddess Fortune. This must have been the place where, according to the legend as told by Cicero, the olive-tree which yielded honey grew, from which the casket was made for the Præstine lots.

Fragments of an inscription which are still visible on the frieze, surmounting two arched chambers under the hemicycle, seem to show that this part was rebuilt by the civic officials and the municipality, but at what period is not discoverable. No traces are now left of this part of the building except the

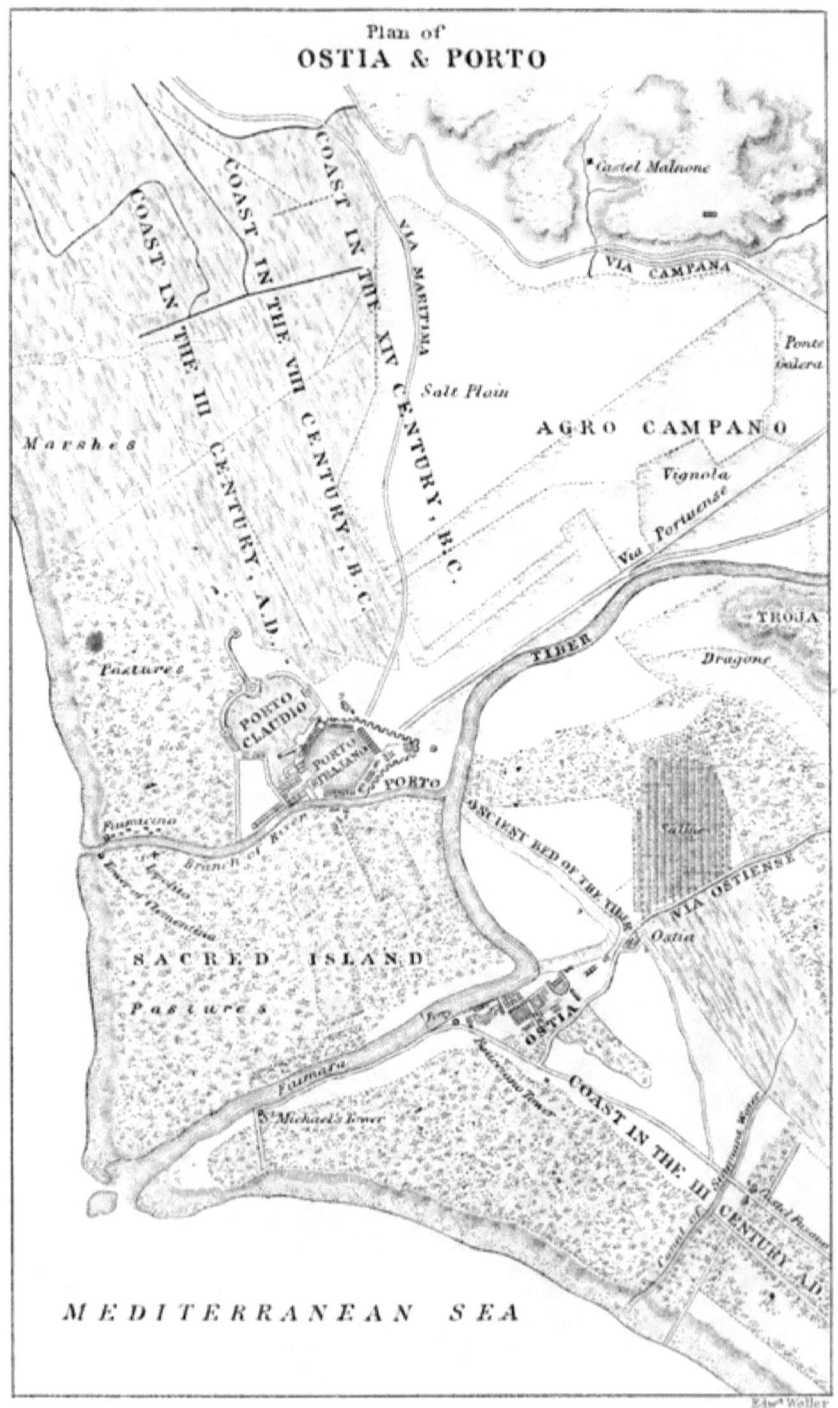

ground-plan of the hemicycle, which may be traced in front of the Barberini Palace, and a few columns belonging to the portico of the great square court. These stand in the public prison, and the house of the sacristan of S. Rosalia.[1]

The ancient town extended to a considerable distance beyond the precincts of the temple. Outside the Porta S. Francesco of the modern town, at about the distance of half a mile, are two huge reservoirs, similar to those described as placed at the foot of the Temple of Fortune; and in the Contrada degli Arconi is the cistern of an aqueduct. This, with other ruins near it, belonged to that part of the town founded by Sylla, which extended to a distance of a mile and a half from the lowest terrace of the great temple.

The forum of the city lay between the western reservoir of the temple, and the churches of S. Lucia and S. Madonna dell' Aquila. This is inferred from numerous inscriptions, and some commemorative pillars and altars found there. The Praenestine Registers of Verrius Flaccus were found in the Contrada delle Quadrelle, a mile and a half from this spot. They may, however, as Nibby suggests, have been moved from the forum, where we should naturally expect to find them.

(D) OSTIA AND PORTO.

Ostia is fifteen miles distant from the Porta di S. Paolo of Rome. The site of the old town is plainly discernible by the hillocks of rubbish with which it is covered, and the ruined brick walls which protrude here and there.

On approaching from the modern village, which is half a mile nearer Rome than the ruins of the old town, we pass between lines of tombs on each side of the road, similar to those which have been excavated at Pompeii. The tombs are very closely packed together, and of different sizes and shapes. On the left-hand side, two sarcophagi remain, with the names of Sex. Carminius Parthenopaeus Eq., and T. Flavius Verus Eq., and a terra-cotta inscription on the tomb of Flavia Caecilia, priestess of Isis at Ostia.[2]

---

[1] See 'Tempio di Fortuna Praenestina,' Thon and Nibby, Roma 1825.
[2] Mon. dell' Inst. VI. tav. xi. Ann. dell' Inst. 1857 p. 281.

At the end of this street of tombs, the gate of the city has been laid bare, and its foundations can be easily traced together with those of a guard-house on the left-hand side, having a rude tabula lusoria marked on the pavement, where the soldiers whiled away their time at some game resembling skittles.

The street which is then entered passes between the ruins of private houses, without anything more remarkable about them than a few common mosaic pavements and two fountains. The principal public buildings which have been excavated, are, I. The house of the priests of Mithras, in which a well-preserved altar still stands with the inscription:

C CAELIVS . HERMAEROS
ANTISTES . HVIVS . LOCI
FECIT

II. The Thermae, consisting of a large court, and several smaller side rooms for vapour-baths, with mosaic pavements of various designs. These baths may possibly be the lavacrum Ostiense of Antoninus Pius. The stamps on the bricks are said to be of the Antonine era.

III. A large rectangular brick edifice with three windows on each side. In the interior are the remains of ornamental niches, Corinthian capitals, and a marble cornice. The walls have rivets upon them, by which it appears that they were covered with a marble casing, and the magnificent block of African marble which serves as the threshold shows that the building was of a costly description. Traces have been found of a front chamber with a portico of grey granite columns. Whether this was a temple or not is uncertain, but it has been supposed that the arrangements in the interior would agree with such a supposition. The masonry may be assigned to the age of Trajan or Hadrian. The name of Vulcan has been usually given to this temple, which was at one end of the ancient forum. Many excavations have been made here within the last ten years, and some valuable works of art have been discovered, and numerous stores and shops of various kinds have been uncovered.

IV. The ruins of a theatre supposed by Nibby to be that

mentioned in the Acta Martyrum, near which S. Quiriacus and S. Maximus, and S. Archelaus, and a number of others were martyred. It is built partly of yellow and red brickwork, and partly of opus reticulatum, and apparently belongs to the restorations and additions made by Hadrian to the city.

V. The ruins of an extensive building, probably an emporium, on the bank of the river near Torre Bovacciano. In this place a great number of works of art were discovered by Fagan in 1797, showing the magnificent decorations with which the building was ornamented; and several inscriptions with the names of Severus and Caracalla found here are given by Nibby.[1]

Fiumicino at the present mouth of the Tiber, and Porto which stands at the site of the ports formed by Claudius and Trajan, may be reached from Rome by steamer down the river, or by carriage. The road which leads to Fiumicino and Porto leaves the city walls at the Porta Portese, and at about the fifth milestone reaches the celebrated grove of the Dea Dia, where the worship of the great collegiate priesthood of the Fratres Arvales was carried on. The railway to Civita Vecchia crosses the road at this spot, to which the modern names of the Monte delle Piche and the Vigna Ceccarelli are given. Discoveries of inscriptions had been made here since the year 1570, but no formal collection of them was made until the publication of Marini's great work in 1785. No effective investigations were, however, carried on until April 1868. The remains of a Christian cemetery were then disinterred on the slope of the hill above the Vigna Ceccarelli, where many of the marble tablets upon which the Arval Brothers had inscribed their records were found to have been used in the graves in lieu of coffins and as gravestones. One tomb was covered with a slab containing the records of the year A.D. 155, and numerous fragments of inscriptions were found scattered in all directions. The cemetery was ascertained to have been adjacent to an oratory founded by Pope Damasus (A.D. 1048), and a subterranean catacomb was found to have been formed, which

Grove of the Arval College.

---

[1] Nibby, Anal. II. 468.

is mentioned in the Acta Martyrum as the Cemeterium Generosae. The inscriptions obtained from this spot refer chiefly to the year A.D. 90, but some fragments belonging to the years 38, 87, and 59 were also found.

These inscriptions are of great interest both archæologically, as containing authentic particulars about the worship of the Arval Brothers, and the places at Rome or elsewhere in which it was held, and also historically, since many of them give the titles of eminent persons, or fix the dates of consuls and other ministers of state, and enable us thereby to correct and compare the statements of Tacitus and Suetonius with those of Dion Cassius. Many points of mythology are also illustrated by the mention of the divinities whom the college worshipped in their ritual.

An instance of the value of these inscriptions in determining the relative accuracy of Dion and Suetonius is afforded by the inscription belonging to the year A.D. 39, which gives us some historical facts about the reign of Caius, a portion of Roman history rendered difficult and obscure by the loss of the central books of the Annals of Tacitus. Suetonius states that the title of Augusta was conferred on Antonia by Claudius, whereas Dion on the contrary attributes the conference of this title to Caius. The inscription decides the question in favour of the account of Dion Cassius. Again, the date of the recognition of Caius by the Senate is fixed by the same inscription as having occurred on the 18th of March, and not on the 16th as recorded by Tacitus and Suetonius, nor the 26th, as Dion Cassius states. Many other interesting corrections or elucidations of the Latin historians will be found in Henzen's learned treatises, or in his articles in the 'Annali dell' Instituto' for 1867, and the 'Hermes' 1867. Besides the grove of the Arval College, which was an extensive wood, four buildings are mentioned in the Records—the Ædes Deæ Diæ, the Cesareum, the Tetrastylon and the Circus.

With regard to the position of these, Pellegrini is of opinion that the Circus was situated on the ridge of the hill on the western side of the Vigna Ceccarelli, in which place some remains apparently belonging to a circus have been found. Henzen leaves the site of the Circus undetermined, thinking that there is not sufficient evidence. The Tetrastylon and the Cesareum were supposed by Mommsen to have been names of the same building, but Henzen thinks that they are mentioned as separate places in the same inscription. The college feasts and meetings were held in one or other of these, which must therefore have been large enough to contain, besides the dining hall, an assembly-room, as the Brothers are said to have met there and to have sat in rows of seats. The Cesareum was a quadrangular building, as the form of the inscriptions which were attached to its walls seems to show, since they could not have been placed on a round surface. The temple of the Dea Dia stood upon a hill, for the priests are described as ascending in order to perform the sacrifices, and descending afterwards. Yet there are no vestiges of a building upon the top of the hill. Henzen therefore concludes that the ruins of the round building, upon which the modern Casa rustica in the Ceccarelli vineyard is placed, must have belonged to this Ædes. It was not decorated with columns but with Corinthian pilasters, and the inscriptions were affixed to the interior until the year 81, when it became necessary from want of space to place them on the pedestals of the columns.[1]

Beyond the site of the Arval Chapel, the road passes by the relics of the papal palace of La Magliana, and then along a causeway six miles in length to Porto. The site of the ancient Portus Trajani on the right branch of the Tiber is now occupied by the town of Porto, mainly consisting of the cathedral, the Villa Pallavicini, and some farm buildings. The sea has here continuously receded for many centuries, and the river deposits of sand and marl have extended. Fiumicino at the present mouth of the river is two miles distant from Porto, and its site was entirely covered by the sea at the time when Claudius, and Trajan after him, constructed their new ports. The large marshy tract to the north of Porto marks the site of the port of Claudius. The hexagonal basin of Trajan lies between this marsh and the town of Porto.

Porto.

[1] Lanciani, 'Scavi nel Bosco Sacro,' Roma 1868.

It is not at all clear when the right arm of the Tiber, or rather the canal which now serves for communication between the sea and the Tiber proper, assumed its present shape. Inundations and occasional repairs and alterations have changed its course, and the constant retreat of the sea must have lengthened it considerably.

Nibby's opinion is that, besides the large harbour, Claudius constructed an inner basin between the harbour and the old course of the river. Into this basin he cut a canal from the bend of the river near modern Ostia, and thus allowed the superfluous waters of the Tiber to escape through the harbour, and at the same time gained a supply of water for his docks. The inscription found in 1837, and now placed by the roadside near the Villa Pallavicini, alludes to this canal. The words of this inscription seem to show that the primary object of the canal was to supply the port with water, and that the advantage of preventing inundations at Rome was only secondary. Trajan probably enlarged and reconstructed the inner basin of Claudius, and surrounded it with the massive quays and warehouses, the ruins of which still remain. This inner basin is referred to by Juvenal.

At the same time the canal was probably enlarged, and it is to this enlargement that Pliny alludes when he speaks of the canal formed by the most provident of all emperors.[1]

Ruins at Torre Paterno.

Passing from Ostia along the sea coast through the woods of Castel Fusano to Torre Paterno, we find the ruins of a large villa, which have been supposed by some to belong to Pliny's Laurentinum. But they are more probably the relics of an imperial villa mentioned by Herodian as the retreat to which Commodus withdrew, by the advice of his physicians, at the time of the great plague in Rome, in the year 187. The neighbourhood of Laurentum was recommended, says the historian, on account of its being cooler than Rome, and also because it was shaded with large woods of laurel and bay trees, the strong scent from which was supposed to counteract the influence of the deadly malaria which was devastating the capital.[2] The present ruins at

---

[1] Plin. Ep. viii. 17.   [2] Herodian i. 12, 2.

Torre Paterno consist of brick walls in two styles, one of which Nibby refers to the age of Nero, and the other to the reign of Commodus or Severus. The central building, which contained the grand suite of rooms, is the only part where work of the first century, analogous to that of Nero's buildings at Rome, is to be seen; the rest, says Nibby, is composed of various courtyards in the style of the Antonine era, which have been altered and partly concealed by later modern edifices. On one side of the ruins are two large cisterns, supplied by an aqueduct which comes from the Tenimento la Santola. The brickwork of this is apparently contemporaneous with other works which we know to have belonged to the age of Commodus or Severus as having very thin bricks and a great quantity of mortar. Near these reservoirs is an enclosed space which was probably a courtyard or garden of a rectangular shape. On the north side it has some ruins in the mode of construction called opus mixtum of the fourth century; and on the east is the principal part of the villa built of large and thick triangular bricks, with thin layers of mortar beautifully laid, and evidently of an early date. On the west there is a large dining-hall looking towards the sea, like that described in Pliny's Laurentinum. Various other rooms and the foundations of a tower can be traced on the sites occupied by the modern guardhouse and the Chapel of S. Filippo.[1]

(E) TIBUR.

The Via Valeria or Tiburtina leading to Tivoli, the ancient Tibur, now leaves Rome at the Porta S. Lorenzo. Traces of the polygonal pavement of the old road can be seen at intervals along the modern road to Tivoli, especially between the eighth and ninth milestones, and here and there elsewhere. In the Basilica of S. Lorenzo, a mile from the gate, are many ancient fragments of architecture. The Ponte Mammolo, by which the Anio is crossed at three and a half miles from Rome, is modern and there are scarcely any relics of the old bridge. Here and there on the road are the naked cores of tombs, but nothing of any interest offers itself to an archaeologist until

[1] Nibby, Anal. ii. p. 205.

the Aquæ Albulæ are reached. Some few remains of an ancient building, which may have belonged to the Thermæ here, have been discovered. They are now built into the walls of a modern farmhouse. These ruins may have belonged to the Thermæ of Agrippa, which Augustus frequented.

The ancient quarries of travertine mentioned by Strabo, whence the stone of the Coliseum came, lie on the right of the road beyond the Solfatara, and the modern quarries on the left. The road then crosses the Anio over an ancient bridge still called the Ponte Lucano, from Marcus Plautius Lucanus, a Tiburtine magistrate, whose memory is preserved in an inscription discovered upon the ancient fourteenth milestone on this road.

The bridge was originally composed of three travertine arches, of which the one next to the left bank remains entire. The central arch has been restored with masonry of the sixth century, similar to that in the Ponte Nomentano and the Ponte Salario. The arch on the right bank was restored in the fifteenth century, and the whole bridge was repaired again about 1836. This bridge was broken down by Totila when he was encamped at Tibur, and Nibby thinks that he destroyed the middle arch, which was then restored by Narses.

Tomb of the Plautian family. Just on the other side of the bridge is the tomb of the gens Plautia, well known from numerous paintings and photographs. It is very similar to that of Cæcilia Metella on the Appian Road, and to the Mausoleum of Hadrian, in its main features. A cylindrical tower of travertine, based on a square foundation, and capped with a cone, was the original design, but a mediæval tower built upon the top now disfigures it.

Two inscriptions placed in a projecting front with Ionic pilasters record the names of M. Plautius Silvanus, consul with Augustus in the year B.C. 2, and his son Ti. Plautius Silvanus, prefect of the city in A.D. 73. A third inscription, which is now destroyed, commemorated a P. Plautius Pulcher. The longer inscription is given with notes in Wilmann's Inscr. Lat. No. 1145. The person whose memory it preserves was the pontifex who officiated at the re-

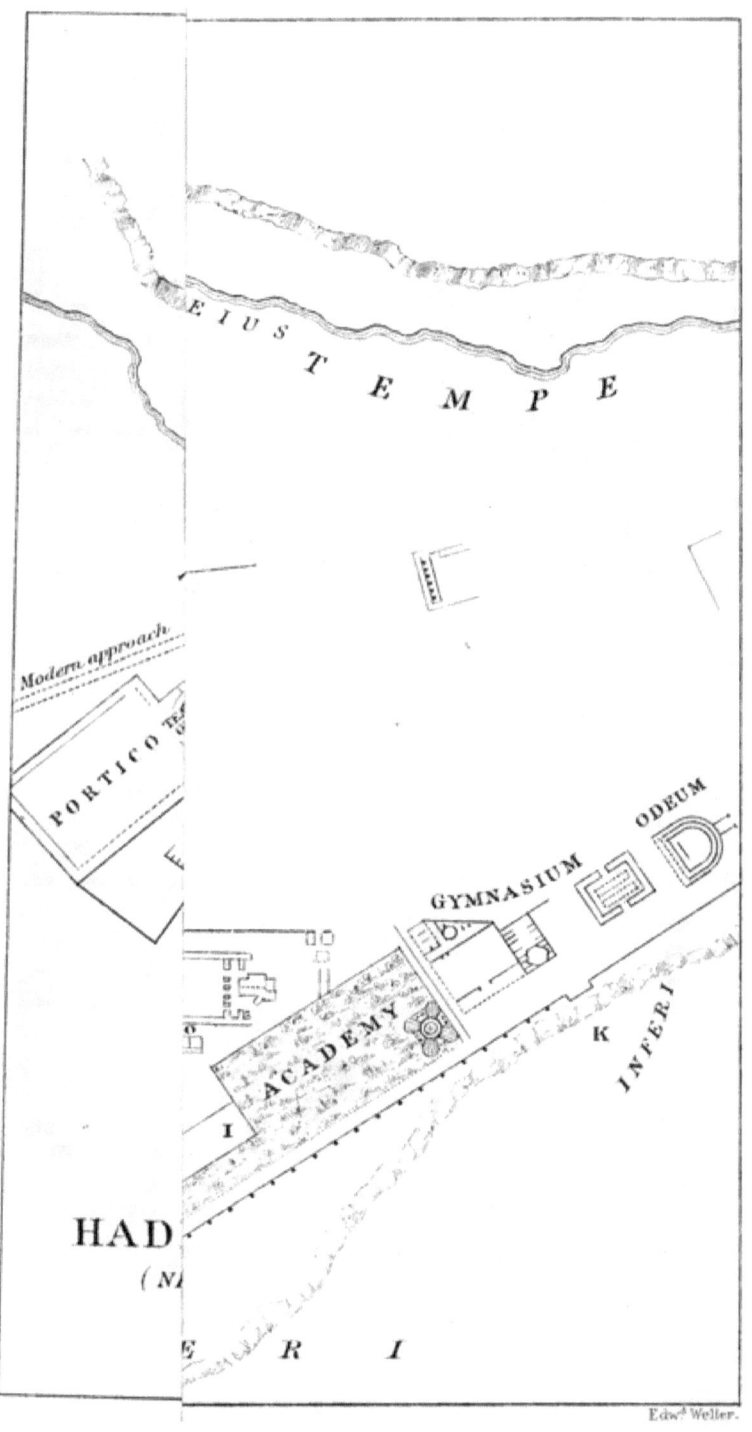

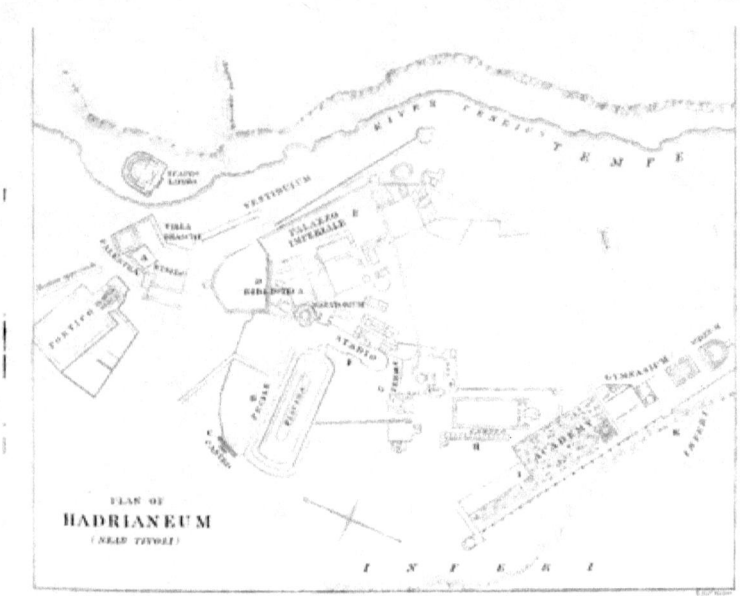

building of the Capitoline Temple in A.D. 70, as recorded by
Tacitus.

Beyond the Ponte Lucano to the right are the ruins of Hadrian's great Tiburtine Villa. They occupy the slopes of a hill of volcanic tufa, which may be called an outlying part of Monte Affliano, extending for about three miles in a direction from south-east to north-west. The various levels afforded by the ground have been formed into terraces adapted to the buildings they were intended to support by means of substructions, which in some places are of vast solidity and gigantic height. "From these terraces," says Nibby, "the views are most varied and picturesque. On one side the horizon is bounded by the pointed heights of the Montes Corniculani, and by the ridges of the Peschiatore, the Ripoli, and the Affliano, and on the other, the eye ranges over the gently undulating expanse of the Ager Romanus, from which rise the towers of the Eternal City; while beyond, the long streak of light reflected from the waters of the Etruscan and Laurentine Sea seems to encircle the whole with a silvery zone. The situation of the villa is open to the healthy breezes of the west wind, but is sheltered by the mountains from the fury of the north wind, the piercing chills of the north-east, and the unwholesome hot summer blasts of the south."

<small>Hadrian's Villa.</small>

The high ground on which the villa stands rises between two valleys, which may be called from their position the north and south valleys. They run down into the plain through which the Anio cuts its bed. The northern valley has been artificially altered, with the view of increasing its picturesque appearance, by cutting the sides so as form perpendicular cliffs of reddish stone. The tints of these rocks, the soft verdure of the plants and trees which grow luxuriantly upon them, the bright colours of the wild flowers scattered here and there, and the lovely hills which rise as a screen behind them, give this valley such a character of soothing and enchanting retirement and beauty, that it has been universally regarded as the spot to which the name of the Vale of Tempe was given by the emperor. The southern valley is less deep and bold, and from its monotonous and

severe aspect it may perhaps have been the spot where
Hadrian placed his imitation of the infernal regions.[1]

The brook which runs at the bottom of the northern valley
(Fosso dell' Acqua Ferrata) has received the name of the
Peneius from antiquaries, and that in the southern valley is
called Fosso di Risicoli by the modern inhabitants. These
streams are now very scantily supplied with water, but in
ancient times, when the villa was watered by a constant flow
from its aqueducts, they must have been of considerable
volume. The ruins, now overgrown with clumps of cypress
and other trees, extend for a space of seven miles in circumference, and in the middle ages were known as Tivoli
Vecchio, from a vague and unfounded idea that the ancient
city of Tibur stood here. It has been remarked that the
Coliseum is strikingly characteristic of the Flavian emperors
who planned and executed it, and with equal truth it may be
said that the Tiburtinum of Hadrian gives a marvellous
picture of the many-sided genius of the great man who was
at once the ruler of the whole known world and had travelled
throughout his vast domains from Britain to the Euphrates,
organising and controlling everywhere, and at the same time
showing an appreciation of and value for literature, philosophy, and the fine arts, which was generally foreign to
the Roman character. Hadrian constructed in his villa at
Tibur a panorama of all the sights which had struck him
most in his world-wide travels, in order that he might in this
realm of enchantment, when no longer able to travel, have
the sights and thoughts in which he had taken such pleasure,
revived for his imagination to feed upon. Considering the
size and magnificence of the place, which almost resembles a
town in its vast extent, it is surprising that so few notices of
it should be found among the Roman historians and bio-
graphers. Dion Cassius, or rather his epitomiser Xiphilinus,
does not even mention it, and Spartianus and Aurelius Victor
pass it over without such special remark as we should expect.
As, however, a great part of the building consisted of the
familiar Thermæ, stadia, theatres and gymnasium, which were
constructed in every large Roman villa, they were perhaps not

[1] Hist. Aug. Hadrian 26. Aur. Vict. Epit. xiv. Tertull. Apol. 5.

noticed, as matters of course, and only the peculiarities of the villa were recorded. After Hadrian's return to Rome at the end of his last journey to the East in A.D. 135, he resigned the care of the empire to Lucius Ælius Verus and retired to this villa, which had probably been built during his absence, and may have been begun in 125 when he returned to Rome from his first journey, and finished during the last three years of his life from 135 to 138.

This opinion as to the date at which the villa was built is confirmed by the stamps found on the bricks, which range from the year 123 to the year A.D. 137, and that the ruins belong to Hadrian's villa is sufficiently attested by universal tradition, and by the number of statues of Antinous, and other works of art found here unquestionably belonging to the reign of Hadrian.

The ruins contain specimens of almost every kind of construction. The most ancient part is a wall of opus incertum, composed of small polygonal fragments of tufa, which stands near the Casino Fede. This wall is probably a remnant of some older villa rustica or farmhouse which occupied the site before Hadrian's time, and may have belonged to the gens Ælia. It apparently belongs to the first half of the first century B.C. The most common mode of construction is opus reticulatum, with squares of tawny coloured tufa cut in the valley adjoining and bonded at the corners with blocks of the same rock, or with red bricks. In those parts of the buildings, which require great durability from being exposed to the action of water, brickwork is used throughout. The Greek theatre and parts of the academy are built of small squared blocks of tufa, or in some cases of irregular fragments of tufa resembling the later opera Saracenesca. These are sometimes strengthened with bands of reticulated work. In most cases the outer covering of the walls has been removed, especially where it consisted of marble slabs. Some of the stucco ornaments are still very beautiful and well preserved.

Each part of the buildings is complete in itself, but they do not seem to have been arranged on any general plan, and now that the roads which conducted from one part to another have disappeared, they present a confused mass which requires some careful attention to unravel. I have been obliged to confine myself to a very general and cursory account of each main feature. To notice every detail would be far beyond the compass of this book. In Ligorio's plan 334 different parts of the villa are marked and separately described, and he spent a year in his investigation of the ruins.

Spartianus gives us the names of the Lyceum, the Academy, the Prytaneum, the Canopus, the Pœcile, the Tempe and the Inferi as the parts of the villa made by Hadrian in imitation of their foreign originals. To these Ligorio has added the name Cynosarges found upon a brick stamp. The sites of the Canopus, the Pœcile, the Academy, Tempe, and the Inferi may be said to be ascertained with tolerable certainty, but those of the Lyceum and Prytaneum have not been discovered.

The other names given by antiquarians to the different buildings are generally founded upon some definite evidence drawn from their shape and situation, and are probably upon the whole fairly applicable. They are the Theatres, the Palæstra, the Nymphæum, the Library, the Imperial Palace, the Hospitals, the Stadium, the Camp, and the Thermæ.

Proceeding from north to south, the ruins may be divided, for the convenience of description, into ten grand groups —A, the Palæstra, including the Greek and Latin Theatres and the Nymphæum; B, the Pœcile; C, the Guards' Barracks; D, the Library; E, the Imperial Palace; F, the Stadium; G, the Thermæ; H, the Canopus; I, the Academy, including the third theatre or Odeum; K, the Inferi. In giving these general divisions, some attempt is made to represent the parts of the villa as they were in Hadrian's time. The ruins are in such different states of preservation—some being entirely destroyed and the ground-plan barely traceable, while others are almost entire—that their real relative importance is completely obscured. The modern alleys and walks also create much confusion, and render the recognition of the ancient arrangement much more difficult.

The ancient grand entrance to the grounds was at the north-western end of the ruins, on the road towards Tibur, about a quarter of a mile beyond the Ponte Lucano. It seems to have consisted of two large pedestals of white marble, between which the carriage-road passed, and which were pierced with arched passages for the footways on each side. One of these is still traceable in the Vigna Gentili, and has the remains of a bas-relief upon it, while the other has been destroyed, and its corresponding bas-relief placed in the Villa Albani at Rome. This gateway has been imitated by the architect of the gateway at the old Villa Borghese. It is erroneously called a tomb by Piranesi and Ligorio (see Piranesi, Ant. Rom. tom. ii. tav. 39.)

The modern entrance to the ruins is at the gate of the Villa Braschi, and leads, through an avenue of cypress-trees, in a direction at right angles to the ancient road of approach. The avenue runs across a space which was formerly a large quadrilateral court, 350 feet by 250 feet, surrounded with porticoes, attached to the theatre which stands a little to the side at the end of the avenue. The ancient road from the Ponte Lucano entered this court at the northern angle. The porticoes have now nearly disappeared, but part of them was remaining in Ligorio's time. They served the same purposes as the great colonnades behind the Theatres of Pompey and Balbus at Rome. The theatre is an oval building, sunk in the slope of the rising ground, the southern side containing the seats for spectators, and the northern being occupied by the orchestra and scena, which has a stage in the form of a long and narrow parallelogram. The plan corresponds exactly to the description by Vitruvius of a Greek theatre, and has, therefore, been called the Greek Theatre by the antiquaries. The Greeks had the orchestra wider and the actual stage much narrower than the Latins. Fragments of the travertine substructions of the scena still remain.

At some distance from this theatre, towards the east, and on the other side of the stream which runs along the Valley of Tempe, is the Latin Theatre, so called because the stage is much broader than that of the theatre just described. Externally it was surrounded with arched porticoes decorated, like the Theatre of Marcellus at Rome, with half-columns.

There were probably two tiers of these arches, corresponding to the two divisions of seats. At the sides of the scena there were rooms for the use of the actors and for the machinery, and behind the scena are three rooms, probably corresponding to the three doors in the wall behind the stage. The spectators' seats are turned towards the south, contrary to the rules of Vitruvius.

Between the two theatres there is a natural rise in the ground, which has been further heightened by the rubbish heaped upon the spot. The ruins here occupy a space in the form of a trapezium, the largest side of which lies towards the north-west, and the shortest towards the south-west. They are now covered with modern buildings belonging to the Villa Braschi.

Palæstra. The northern angle of these ruins shows the remains of a quadrilateral area surrounded by a covered way; and at the eastern angle there is another smaller court, surrounded with a portico, which has a double row of columns on the south-west side. This court is called the Palæstra by Ligorio and Piranesi, and it is supposed by them that the double portico was intended to be used in bad weather, when the athletes could not take their exercise in the unsheltered part of the court. Several statues of athletes, the colossal bust of Isis, now in the Museo Chiaromonti, and a statue of Ceres, were found here. There is a suite of rooms on the north-west side, intended, perhaps, for anointing-rooms, dust rooms, or sparring-courts. On the southern side there is a spacious recess, with niches for statues, and attached to it are two large halls, in the form of a Greek cross, with small recesses at the sides, still retaining some marks of their ancient decorations in stucco and paint. The western angle of these ruins is conjectured to have been the site of the Xystus or covered Palæstra, a cloistered court, with a small square opening in the centre.

The ruins of the Nymphaeum lie on the south side of the Palæstra, and are connected with it by some chambers in which the stucco ornaments are still well preserved, and show what elegance of design and workmanship was bestowed even on the inferior parts of the villa. The curved basin of the Nymphæum can be traced, though it is now overgrown with trees, and some of the niches still covered with stucco-work remain. The western side of one of the adjacent rooms, now used as a granary, is ornamented with niches, and Nibby thinks that this, which was the back of the Nymphæum, was arranged so as to present a fountain supplied from the main pipe of the aqueduct. A similar arrangement, he says, may be seen in the remains of the Nymphæum at Ampiglione. The great vase now at Warwick Castle came from Hadrian's Villa.

The Pœcile lies to the south of the Nymphæum. Between them is a reservoir and the remains of a fountain belonging to some building now entirely destroyed.

The Athenian Pœcile, of which this is an imitation, was a portico, the walls of which were decorated with the paintings of Polygnotus and Micon. From the description given of it by Pausanias, the Athenian building appears to have been a portico with three sides at least, on one of which the battle of Oenoe was represented; on the second, and longest, the wars of Theseus against the Amazons, and the council of the Greek chiefs after the capture of Troy; and on the third, the battle of Marathon. It thus appears that one of the sides was much longer than the others; and this is the case with the ruin in the Villa of Hadrian, which has three sides, one, 640, on the north, and the others, on the east and west, each 240 feet in length. In Ligorio's time, 1550, a part of the porticoes, which were of brick, still remained, and some of the paintings corresponding to the Athenian pattern. It is not certain whether there was a similar wall and portico on the southern side. The wall of the northern side, which is the longest, still remains entire. It had a portico on the exterior, which terminated in two circular buildings; and in the centre was the principal entrance to the Pœcile. The present entrance is modern. Both the eastern and western sides are slightly curved. The former contains a recess in the centre connected with the buildings behind. In the centre was an open reservoir of the same shape as the building surrounding it. On the western and southern sides the area of the Pœcile is supported by substructions of masonry, against which are built a number of soldiers' rooms commonly called the Cento Camarelle. At the corner towards the south-west is a public washhouse, the tubes of which are still in good preservation.

Attached to the north-eastern corner of the Pœcile is a fine building, in the form of a recess, with a semicircular niche turned towards the north, which, from the connection of the Stoic philosophy with the Stoa Pœcile at Athens, has been called the Temple or School of the Stoics. It was possibly a hall for conversation and discussion.

Opening from this school, towards the north-east, is a building in the form of two concentric circles. Between the two circular parts there was a canal filled with water. This edifice was probably a swimming-bath. It appears to have been very highly ornamented with precious marbles and sculptures, most of which were taken to Rome by Cardinal Alessandro Farnese, and others to Tivoli by Cardinal Ippolito d'Este. The ruin commonly goes by the name of Theatrum Maritimum. A little farther to the north east is a quadrilateral court, 200 feet wide, which was surrounded by a portico with Corinthian columns. On the north-west side of this court are the buildings usually supposed to belong to the library, and called the Greek and Latin libraries. They consist of a large number of rooms, more or less preserved, which may have been ante-rooms and chambers for the attendants and librarians. In the centre of the north-western side of the court is a well-preserved Nymphæum, and on the north-east a long corridor with windows towards the south, which may be called a Helio Caminus, or room for basking in the sun, from its resemblance to the place so called by Pliny at his Laurentine villa. The ruins to the north-east of these, towards the Valley of Tempe, are thought by Nibby to be the remains of a suite of rooms belonging to one wing of the imperial palace, but their plan is very imperfectly known.

Library.

The great mass of the imperial apartments were farther to the south-east, and were grouped round three large courts of dazzling magnificence. The most splendid of these, which afforded spoil for generations of plunderers, is called by

Palace.

Piranesi, from the richness of its decorative work, the Piazza d'Oro. Round the courts were numberless suites of rooms and several large recesses, a basilica, and a great hall now called Eco Corintio, formerly supported on vast granite columns, and cased with slabs of the choicest marbles.

The Stadium lies in a direction at right-angles to the southern side of the Pœcile. The curved end is towards the south. Between the swimming-bath and the northern, or square end of the Stadium, are some bath-rooms for the use of the athletes, and on the west side stands a temple surrounded by a sacred enclosure formed by two vast semicircular walls ornamented with niches. On the eastern side are more rooms, and a magnificent quadrilateral covered way. Stadium.

The Thermæ stand between the Stadium and the Canopus. Numerous pipes and conduits for water, and also the arrangement of the various parts of the buildings, show that they have been rightly placed here. There seem to have been two distinct sets of bath-rooms, which are generally called the Terme virili and the Terme muliebri by the Italian antiquaries. The northern group of buildings is connected with the curved end of the Stadium, and contains the usual number of halls and an elliptical Laconicum. The Laconicum of the southern wing is circular, and is connected with a grand central hall similar to that in the Baths of Caracalla at Rome. Thermæ.

The place called Canopus lies to the south of the Thermæ, and close to a mass of buildings now utterly destroyed, but in Piranesi's time thought to be a vestibule of the villa. The Canopus itself consists of an oblong pool of water or euripus excavated in the tufa, with a row of buildings on the west side, and a magnificent nymphæum at the southern end, containing a great number of niches for statuary, and holes for jets of water. At the back of the Nymphæum is a hall called the Sacrarium, in which it is supposed the statue of Serapis stood. A passage of Strabo explains the idea which Hadrian had in forming this canal and Nymphæum. He says that on the grand festival of Serapis, whose temple and oracle were at Canopus, 120 stadia from Alexandria, immense crowds of men and women go down to Canopus from Alexandria by Canopus.

boats on the canal, on the banks of which are pleasant houses of entertainment, where the worshippers stop on their way to feast and dance.[1] The long, broad pool was intended to represent the Canopic canal, and the rooms ranged along the side, the houses of refreshment. A confirmation of this is derived from the character of the statues found here which were almost all those of Egyptian deities.

Academy.   To the south-west of the Canopus rise the immense substructions, 1755 feet in length, which supported the highest terrace on this side of the villa. They extend as far as the square tower called Rocca Bruna in Ligorio's plan. This terrace and hill are supposed to have been the imitation of the Athenian Academy mentioned by Spartianus. There was a gymnasium here, the ruins of which are to be seen in a vineyard at the southern end of the hill, consisting of a large court, a circular temple, and a large recess. Beyond these there was a large square block of buildings supposed by Nibby to have been used for the students and masters of the School of Art maintained by Hadrian, and beyond this again was a spacious Odeum or theatre for musical performances. The raised seat of this is now converted into a vineyard, but the stage is still well preserved. There were, as in the Odeum of Catania, two divisions, and at the top of the central division was a round temple dedicated to the presiding genius of the Odeum; just as in the Theatre of Pompey the Chapel of Victory stood above the seats.

Close to this Odeum are the vast subterranean passages supposed to be the Inferi which Spartianus mentions. The depth at which these lie is only fourteen feet, but they occupy a trapezoidal area, the longest side of which is about one thousand and fifty feet, and the shortest two hundred. Most of these corridors are excavated like catacombs in the natural rock. A brick stamped with the name Cynosarges was found near the aqueduct which runs to the south of the Inferi. There are two other names found in Spartianus, the Lyceum, and the Prytaneum, and Piranesi identifies the Lyceum with a ruined portico at a little distance to the south

[1] Strabo, xvii. 17.

of the Inferi, and the Prytaneum with some more extensive ruins to the south-east.

After Constantine's time, the Villa of Hadrian remained in a desolate state, and was abandoned to the caprices of the imbecile Cæsars, who tormented the empire in the fourth and fifth centuries, and to occasional visits from the plundering hordes of Goths, Vandals, and Heruli, who successively ravaged the neighbouring country. In the middle of the sixth century it was completely pillaged and ruined. In the Gothic wars of 546–556 Totila took Tibur after a siege of some months, and revenged himself for the resistance of the Isaurian garrison by putting all to the sword without sparing even the bishop. At the same time Totila broke down all the bridges on the Anio. During that long siege, the Villa of Hadrian with its enormous halls, its vast ranges of rooms, and its advantageous and commanding site at the junction of several roads, offered convenient quarters to the barbarian king and his host. It may be imagined what devastation such tenants would inflict upon the place. In the sixth century the villa fell more and more into ruins; to the disasters of the Gothic wars were added those incurred during the Lombard wars under Astulf. The Lombards were a more savage horde than the Goths, and their object was to destroy the Roman empire utterly, and to divide Italy into dukedoms. These barbarians attacked Rome many times, and ravaged the Campagna, but Astulf distinguished himself above all the rest in these incursions, massacring and burning everywhere without distinction. As we hear that he was encamped near Tivoli, we may conclude that the Villa of Hadrian suffered severely in or about the year 755.

The wars between emperors and popes, and the quarrels between the factions in Rome itself which followed, injured Rome perhaps rather more than the cities of the Campagna. But the greatest damage of all was done to the villa by its being made the quarry whence the churches, the monasteries, and the houses of the wealthy Tiburtines were decorated with marbles, columns, and costly stonework, and when these were filled and could hold no more of the innumerable marble sculptures and statues, they were condemned to the lime-kiln and converted into mortar. After the revival of letters and arts in the fifteenth century, the lamentations poured out in the time of Pius II. (A.D. 1458) over the ruins of the villa are most pathetic. "The lofty vaults of the temples are still standing, and the wonderful columns of the cloisters and magnificent porticoes. The swimming-baths and Thermae can be traced, where the water of the Anio once mitigated the summer heats. But the hand of time has defaced all these, and the walls once draped with embroidered tapestry and cloth of gold are now clad with ivy; the thorns and briar grow where tribunes sat in purple robes, and serpents crawl, in their kings' chambers." In spite of the existence here and there of such love of antiquity, the burning of the Tiburtine marbles into lime continued throughout the sixteenth century, and the levelling of the ground for cultivation has gone on even to the present century.[1]

The same fate attended all the other grand monuments of the Campagna. Rutilius Numatianus, writing probably in 417 in the reign of Honorius, speaks of the buildings of Rome and the aqueducts of the Campagna as if they were still uninjured, but he prefers to return to his native home in Gaul by sea, on account of the bad state of the roads on the coast caused by the Gothic devastations.

Tibur.

Ascending from Hadrian's Villa to the point where the Anio issues from a valley dividing the Æquian from the Sabine Mountains, we find the river winding round a considerable hill, partly clothed with groves of olive, and rising to the height of 830 feet. At the back of this hill the river has forced a passage for itself through the limestone rocks which threaten to impede its exit from the upper valley, and falls in a tremendous cataract down a precipitous cliff of 320 feet in height to the lower level. The water is strongly charged with carbonate of lime, which is constantly being deposited in the shape of masses of travertine in the channels through which the stream runs, especially where the water, in consequence of the violent agitation caused by its rapid descent, parts quickly with the carbonic acid gas contained in it. The course of the stream is from time to time blocked up by its own

[1] Nibby, Anal. iii. 655.

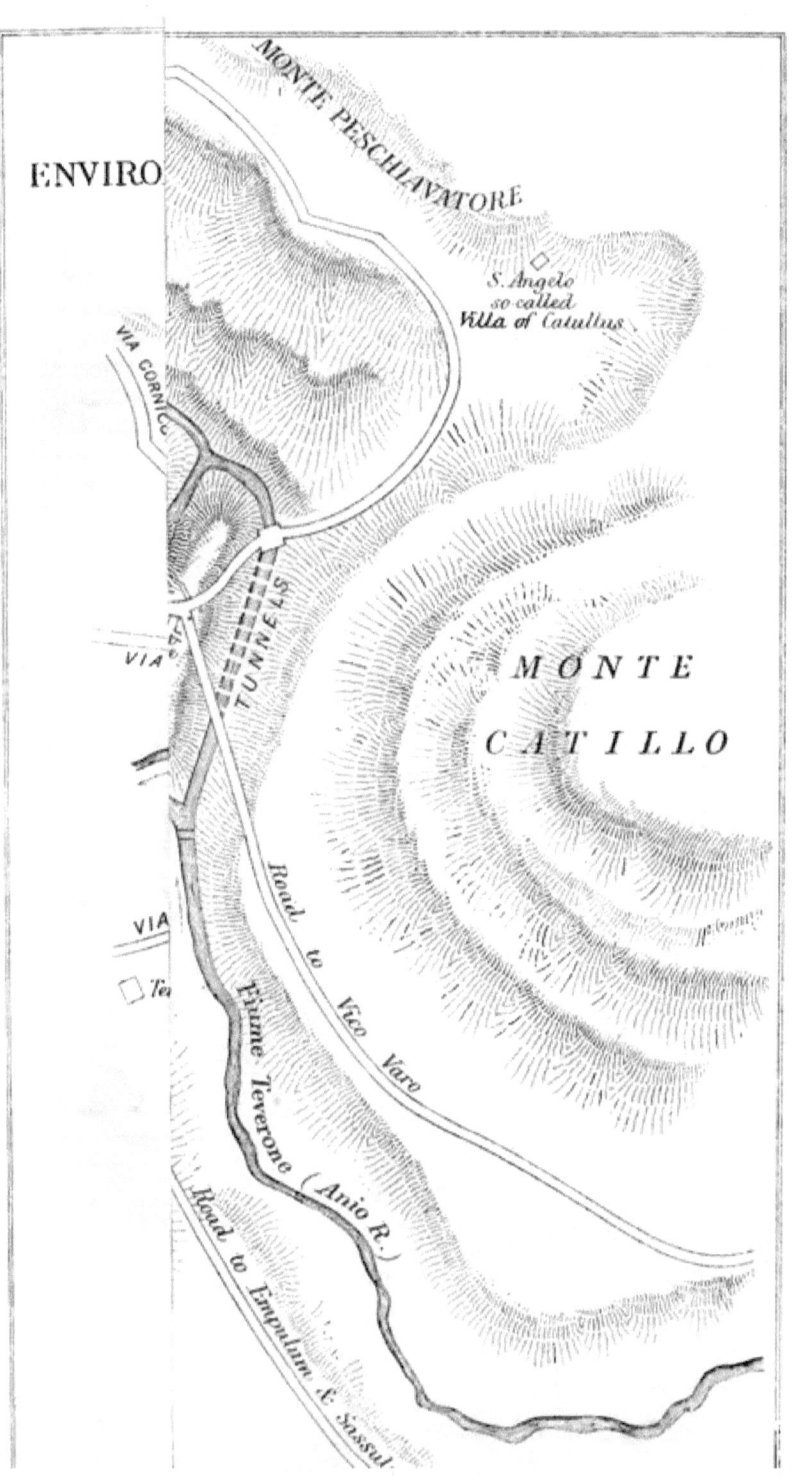

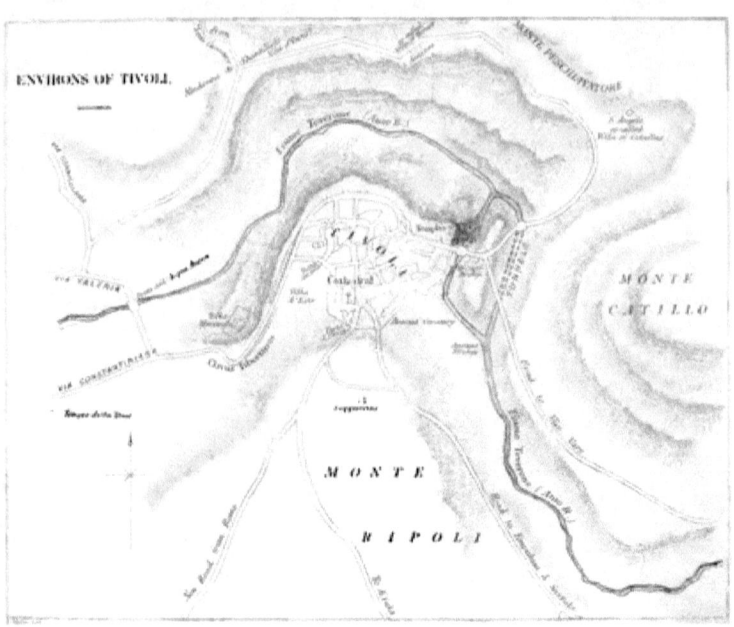

formations of stone, and it is forced to open new passages for itself. From this cause the city of Tibur, which stands on the hill, close to the point where the river falls to its lower level, has always been subject to violent and dangerous inundations. The great inundation of 1826 proved so formidable that it was at once resolved to divert the course of part of the river and provide it with an artificial outlet. This was effected by boring two tunnels through Monte Catillo on the east of the city, through which any rush of water can be allowed to pass and fall harmlessly into the lower valley. A part of the river water is always allowed to pass through these tunnels, and forms at their lower end a magnificent cascade. Another part passes under the bridge called Ponte S. Gregorio and then rushes through a fantastic grotto of travertine blocks called by the local guides Grotta di Nettuno, and joins the stream from the tunnels at the bottom of the valley. A third portion of the Anio is diverted just above the bridge into canals apparently of very ancient date, which, passing completely through the centre of the town, are used as the motive power of water-mills and factories of various kinds, and then fall again into the main stream at various points of the romantic cliffs on the western hill side. These form the wreaths of "snow white foam" so celebrated as the cascades of the Anio, and explain perfectly the expression of Horace:

> O headlong Anio, O Tiburnian groves,
> And orchards saturate with shifting streams.

But few traces of the ancient walls of the city are left. Nibby is however doubtless right in saying that there can be no question about their course along the northern and eastern sides of the city, where the brow of the hill is steep and perfectly adapted for defence by a wall placed on the edge of the rocky valley of the Anio. The citadel was probably situated in the quarter called Castro Vetere—where the two temples commonly called the temples of the Sibyl and of Drusilla stand, for it is plain that some pains have been taken to isolate this from the remainder of the site. On the western side the limit of the ancient walls is marked by the

Temple of Vesta at Tibur.

old gate, and by the fragments of walls which still exist at the point where the direct road from Rome enters the city by the modern Porta del Colle. The course of the walls then excludes the Villa d'Este, and runs across the hill to the Church of the Annunziata and the Porta Santa Croce and the citadel built by Pius II. on the site of the ancient amphitheatre. From thence the walls passed in a straight line down to the river near the Church of S. Bartolommeo. The ancient town did not extend to the right bank of the Anio.

Two ancient temples are still standing in tolerable preservation at Tibur. The first of these is a small round temple perched on the very edge of the precipitous ravine through which the Anio dashes. It has been protected against the violence of the furious torrent by massive substructions, which apparently existed in ancient times and have often been renewed. Ten of the eighteen columns which formerly surrounded the inner chamber still remain. *Temple of Vesta.*

The details of this temple are rather peculiar in style, and show an originality of invention very rare in Roman architecture. The columns have Attic bases, but the grooves of the fluting are cut in a style which is neither Doric nor Ionic. They terminate above in an abrupt horizontal line, and reach at the foot of the column quite down to the base without any intermediate cylinder. The capitals exhibit a fantastic variety of the Corinthian order, having the second row of acanthus leaves nearly hidden behind the first, and a lotus blossom as the decoration of the abacus. The frieze is ornamented with the skulls of oxen and festoons, in the loops of which are rosettes and pateræ placed alternately. The inner chamber, which is built of opus incertum, is partly destroyed, but the lower half of the door and a window still remain.

From the above description it will be seen that the architecture of the temple appears to belong to the end of the Republican era, but the inscription on the architecture gives us no further hint of the exact date, as the whole of it; with the exception of the words L. CELLIO. L. F., has disappeared. The most probable conjecture as to the deity to whom it was dedicated is that based upon the fact that Vesta was worshipped at Tibur, as is shown not only by two inscriptions found near the spot, but also by the mediaeval name of this quarter of the town. The form of the temple also confirms such an opinion.

Temple of Albunea.

The second temple stands quite close to this round building, and is now consecrated as the Church of S. Giorgio. Its shape was that of a pseudoperipteral temple, i.e. with the side columns half sunk in the walls, raised on a meagre base of tufa blocks. It had a front, with four Ionic columns, one of which still remains, forming a support to the Campanile. An inscription dedicated to Drusilla, the sister of Caligula, was found here, but no reference as to the name of the temple can be drawn from it. A bas-relief, also found on the spot, represents the Tiburtine Sibyl sitting, and in the act of delivering an oracle. Hence it has been thought that we have in the Church of S. Giorgio the Temple of the Sibyl Albunea mentioned by Horace, Tibullus, and Lactantius, and this seems to be the most probable of the various conjectures which have been hazarded on the subject. The Grove of Tiburnus mentioned by Horace was probably on the right bank of the Anio, but further than this it is impossible to determine its exact position. There was also a grove dedicated to Diana. The Mons Catillus, now Monte Catillo or Monte della Croce, is the height on the right bank of the Anio. The name is at least as early as the time of Servius.

Villas.

As may easily be imagined there are numerous remains of ancient villas scattered about the immediate neighbourhood of Tibur, and the local guides, in order to please travellers but without the slightest evidence in support of their assertions, have dubbed them the Villas of Catullus, Horace, Ventidius, Quintilius Varus, Maecenas, Sallust, Piso, Capito, Brutus, Popillius, and other celebrated Romans.

The most remarkable ruins are those to which the name of Maecenas has been attached. The greater part of these have been now unfortunately concealed by new buildings and by an iron manufactory, but a fine terrace and parts of the porticoes still remain on the lofty bank of the Anio.

The rest is a mere confused mass of vaulted chambers and archways. The Via Tecta, or Porta Oscura, as it is sometimes called, by which the road passes underneath these ruins, was built, as we learn from an inscription now in the Vatican collection, by O. Vitulus and Rustius Flavos. The materials and style show that it can hardly be of a later date than the first century A.D.

The Tempio della Tosse which probably obtains its name from a vulgar interpretation of the name of the gens Tossia, is a ruin standing in a vineyard at the side of the old road, called the Via Constantina, below the Villa d'Este. It has none of the characteristic marks of an ancient temple, and the large number of windows it contains forbid us to suppose it to be a tomb. The interior of the building is round, the exterior octagonal. It is built of layers of small fragments of tufa intermixed with courses of bricks, materials which point to the fourth century as the earliest possible date of its erection. On the walls are the remains of frescoes of the Saviour and the Virgin, dating probably from the 13th century. These show that, if it was not originally a Christian Church, it was used as one at the time the frescoes were painted.

Tempio della Tosse.

The ruins of a considerable villa lie near the Porta S. Croce of Tivoli, in the estate called Carciano, from the mediæval name of the Fundus Cassianus, which is stated in a list of the estates belonging to the cathedral at Tivoli to have been the site of a villa of Caius Cassius. Part of these ruins consist of a very ancient structure of polygonal work, but the rest is pronounced by Nibby to belong to the time of the later republic. The casino of the Collegio Greco is now built on the spot, but the plan of the ancient villa can be so far traced as to show that it had several terraces, and looked towards the south-west. In the 16th century there were still eighteen large apartments existing, surrounded with a portico of Doric columns, and also some temples, a theatre, some fountains, and fish ponds. The opus reticulatum of these ruins is peculiar for the alternate arrangement of coloured tufa in its lozenges. An immense number of works of art were dug up here, and the nearly complete destruction

Villa of Cassius.

of what still remained of the villa in the 16th century, is probably due to the fact of its having been found to be so rich a mine of sculpture.

Sabine Farm of Horace.

The Sabine farm of Horace can hardly be passed over here, though it is not strictly included within the district of Tibur. There is no evidence to show that Horace ever had any villa at Tibur in addition to his Sabine farm; indeed his own words seem expressly to imply the contrary. The estate he had was plainly usually called a Sabinum, not a Tiburtinum, and must therefore be looked for at some distance from Tibur. Horace mentions two places in its neighbourhood, Varia, and Mandela, the sites of which can be exactly determined. The ancient list of towns places Varia on the Via Valeria, eight miles beyond Tibur, and precisely at this distance are the remains of an ancient town now covered by the modern village of Vico Varo. But the position of Mandela is more important for ascertaining the site of Horace's farm, because if we can fix upon it, we then can discover to which of the mountain streams which flow into the Anio the name Digentia belonged. An inscription dug up in 1757 near the Church of S. Cosimato on the Via Valeria, two miles from the village of Bardella, shows that an estate in the modern district formed by the union of Cantalupo and Bardella was called in the later imperial times, or the early Middle Ages, Massa Mandelana.

From this it is plain that the Digentia was the torrent called Mariscella, which joins the Anio between Cantalupo, Bardella and Vico Varo, descending from near Licenza, a small village about six miles from Vico Varo. As to the exact spot where the farm of Horace itself stood in the valley of the Digentia, we cannot be quite certain. The ruins usually pointed out are on a little knoll opposite to the village of Licenza, and on the other side of the stream. These are possibly situated on the spot on which the farmhouse stood, if they do not date so far back as the lifetime of the poet himself. Dennis in Milman's Horace says, "The ruins consist only of a mosaic pavement, and of two capitals and two fragments of Doric columns lying among the bushes. The pavement has been much ruined by the planting of a vineyard, and can only be seen on removing the earth which covers it. The groundwork is white with a border of animals in black.

Vico Varo and Lucretilis.

These are the sole traces now visible (1842), but some fifty years ago, the mosaic floors of six chambers were brought to light, but were covered again with earth, as nothing was found to tempt any further excavation. The farm is situated on a rising ground which sinks with a gentle slope to the stream, leaving a level intervening strip now yellow with the harvest. In this I recognised the sunny meadow which, as the poet says, was in danger of being inundated. The sunny fields were probably then, as now, sown with corn. Here it must have been that the poet was wont to repose on the grass after his meal, and here his personal efforts perhaps to dam out the stream provoked his neighbours' smiles." The place is surrounded on all sides by hills, except where the main valley of the Digentia separates them, running nearly due north and south, so that facing down the valley, the sun before midday rests on the right-hand slopes, and in the afternoon on the left hand, thus corresponding exactly to the poet's description of the site.[1]

The other spots mentioned by Horace as near his farm, are the Chapel of Vacuna, the slopes of Ustica, and the mountain of Lucretilis. The first of these has been placed by the Italian topographers at Rocca Giovane, a village perched on a hill on the west side of the valley about two miles above Cantalupo Bardella. The evidence for this identification is, however, very doubtful.

The Ustica cubans of the poet is commonly with some probability supposed to be La Rustica, which lies on the hill close to Licenza on the eastern side of the valley. Lucretilis is probably a name applied to the whole range of hills connected with Monte Gennaro. Cav. Rosa, however, places it at Monte del Corynaleto just above Rocca Giovane. The name of Fons Bandusiæ has been given to most of the springs in this valley by the enthusiastic admirers of Horace, but it is quite uncertain whether the Fons Bandusiæ was not in Apulia.

(F) THE NORTH-WESTERN DISTRICT.

The principal roads which traversed the Campagna to the north and north-west of Rome are the Nomentana, the

---

[1] Dennis in Milman's Horace, p. 101; pratum apricum, Ep. i. 14, 30; aprica rura, Od. iii. 18, 2. See also, Od. iii. 16, 30; Ep. i. 14, 35, 39. 'Rome and the Campagna,' p. 430.

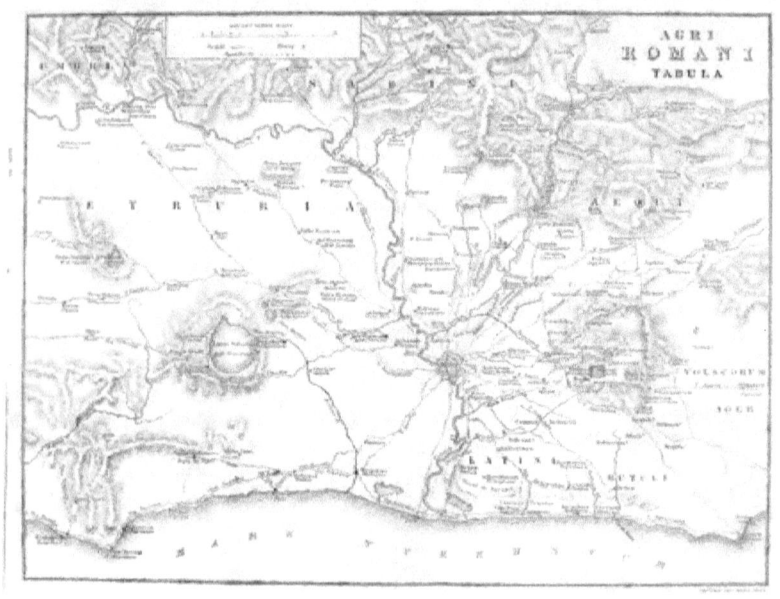

Salaria and the Flaminia. These roads offer but little, within the bounds of ancient Latium, which calls for remark.

The Via Nomentana diverged from the Via Salaria at the Collina gate in the Servian walls, and passed through the Aurelian wall at a gate which now stands a little to the south of the modern Porta Pia. The present road follows the line of the ancient Via Nomentana, as may be seen by the ruins of tombs which fringe it beyond S. Agnese. The Chapel of S. Constanza, opposite S. Agnese, is an interesting building of the Constantinian epoch, and the mosaics it contains, including a mixture of Christian and pagan emblems, are very remarkable. The Mons Sacer stands just beyond the bridge over the Anio, and the Villa of Phaon, where Nero ended his life, was at the Vigne Nuove, on a side road which branches off to the right, just beyond the Ponte Nomentano.

The Via Salaria is said to have been so named from the supplies of salt conveyed along it to the Sabine district at the time when the Romans and Sabines were confederates. It is first mentioned in history as the scene of the single combat between Manlius and the gigantic Gaul. The ancient road passed out at the Collina gate, and followed very nearly the same line as the present road along the left bank of the Tiber, as may be seen by the ruins near Serpentara, and by the position of the ancient bridge, the Ponte Salaro, which carries it over the Anio close to Antemnæ. Beyond this, Fidenæ and the Allia are the most remarkable points of interest upon the road in the neighbourhood of Rome. Beyond Malpasso, the ancient road, according to Nibby, diverges to the right, crossing the railway to Ancona.

The Via Flaminia, after passing through the Porta Ratumena at the Tomb of Bibulus, left the Aurelian fortifications at the Porta Flaminia, which stood a little nearer the slope of Monte Pincio than the present Porta del Popolo. It ran to the right of the present street, and then crossed the Tiber at the well-known Milvian bridge, and then diverged to the right along the Tiber valley, while the Via Cassia ascended to the left among the Etruscan hills towards Veii, which lay to the right at the twelfth milestone. The old Flaminian Road lay closer to the river than the modern, which is carried through a cutting in the hills and rejoins it at Tor di

Ponte Nomentano.

Quinto. There are a few rock tombs on the left hand, between the fifth and sixth milestones. One of them has been connected with the poet Ovid by a mistaken inference drawn from the inscription found upon it which bears the name of Q. Nasonius Ambrosius.

The Ponte Molle, which derives its name from an unknown Roman Mulvius, or from the neighbouring hills, carries the Flaminian Road over the Tiber at a distance of two miles from the Porta del Popolo. Some of the foundations of the bridge, and parts of the peperino and travertine stonework in the smaller arches, are ancient. The victory of Constantine over Maxentius, which is usually called the battle of the Pons Mulvius, was gained six miles further along the road.

An inscription cut in a block of travertine has been fixed in the right-hand parapet of the bridge. This inscription records the inspection of the banks of the Tiber by the Censors of M. Valerius and Publius Serveilius, who were Censors in the year B.C. 55.

One of the imperial villas of an early date was placed on the right bank of the Tiber at the ninth milestone on the Via Flaminia in the Veientine territory. *Villa of Livia at Prima Porta.*

The Via Flaminia is here bordered for a long distance on the left-hand side by tufa rocks of a reddish hue, whence the district had obtained, in Livy's time, the name of Saxa Rubra. The Cremera, now the Valca, is one of the streams which enter the Tiber in this district, and beyond it, where the road turns to the left, and, leaving the valley of the Tiber, ascends the hill through a cutting, is the stream and hamlet of Prima Porta. On the right of the road here, and between it and the Tiber, lie the ruins of a large villa, the various terraces of which, raised one above the other, occupy the whole of the top of the hill, and command magnificent views of the Sabine and Æquian highlands. There can be no doubt that these ruins are the remains of the villa of Livia called ad Gallinas, mentioned by Pliny and by Suetonius as situated at the ninth milestone on the Via Flaminia. The style of construction in the walls which remain corresponds to that of the Mausoleum of Augustus in the Campus Martius. The reticulated work has that peculiar irregularity about it which indicates the transition from the opus incertum to the more regularly

T

formed opus reticulatum. Nibby had pointed out this spot in 1837 as one in which a rich harvest might be reaped from excavating, but it was not till 1863 that the splendid Statue of Augustus, now in the Braccio Nuovo of the Vatican with other interesting sculptures, was dug up here.[1]

At the same time some rooms were excavated at a depth of ten feet, under the level of the ancient villa. They had apparently been closed at a very early time and filled with earth, in order to erect a building over them. The largest of these was apparently intended as a cool retreat during the summer heats, and the walls are painted with trees and birds, in imitation of a rustic bower. These paintings have attracted great attention as being some of the most ancient now in existence, and also on account of their intrinsic beauty, and the wonderful way in which they have preserved their freshness of colour. The pavement of this painted room was of marble, which was, however, removed when the earth was thrown in at the time of building the rooms above.

The legend about this villa connects it with the death of Nero, relating that the laurel bushes and the white fowls, for which the villa had been celebrated since the days of Livia, withered and died out during Nero's last days.

Veii.

Beyond Prima Porta, to the west, is the site of Veii. This is about twelve miles from Rome, and now bears the name of Isola Farnese. But little remains of the ancient city have been found, but no doubt is now felt by antiquaries that the city occupied the rocky ground between the Cremera and the Fosso de' due Fossi.

Inscriptions bearing the names of some Etruscan families, especially the Tarquitii, have been found here, and the remains of the ancient citadel, on the spot now called the Piazza d'Armi, are mentioned in some old ecclesiastical documents.

One of the gates must have been at the spot now called the Porta de' Sette Pagi as the road from Veii to Sutri probably passed out here, and another gate was opposite Isola called the Porta dell' Arco. A third may have stood towards Fidenæ, where the ancient postern and flight of steps is now

[1] Nibby, Anal. iii. 31. Bull. dell' Inst. 1863, pp. 72, 81.

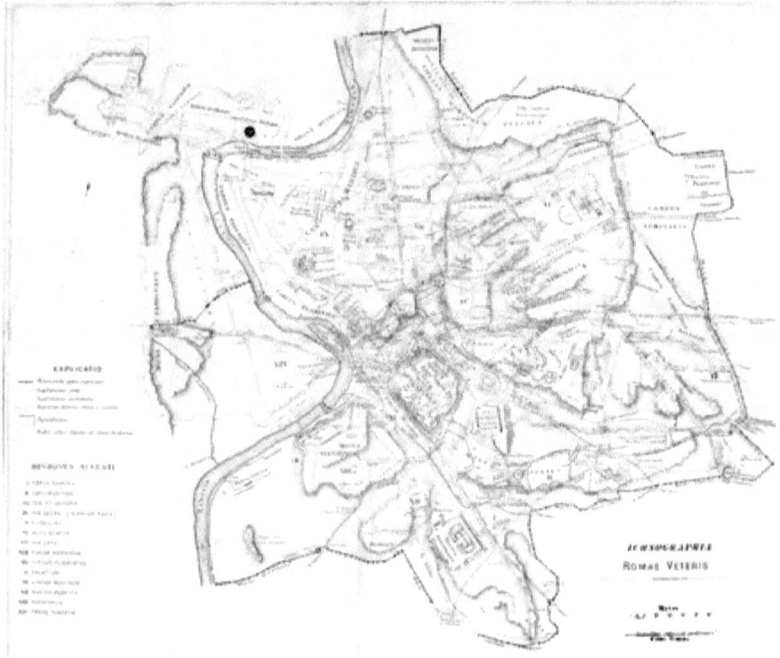

to be seen, called La Scaletta. Other remains are to be seen near the site of a gate called by Canina La Spezieria. The Ponte Sodo and the tombs near it are worth attention, as is also the ancient Etruscan tomb called the Grotta Campana, in which a most interesting set of sepulchral ornamentations and cinerary urns has been preserved. The chief monuments of Veii, which have been taken to Rome, are the Ionic columns in front of the Post Office in the Piazza Colonna, the Statue of Tiberius, and the colossal heads of Tiberius and Augustus, now in the Vatican Museum.[1]

[1] See Dennis, 'Etruria,' ch. i.

INDEX.

A.

Academia, 21, 246
Ædes Publicæ, Flavian, 22, 24
Æsculapius, temple of, 116
Agger of Servius, 157
Agon Capitolinus, 181
Agrippina, pedestal of, 146, 178
Alba Longa, 207
Alban Hills, 192, 194; Emissarium or tunnel of, 204
—— Lake, 203
—— Mount, 206
Albanum Cæsarum, 202
Albula, 189
Albulæ Aquæ, 236
Alexamenus, 18
Allia, 257
Altar of Sextius, 16
Amphitheatrum Castrense, 173
Ancient stone work, 163
Anio, falls of, 249
Antoninus Pius, pedestal of column, 178
Appian Road, 194
Aqua Virgo, 135
Arches, 9
Arch of Constantine, 59
—— Dolabella, 174
—— Drusus, 171
—— Gallienus, 77
—— M. Aurelius, 177
—— Severus, 52
—— Silversmiths, 104
—— Tiberius, 46
—— Titus, 31
Architectural styles, 5, 11
Arco dei Pantani, 92
Area Flacciana, 15
Arena of Coliseum, 67
Arricia, causeway at, 208
Arval College, 231
Atta, tomb of, 219
Atticus, tomb of, 198
Atrium, Palatine, 23
Auguratorium, on Palatine, 30
Augustan buildings, 21
Aurelius, M., bas-reliefs from arch, 177
Aventine and Cælian Hills, 161.

B.

Bandusiæ Fons, 256
Basilica, Constantine, 34, 35, 183
—— Julia, 44
——, Palatine, 24
——, Ulpia, 83
Bas-reliefs in Forum, 42, 43
Baths of Agrippa, 134
—— Caracalla, 166, 183
—— Constantine, 100, 183
—— Diocletian, 153
—— Titus, 75
Bibliotheca, 21
Bibulus, tomb of, 97
Brickwork, 12
Bronze cone, 149, 178; peacocks, 150, 178
Bovillæ, 200

C.

Cæcilia Metella, tomb of, 197
Cælian, houses on, 176
Caffarelli Palace, 98
Caligula, Palace of, 31
Calydonian boar hunt, 181
Campagna, hills of, 191; population, 192

Capitoline map, 120, 181
Capitolium, 98
Casale Rotondo, 200
Cestius, tomb of, 165
Cicero's Villa, 218
Circus Flaminius, 123;
—— Maximus, Carceres of, 112
Claudian Aqueduct, 20, 81, 174
Climate, 189
Clivus Victoriæ, 14
Cloaca Maxima, 46, 105
Clodius, Villa of, 201
Cluilia Fossa, 197
Coliseum, 61; architecture of, 72; characteristic of builder, 70
Colonnacce, 94,
Colossus of Nero, 63
Columbaria, 73, 170
Columns, 10
Column of Marcus Aurelius, 138
—— Phocas, 41
—— Trajan, 84; cast of, 89
Columna Centenaria, 142
Commodus, Palace of, 176
Constantine, Baths of, 100
Cornelia Gracchorum, 121
Cosmedin, S. Maria in, 111
Cremera, 259
Cryptoporticus, 25
Curtius, bas-relief, 179

D.

Dacian campaigns, Trajan's, 87
Decebalus, 88
Demosthenes, statue of, 182
Digentia, 254
Dii Consentes, area of, 48
Dogana, in Piazza di Pietra, 136
Domitius Calvinus, pedestal, 26, 28
Domus Aurea of Nero, 73
Doria Palace, 127
Duilian column, inscription on, 179

E.

Egeria, grotto of, 195
Egyptian antiquities, 129, 177

Einsiedlen MS., 51, 76, 100, 125, 138, 148
Eurysaces, tomb of, 81

F.

Fasti Consulares, 179
—— Prænestini, 229
Faustina, the younger, 178
Fidenæ, 257
Fiumicino, 231
Flaminia, Via, 257
Forum Augusti, 92
—— Julium, 91
——, Nerva's, 94
—— Romanum, 38
——, Trajan's, 83
Fratres Arvales, 231; buildings of, 232
Freshwater strata, 187
Frontispicium Neronis, 100

G.

Gabii, 221
Gabinius, Villa of, 218
Galuzze, 79
Gelotiana, Domus, 17
Geology of Campagna, 185
Germalus, 17, 29
Germanicus, House of, 26
Geta, erased, 104, 119
Gladiator or Gaul, dying, 181
Gnomon Obelisk, 137
Gordiana, Villa, 219
Gradus Concordiæ, 51
Graffiti, 18, 70

H.

Hadrian, colossal head of, 178
Hadrian's Villa, 237; antiquities from, 181, 183
Heliogabalus, Lavacrum, 36, 58
Horace, Sabine farm, 254
House of Laterani, 173

I.

Imperial monuments, 3

J.

Janus Quadrifrons, 103
Julius Cæsar, Heroon of, 39
Jupiter Pluvius, 141
—— Propugnator, 28
—— Redux, 176
—— Stator, 25
—— Victor, 28

L.

Labicum, 223
Laconicum, 134, 155, 168
Laocoon, 182
Lararium, Palatine, 24
Latifundia, 192
Latin road, tombs on, 211
Latium, towns of, 191, 192
Lautumiæ, 56
Legio fulminata, 141
Lucretilis, 256

M.

Mæcenas, Auditorium of, 80; Tower of, 102
Mamertine Prison, 55
Mandela, 254
Marcus Aurelius, statue of, 183
Marine strata, 185
Masonry, Roman, 4
Mausoleum of Augustus, 143
—— Hadrian, 148
Maxentius, Circus of, 196
Meta Sudans, 58
Milestones on Appian Road, 183
Miliarium Aureum, 54
Minerva Medica, 78
Mons Sacer, 257
Monte Cavallo, 183
—— Testaccio, 164
Monumental History, 2
Monumentum Ancyranum, 145
Muro Torto, 147
Museum, Kircherian, antiquities in, 183

N.

Navicella, 174
Nemi, Lake of, 208; Cæsar's Villa at, 210
Nomentana, Via, 257
Nymphæum, Palatine, 23

O.

Obelisks, 12, 129, 145
Oligarchical monuments, 2
Ostia, 229; antiquities from, 182

P.

Palatine, Belvedere on, 20; entrance, 14; paintings on peristylium, 23, 27; walls, 16, 17
Pantheon, 130; plundered, 135
Pedestals, in Forum, 41, 42
Phaon, Villa of, 257
Piazza Navona, 143
Pillar of Antoninus Pius, 138
Plautian Tomb, 236
Pompey, Villa and Tomb of, 201
Pons Ælius, 148
Ponte Lucano, 236
—— Molle, or Milvian bridge, 257
—— di Nono, 221
—— Rotto, 115
—— S. Sisto, 126
Porphyry basin, 182
Porta Capena, 163
—— Chiusa, 159
—— Collina, 257
—— Maggiore, 81
—— Mugionia, 24
—— Ratumena, 97
—— Romanula, 15
—— S. Lorenzo, 81
—— Viminalis, 153
Porticus Catuli, 15
—— Metelli, 120
—— Octaviæ, 119
Portland Vase, 181
Porto, 233
Præneste, 223

Prætorian Camp, 158
Prima Porta, statue of Augustus from, 260; Villa of Livia, 259
Puteal, in Forum, 39

Q.

Quintiliana, Villa of Commodus, 198, 212; sculpture from, 200
Quirinal Hill, 101
Quirinale, or Monte Cavallo, Piazza, 101, 183

R.

Rediculus, Divus, 195
Regal Monuments, 2
Republican Monuments, 2
Rienzi, 147
Roma Vecchia, 197, 212
Rostra of Empire, 54
Rutilius, 248

S.

Salaria Via, 257
Salita del Grillo, ruin in, 83
Sallustii, statue of, 172
S. Andrea della Valle, 123
S. Angelo, bridge of, 148
S. Constanza, Chapel of, 257
SS. Cosma and Damiano, 36
S. Maria degli Angeli, 153, 155
S. Maria in Via Lata, 127
S. Nicola in Carcere, ruins in, 117
S. Urbano, 195
Sarcophagi and cippus, 182
Saxa Rubra, 259
Scala Cœli, 29
Schola Xanthi, 49
Scipio, Sarcophagus, 182
Scipios, Tomb of, 170
Sculpture, ancient specimens of, 184
Seneca, Villa of, 197
Septa, 127
Septizonium, 20, 151
Servian Walls, 161
Sessorium, 172

Sette Basse, 212
——— Sale, 75
Site of Rome, 1
Sortes Præuestinæ, 225, 228
Stadium Palatinum, 18
Suovetaurilia, 42, 60, 88

T.

Tabularium, 56
Tarpeian Rock, 99
Tarquin Dynasty, 106, 157, 161
Teatro Correa, 143
Temple of Albunea at Tivoli, 252
——— Antoninus and Faustina, 40
——— Artemis at Nemi, 210
——— Bacchus or Honos, 195
——— Castor, 38
——— Ceres, 110
——— Concord, 50
——— Cybele, 29
——— Fortuna Prænestina, 225
——— Fortuna Virilis, 107
——— Hadrian, 137
——— Isis, 128
——— Jupiter Capitolinus, 98
——— Jupiter Feretrius, 29
——— Jupiter Latiaris, 207
——— Lares Præstites, 29
——— Marcus Aurelius, 139
——— Mars Ultor, 92
——— Minerva, 96
——— Penates, 36
——— Romulus, 196
——— Saturn, 46
——— Serapis, 128
——— Sibyl, or Vesta, at Tivoli, 251
——— Sun, Aurelian's, 100
——— Venus and Cupid, 172
——— Venus and Rome, 32
——— Vespasian, 49
——— Vesta, 39
——— Vesta or Hercules, 108
Temples, on Palatine, 28
Theatre of Balbus, 122, 183
——— Marcellus, 112
——— Pompey, 123
Theseus and Amazons, 184

Tiber, Island of, 115; bridges, 116; water of, 188
Tiberius, House of, 26, 30
Tivoli, or Tibur, 235; Villas at, 252
Torre Fiscale, 212
—— Paterno, ruins at, 234
—— Pignatara, 221
Torso Belvedere, 182
Totilas, 152, 236, 247
Transitoria, Domus, 34
Transtiberine Walls, 4
Travertine, quarries, 236
Triclinium, Palatine, 22
Trophies, of Marius, 76, 183
Tufaceous stone, 186
Tunnels, subterranean, 206
Tusculum, 214; gate and walls, 216; history of city, 217; theatre at, 215

U.

Ustica, 256
Ustrina Cæsarum, 144, 146

V.

Vacuna, Chapel of, 256
Varia, 254
Vatican Hill, enclosed, 4
V. D. N., 18
Veii, 260
Veii and Campagna, antiquities from, 182
Velabrum, 103
Velia, 31
Vettius Prætextatus, 49
Vicus Tuscus, 39
Vigna Guidi, 169
Villa Mills, 21
Villas, ancient, 190, 193
Vitiges, 149, 152, 193
Volcanic strata, 186
Vota, 60

W.

Wolf, bronze figure, 17, 180

HISTORICAL WORKS.

MODERN EUROPE. From the Fall of Constantinople to the Establishment of the German Empire, A.D. 1453-1870. By THOMAS HENRY DYER, M.A. Second Edition, revised and continued. In 5 vols. demy 8vo. 2*l*. 12*s*. 6*d*.

HISTORY OF ENGLAND, during the Early and Middle Ages. By C. H. PEARSON, M.A., Fellow of Oriel College, Oxford. Second Edition, much enlarged. Vol. I. 8vo. 16*s*. Vol. II. 8vo. 14*s*.

HISTORICAL MAPS of ENGLAND during the first Thirteen Centuries. With Explanatory Essays and Indices. By C. H. PEARSON, M.A. Imp. folio. Second Edition. 31*s*. 6*d*.

THE BARONS' WAR. Including the Battles of Lewes and Evesham. By W. H. BLAAUW, M.A. Second Edition, with Additions and Corrections by C. H. PEARSON, M.A. Demy 8vo. 10*s*. 6*d*.

MARTINEAU'S (HARRIET) HISTORY OF ENGLAND FROM 1800-15. Being a Reprint of 'The Introduction to the History of the Peace.' With new and full Index. 1 vol. 3*s*. 6*d*.

MARTINEAU'S (HARRIET) HISTORY OF THE THIRTY YEARS' PEACE, 1815-46. With new and copious Index. 4 vols. 3*s*. 6*d*. each.

These histories contain a vast store of information, only with much labour attainable elsewhere, on all the great social and political questions of the important and interesting period of which they treat—a period separated by so short an interval from our own time that to every educated person who takes an intelligent interest in the questions of the present day a thorough knowledge of its history is indispensable.

LIVES OF THE QUEENS OF ENGLAND, from the Norman Conquest to the Reign of Queen Anne. By AGNES STRICKLAND. Library Edition. With Portraits, Autographs, and Vignettes. 8 vols. post 8vo. 7*s*. 6*d*. each. Also a Cheaper Edition in 6 vols. 5*s*. each.

LIVES OF THE LAST FOUR PRINCESSES OF THE ROYAL HOUSE OF STUART. Forming an appropriate Sequel to the 'Lives of the Queens of England.' With a Photograph of the Princess Mary, after a picture by Honthorst. Crown 8vo. 12*s*.

THE LIFE OF MARY, QUEEN OF SCOTS. By AGNES STRICKLAND. 2 vols. post 8vo. 5*s*. each.

HUME, SMOLLETT, & HUGHES' HISTORY OF ENGLAND. 18 vols. [sold separately] post 8vo. 4*s*. each.

THE STORY OF THE IRISH BEFORE THE CONQUEST. From the Mythical Period to the Invasion under Strongbow. By LADY FERGUSON. Fcap. 8vo. 5*s*.

HISTORY OF THE IRISH REBELLION IN 1798. By W. H. MAXWELL. With Portraits and Etchings on Steel by George Cruikshank. Tenth Edition. 7*s*. 6*d*.

THIERRY'S HISTORY OF THE CONQUEST OF ENGLAND BY THE NORMANS; its Causes, and its Consequences in England, Scotland, Ireland, and the Continent. Translated from the 7th Paris edition by WILLIAM HAZLITT. With short Memoir of Thierry, Index, and Portraits of Thierry and William the Conqueror. 2 vols. 3*s*. 6*d*. each.

JESSE'S MEMOIRS OF THE PRETENDERS AND THEIR ADHERENTS. With Index and Portraits. Post 8vo. 5*s*.

JESSE'S MEMOIRS OF THE COURT OF ENGLAND DURING THE REIGN OF THE STUARTS, including the Protectorate. 3 vols. With Index and 42 Portraits. 5*s*. each.

NUGENT'S (LORD) MEMORIALS OF HAMPDEN, HIS PARTY AND TIMES. With a Memoir of the Author, copious Index, an Autograph Letter, and Portraits. Post 8vo. 5*s*.

CARREL'S HISTORY OF THE COUNTER-REVOLUTION IN ENGLAND for the Re-establishment of Popery under Charles II. and James II. By ARMAND CARREL. Together with Fox's (Right Hon. C. J.) History of the Reign of James II., and Lord Lonsdale's Memoir of the Reign of James II. With Portrait of Carrel after Viardot. 3*s*. 6*d*.

JAMES'S (G. P. R.) HISTORY OF THE LIFE OF RICHARD CŒUR DE LION, King of England. With Index and Portraits of Richard and Philip Augustus. 2 vols. 3*s*. 6*d*. each.

COXE'S MEMOIRS OF THE DUKE OF MARLBOROUGH. With his original Correspondence, collected from the family records at Blenheim. Edited by Archdeacon W. COXE, M.A., F.R.S. Revised Edition by JOHN WADE. With Portraits and Index. 3 vols. post 8vo. 3s. 6d. each.

*** An Atlas of the plans of Marlborough's campaigns, 4to. 10s. 6d.

COXE'S HISTORY of the HOUSE OF AUSTRIA. From the Foundation of the Monarchy by Rhodolph of Hapsburgh to the Death of Leopold II., 1218-1792. By Archdeacon COXE. Together with a Continuation from the Accession of Francis I. to the Revolution of 1848. To which is added Genesis, or Details of the late Austrian Revolution (translated from the German). With Portraits of Maximilian, Rhodolph, Maria Theresa, and Francis Joseph. 4 vols. with Indexes. 3s. 6d. each.

LIFE OF THE EMPEROR KARL THE GREAT [Charlemagne]. Translated from the Contemporary History of Eginhard, with Notes and Chapters on Eginhard, the Franks, Karl, and the Breaking-up of the Empire. With a Map. By WILLIAM GLAISTER, M.A., B.C.L., University College, Oxford. Crown 8vo. 4s. 6d.

GERMANY, MENZEL'S HISTORY OF, from the Earliest Period to a recent date. With Index and Portraits of Charlemagne, Charles V., and Metternich. 3 vols. 3s. 6d. each.

RUSSIA, HISTORY OF, from the Earliest Period. Compiled from the most authentic sources, including Karamsin, Tooke, and Ségur. By WALTER K. KELLY. With Index and Portraits of Catherine, Nicholas, and Menschikoff. 2 vols. 3s. 6d. each.

OCKLEY'S HISTORY OF THE SARACENS and THEIR CONQUESTS IN SYRIA, PERSIA, AND EGYPT. Comprising the Lives of Mohammed and his Successors to the Death of Abdalmelik, the Eleventh Caliph. By SIMON OCKLEY, B.D., Professor of Arabic in the University of Cambridge. Sixth Edition. With Portrait of Mohammed. 3s. 6d.

CONDÉ'S HISTORY OF THE DOMINION of THE ARABS IN SPAIN. Translated from the Spanish by Mrs. FOSTER. With Engraving of Abderahmen Ben Moavia, and Index. 3 vols. 3s. 6d. each.

MACHIAVELLI'S HISTORY OF FLORENCE and of the Affairs of Italy, from the Earliest Times to the Death of Lorenzo the Magnificent; together with the Prince, Savonarola, various Historical Tracts, and a Memoir of Machiavelli. With Index and Portrait. 3s. 6d.

HUNGARY, its History and Revolution: together with a copious Memoir of Kossuth from authentic sources. With Index and Portrait of Kossuth. 3s. 6d.

ROSCOE'S (W.) LIFE of LORENZO DE MEDICI, called 'the Magnificent,' including the Copyright Notes and Illustrations, and Index. With his Poems, Letters, &c. Tenth Edition revised, with Memoir of Roscoe by his Son, and Portrait of Lorenzo (after Vasari). 3s. 6d.

ROSCOE'S (W.) LIFE and PONTIFICATE OF LEO X., with the Copyright Notes, Appendices of Historical Documents, the Dissertation on Lucretia Borgia. Final Edition, revised by THOMAS ROSCOE, with Index, and two Portraits of Roscoe, and one of Leo X. 2 vols. 3s. 6d. each.

RANKE'S HISTORY OF THE POPES, their Church and State, and especially of their Conflicts with Protestantism in the 16th and 17th Centuries. Translated by E. FOSTER. With Portraits of Julius II., Innocent X., and Clement VII. 3 vols. 3s. 6d. each.

RANKE'S HISTORY OF SERVIA AND THE SERVIAN REVOLUTION. With an Account of the Insurrection in Bosnia. Translated by Mrs. KERR. To which is added, The Slave Provinces of Turkey, from the French of Cyprien Robert and other sources. 1 vol. 3s. 6d.

KINGS OF ROME, History of the. By T. H. DYER, LL.D. With a Prefatory Dissertation on the Sources and Evidences of Early Roman History. Demy 8vo. 16s.

DECLINE OF THE ROMAN REPUBLIC. From the Destruction of Carthage to the Consulship of Julius Cæsar. By GEORGE LONG, M.A. 5 vols. 8vo. 14s. per vol.

'If any one can guide us through the almost inextricable mazes of this labyrinth, it is Mr. Long.'—*Saturday Review.*

MASON (A. J.). THE PERSECUTION OF DIOCLETIAN; an Historical Essay. By ARTHUR JAMES MASON, M.A., Fellow of Trinity College, Cambridge. Demy 8vo. 10s. 6d.

'This is one of the most striking and original contributions to ecclesiastical history which has come under our notice for some time.'—*Spectator.*

'Mr. Mason has worked vigorously and independently, and in a right direction. We do not pretend to be convinced by him on all points, but he has given us, at least, a good deal of matter for thought.'—*Saturday Review.*

GIBBON'S ROMAN EMPIRE, Complete and Unabridged, with Variorum Notes, including, in addition to the Author's own, those of Guizot, Wenck, Niebuhr, Hugo, Neander, and other Scholars. Edited by an English Churchman. 7 vols. With copious Index, and two Maps and a Portrait of Gibbon. 3s. 6d. each.

HISTORICAL WORKS.

GUIZOT'S HISTORY OF THE ORIGIN OF REPRESENTATIVE GOVERNMENT IN EUROPE. Translated by A. R. SCOBLE. With Index. 3s. 6d.

GUIZOT'S HISTORY OF THE ENGLISH REVOLUTION OF 1640. From the Accession of Charles I. to his Death. With a Preliminary Essay on its Causes and Success. Translated by WILLIAM HAZLITT. With Portrait of Charles, after Vandyke. With Index. 3s. 6d.

GUIZOT'S HISTORY OF CIVILISATION, from the Fall of the Roman Empire to the French Revolution. Translated by WILLIAM HAZLITT. With Portraits of Guizot, Charlemagne, and Louis IX. 3 vols. with Index, 3s. 6d. each.

JAMES (G. P. R.), THE LIFE and TIME OF LOUIS XIV. With Index, and Portraits of Louis XIV. and Mazarin. 2 vols. 3s. 6d. each.

DE LOLME ON THE CONSTITUTION OF ENGLAND; or an Account of the English Government, in which it is compared both with the Republican form of Government and the other Monarchies of Europe. Edited, with Life of the Author and Notes, by JOHN MACGREGOR, M.P. 3s. 6d.

LAMARTINE'S HISTORY of THE GIRONDISTS; or, Personal Memoirs of the Patriots of the French Revolution, from unpublished sources. Translated by H. T. RYDE. With Index, and Portraits of Robespierre, Madame Roland, and Charlotte Corday. 3 vols. 3s. 6d. each.

LAMARTINE'S HISTORY of THE RESTORATION of MONARCHY in FRANCE (a Sequel to his History of the Girondists). With Index, and Portraits of Lamartine, Talleyrand, Lafayette, Ney, and Louis XVII. 4 vols. 3s. 6d. each.

LAMARTINE'S HISTORY of THE FRENCH REVOLUTION OF 1848. With Index and Frontispiece. 3s. 6d.

MICHELET'S HISTORY of THE ROMAN REPUBLIC. Translated by W. HAZLITT. With Appendix, Index, and a Portrait of Michelet. 3s. 6d.

MICHELET'S HISTORY of THE FRENCH REVOLUTION, from its earliest indications to the flight of the King in 1791. With Index and Frontispiece. 3s. 6d.

MIGNET'S HISTORY OF THE FRENCH REVOLUTION, from 1789-1814. With Index and Portrait of Napoleon. 3s. 6d.

PHILIP DE COMMINES, MEMOIRS OF. Containing the Histories of Louis XI. and Charles VIII., Kings of France, and Charles the Bold, Duke of Burgundy. Together with the Scandalous Chronicle, or Secret History of Louis XI., by JEAN DE TROYES. Edited, with a Life of De Commines and Notes, by Andrew R. SCOBLE. With Index, and Portraits of Charles the Bold and Louis XI. 2 vols. 3s. 6d. each.

SULLY, MEMOIRS OF THE DUKE OF, Prime Minister to Henry the Great. Translated from the French, with Notes, an Historical Introduction, Index, and Portraits of Sully, Henry IV., Coligny, and Marie de Medicis. 4 vols. 3s. 6d. each.

SCHLEGEL'S (F.) LECTURES ON THE PHILOSOPHY OF LIFE and THE PHILOSOPHY OF LANGUAGE. Translated by A. J. W. MORRISON. With Index. 3s. 6d.

SCHLEGEL'S (F.) LECTURES ON THE PHILOSOPHY OF HISTORY Translated from the German, with a Memoir of the Author, by J. B. ROBERTSON. With Index and Portrait. 3s. 6d.

SCHLEGEL'S (F.) LECTURES ON MODERN HISTORY, together with the Lectures entitled Cæsar and Alexander, and The Beginning of Our History. Translated by L. PURCELL and R. H. WHITELOCK. With Index. 3s. 6d.

TYTLER'S (PROF.) THE ELEMENTS OF GENERAL HISTORY. New Edition. Revised and brought down to Christmas, 1874. Small post 8vo. 3s. 6d.

THE STUDENT'S TEXT-BOOK OF ENGLISH AND GENERAL HISTORY, from B.C. 100 to the Present Time, with Genealogical and Literary Tables, and Sketch of the English Constitution. By D. BEALE. Crown 8vo. 2s. 6d.

THE STUDENT'S CHRONOLOGICAL MAPS OF ANCIENT AND MODERN HISTORY. By D. BEALE. Medium 8vo. 3s. 6d.

A PRACTICAL SYNOPSIS OF ENGLISH HISTORY; or, A General Summary of Dates and Events for the use of Schools, Families, and Candidates for Public Examinations. By Arthur Bowes. 4th edition. Demy 8vo. 2s.

[TURN OVER.

ENGLISH CHRONICLES.

Post 8vo. 5s. per Volume.

BEDE'S ECCLESIASTICAL HISTORY, and the Anglo-Saxon Chronicle. With Notes, Analysis, Index, and Map. By Dr. GILES.

CHRONICLES OF THE CRUSADERS. Richard of Devizes, Geoffrey de Vinsauf, Lord de Joinville.

FLORENCE OF WORCESTER'S CHRONICLE, with the Two Continuations; comprising Annals of English History to the Reign of Edward I.

GIRALDUS CAMBRENSIS' HISTORICAL WORKS: Topography of Ireland; History of the Conquest of Ireland; Itinerary through Wales; and Description of Wales. With Index. Edited by THOMAS WRIGHT.

HENRY OF HUNTINGDON'S HISTORY OF THE ENGLISH, from the Roman Invasion to Henry II.; with the Acts of King Stephen, &c.

INGULPH'S CHRONICLE of the ABBEY OF CROYLAND, with the Continuations by Peter of Blois and other Writers. By H. T. RILEY.

MATTHEW PARIS'S CHRONICLE. In 5 vols. FIRST SECTION: Roger of Wendover's Flowers of English History, from the Descent of the Saxons to A.D. 1235. Translated by Dr. GILES. 2 vols. SECOND SECTION: From 1235-1273. With index to the entire Work. 3 vols.

MATTHEW of WESTMINSTER'S FLOWERS OF HISTORY, especially such as relate to the affairs of Britain, to A.D. 1307. Translated by C. D. YONGE. In 2 vols.

ORDERICUS VITALIS' ECCLESIASTICAL HISTORY OF ENGLAND AND NORMANDY. With Chronicle of St. Evroult. Translated, with Notes, by T. FORESTER, M.A. In 4 vols.

ROGER DE HOVEDEN'S ANNALS OF ENGLISH HISTORY; from A.D. 732 to A.D. 1201. Edited by H. T. RILEY. In 2 vols.

ROGER OF WENDOVER. See *Matthew Paris.*

SIX OLD ENGLISH CHRONICLES, viz.:—Asser's Life of Alfred, and the Chronicles of Ethelwerd, Gildas, Nennius, Geoffrey of Monmouth, and Richard of Cirencester.

WILLIAM OF MALMESBURY, CHRONICLE OF THE KINGS OF ENGLAND. Translated by SHARPE.

PAULI'S (Dr. R.) LIFE of ALFRED THE GREAT. Translated from the German. To which is appended Alfred's Anglo-Saxon Version of Crosius, with a literal Translation, and an Anglo-Saxon Grammar and Glossary.

COOPER'S BIOGRAPHICAL DICTIONARY. Containing concise Notices (upwards of 15,000) of Eminent Persons of all Ages and Countries, and more particularly of distinguished Natives of Great Britain and Ireland. By THOMPSON COOPER, F.R.S., Editor of 'Men of the Time,' and Joint Editor of 'Athenæ Cantabrigienses.' 1 vol. 8vo. 12s.

'It is an important original contribution to the literature of its class by a painstaking scholar.... It seems in every way admirable, and fully to justify the claims on its behalf put forth by its editor.'—*British Quarterly Review.*

'The mass of information which it contains, especially as regards a number of authors, more or less obscure, is simply astonishing.'—*Spectator.*

'Comprises in 1210 pages, printed very closely in double columns, an enormous amount of information.'—*Examiner.*

THE ONLY AUTHORIZED AND UNABRIDGED EDITION.

WEBSTER'S DICTIONARY OF THE ENGLISH LANGUAGE. Including Scientific, Technical, and Biblical Words and Terms, with their Significations, Pronunciations, Alternative Spellings, Derivations, Synonyms, and numerous Illustrative Quotations. In 1 volume of 1576 pages, with 3000 Illustrations. 4to. cloth, 21s.

THE COMPLETE DICTIONARY contains, in addition to the above matter, several valuable Literary Appendices, and 70 extra pages of Illustrations, grouped and classified. Price, in cloth, 31s. 6d.

'Certainly the best practical English Dictionary extant.'—*Quarterly Review,* Oct. 1873.

Prospectuses, with Specimen Pages, sent post free on application.

LONDON: GEORGE BELL & SONS, YORK STREET, COVENT GARDEN.

www.ingramcontent.com/pod-product-compliance
Lightning Source LLC
Chambersburg PA
CBHW030736230426
43667CB00007B/739